THE
GUARDIANS

THE
GUARDIANS

100 YEARS OF AN GARDA SÍOCHÁNA
1922–2022

COMPILED BY GARDA STEPHEN MOORE

IN CONJUNCTION WITH *THE GUARDIANS* EDITORIAL BOARD

ON BEHALF OF AN GARDA SÍOCHÁNA

THE O'BRIEN PRESS
DUBLIN

CONTENTS

Forewords   7

    Commissioner Drew Harris   7

    An Taoiseach, Mícheál Martin   8

    Helen McEntee, TD, Minister for Justice   10

Preface – *John Twomey, Chair of* The Guardians *editorial board*   13

Significant Events in 100 Years of An Garda Síochána – *Garda Tom Daly*   15

A Reflection – *Assistant Commissioner John O'Driscoll*   20

SECTION 1: THE FIRST GENERATION   23

1. A New Force – *Garda Stephen Moore and Garda Tom Daly*   26

2. The First Generation – A Family in Service – *Garda Stephen Moore and*

    Retired Sergeant Martin Drew   36

3. General Eoin O'Duffy – *Retired Inspector John Duffy*   43

4. Oriel House – *Inspector Paul Maher*   49

5. Eamon Broy – *Áine Broy*   55

6. Progress and Goodwill – *Retired Inspector Phelim Patrick (Pat) McGee*   60

7. Women in An Garda Síochána – *Retired Chief Superintendent Lorraine Wheatley*

    and Garda Stephen Moore   67

8. Jim 'Lugs' Branigan (1910–86) – *Garda Stephen Moore*   77

9. Policing in Cork – *Retired Sergeant Tim Bowe*   80

SECTION 2: THE SECOND GENERATION   89

10. New Generation – New Challenges – *Retired Inspector Tim Doyle*   92

11. Policing the Troubles – *Sheelagh Brady, Former Garda Sergeant*   98

    The Burning of the British Embassy – *Retired Chief Superintendent Paul Smyth*   103

12. A Border Beat – *Retired Garda Pat O'Donoghue*   106

13. The Technical Bureau: The Beginning and the Early Years

    – *Retired Inspector Edwin S. Handcock*   115

14. The JFK Visit – *Retired Sergeant Fachtna O'Donovan*   122

15. 'Two Depots': A Brief History of Garda Headquarters and the Garda College

    – *Sergeant John Reynolds and Michael Reynolds*   129

16. The Scott Medal – *Geraldine Du Berry*   136

17. The United Nations – *Garda Stephen Moore and Retired Sergeant Martin Drew*   139

18. A History of Legal Powers – *Detective Garda Darren Martin*   152

19. A Life in the Guards – *Retired Assistant Commissioner Pat Leahy*   159

SECTION 3: MODERN POLICING   167

20. 'The Perfect Murder' – *Retired Detective John Cribbin*   170

21. The Investigator – *Assistant Commissioner John O'Driscoll with Garda Stephen Moore*   178

22. Roads Policing – *Garda Damien Duffy*   186

23. Tackling the Scourge of Drugs – *Retired Assistant Commissioner Michael O'Sullivan*   193

24. CAB – A Success Story – *Garda Stephen Moore in conversation with*

  former Minister for Justice Nora Owen, and Retired Garda Commissioner Fachtna Murphy   199

25. Rural Policing – *Garda Brendan O'Connor*   205

26. The Super, the Inspector, the Sergeant, and the Guard – *Superintendent Chris Grogan,*

  Inspector Ailish Myles, Detective Sergeant Dara Kenny and Garda Billy Horan   212

27. 'Sure, you can't be doing that!' A Crimecall Story – *Sergeant Kelvin Courtney*   221

28. Operational Support Services – *Garda Stephen Moore, Garda Alan Cummins*   229

29. 'The House of Horrors' – *Retired Sergeant John Hynes*   237

30. Policing with Diverse Communities – *Inspector David McInerney*   244

31. G-Forcing Change – *Superintendent Paul Franey*   252

32. The First Female Commissioner – *Retired Garda Commissioner Nóirín O'Sullivan*   257

33. Cybercrime – *Garda Stephen Moore interviews Detective Chief Superintendent Paul Cleary*   261

34. Garda Staff – *Andrew McLindon*   266

35. The Garda Reserve – *Garda Stephen Moore, Garda Reserves Sean O'Sullivan, Mick Kenneally*

  and Ravinder Singh Oberoi   268

36. Policing a Pandemic – *Retired Deputy Commissioner John Twomey and*

  Detective Sergeant Brendan Tighe   273

37. An Garda Síochána – A Changing Force – *Conor Brady*   280

38. Guardians of the Peace – An Assessment – *Myles Dungan*   286

39. An Garda Síochána Roll of Honour

  – *Reflections by Fr Joe Kennedy and Archdeacon David Pierpoint*   291

About the Contributors   295

Acknowledgements   299

Bibliography   301

FOREWORDS

FOREWORD BY COMMISSIONER DREW HARRIS

T his book is not a traditional history of An Garda Síochána. There are authors who have done that already to great effect. Instead, *The Guardians: 100 Years of An Garda Síochána, 1922–2022* details not only some of the key dates and events in our 100-year history, but also the impact the organisation and its personnel have had on this society in fulfilling our mission of keeping people safe across the last century. This insight is provided by historians and academics, but also by those who have served in the organisation. I want to thank them for their contributions, the publisher O'Brien Press, and the editorial team.

As is written by others in this book, An Garda Síochána is a unique police and security service in global terms. Born from the chaos and confusion as the new state struggled to establish itself, and in the midst of a civil war, An Garda Síochána could easily have rapidly failed through a lack of organisation and public support in a bitterly divided society. And it very nearly did. However, against the odds, it prevailed, and as an unarmed police service has gone on to become an integral and trusted part of Irish society.

For me, the reason for its success goes back to the ethos espoused by the first holder of the office that I am so proud to hold, Commissioner Michael Staines, when he said: 'The Garda Síochána will succeed, not by force of arms or numbers, but on their moral authority as servants of the people.'

Over decades, this has developed into a connection with the communities we serve that is the envy of many police services across the world. The development and importance of that connection runs like a golden thread through this book. It is that connection that enabled an unarmed police service to establish its credibility as independent, fair and trusted. It is that connection that has seen us become the organisation people turn to at their most difficult times for help, safety and reassurance. There are countless examples over the past 100 years, with the most recent being our work during the COVID-19 pandemic. It is this connection that means we have one of the highest public trust levels in the world for a police service and are regarded globally as a model of community policing. It is this connection that makes An Garda Síochána truly unique.

Combined with that connection, this book is also a reminder of the sacrifices, dedication and professionalism of Garda personnel – including the Gardaí who made the ultimate sacrifice, to protect others and this State.

Of course, there have been times in our history when we have not lived up to the high standards that the public expect of us. Where this has happened, it is very much regretted. It is important that we learn the lessons from our history to ensure that we maintain those high standards now and into the future.

This book showcases all that is good about An Garda Síochána – its dedicated and professional personnel, its commitment to working with the community, its can-do attitude, its pride in protecting and supporting people.

Then there is the work that is not public facing, but vital to the security of the State. The bravery, resilience and expertise in An Garda Síochána protecting this State and its people from terrorist organisations determined to violently overthrow democracy is one of our most important achievements over the past hundred years.

While reflecting on the past, it is also important to focus on the future. An Garda Síochána has evolved over the last hundred years to adapt to changes in society, and this will continue over the next century, particularly in areas such as technology, training, and diversity. But what will not change is the foundation to our success – connection to community.

FOREWORD BY AN TAOISEACH, MÍCHEÁL MARTIN

Is cúis an-áthais dom réamhrá a chur ar fáil don fhoilseachán speisialta seo ar chomóradh céad bliain An Gharda Síochána.

Is é ceann de na céad bliain is suntasaí a dhéanfaidh muid comóradh ar le linn an Deich mBliana de Chomóradh é céad bliain An Garda Síochána. Cé go raibh tionchar buan ag na himeachtaí seo ar ár saol agus ar stair an Stáit, bhí tábhacht faoi leith ag baint le bunú An Gharda Síochána. Chuir seo tús le caidreamh speisialta idir muintir na hÉireann agus seirbhís phóilíneachta nua an Stáit.

As the first Garda Commissioner, Michael Staines, famously said in 1922:

> The Garda Síochána will succeed, not by the force of arms or numbers, but on their moral authority as servants of the people.

Throughout the past century, these principles

An Taoiseach, Mícheál Martin.

have guided the organisation, with its defining characteristic being its unique connection to our communities. This relationship, which is the envy of many police services across the world, is rooted in serving our communities and keeping people safe.

We have seen this connectedness again during the most trying times of the COVID-19 pandemic. An Garda Síochána, alongside other public-sector bodies and community groups, responded to protect the elderly and vulnerable by delivering food parcels and medicines and calling in on the isolated. In some respects, this represented a renewal of their historical relationship with the people when they carried out a range of administrative and non-crime-related tasks. It also exemplifies a positive bond with local communities upon which much can be built. The Gardaí are often the people we turn to in our most difficult moments. The Gardaí are often the ones to bring sad news and to provide support in our most intense moments of grief.

While the types of crime Gardaí face have changed over the decades, with many existing now that could not have been dreamed of 100 years ago, the relationship of service remains as strong as ever. The strength of the connection between local Gardaí and their communities is why we all feel such deep collective hurt on each occasion when a Garda has given their life in the service of the State. The death of each and every Garda in the line of duty represents a devastating and traumatic loss to their families, friends and colleagues, but also to the wider communities in which they lived and served.

Each of the eighty-nine men on the Garda Roll of Honour died in the service of the State and for the people of Ireland. Reading their names and recalling the circumstances of so many of their deaths, we cannot but be struck by the dedication that Gardaí have shown in preserving peace and protecting the security of our country. So many individual members of An Garda Síochána have provided an immense and valuable frontline service throughout the most challenging years in the State's history. Their commitment and loyalty have never faltered.

This book provides a diverse, informative and engaging compendium of organisational and individual histories of the first hundred years of the life of An Garda Síochána. I hope that all who read it will be reminded of the contribution that Gardaí make to our lives and of the risks that they take for us on a daily basis.

As an organisation, An Garda Síochána has grown and developed hand in hand with our state. It has embarked on a significant programme of reform, which will enshrine human rights at the heart of policing and deliver a new policing model dedicated to keeping communities safe. There is much to be proud of in its past. Let us work together to ensure that it has an even prouder future.

On behalf of the people of Ireland, I would like to thank all Gardaí, past and present, for their service and sacrifice, and to wish An Garda Síochána well for the next hundred years.

Foreword by Helen McEntee, TD, Minister for Justice

On this special occasion of the centenary of An Garda Síochána, I would like to congratulate and thank all those who have served in the organisation over the past hundred years.

'The Civic Guard', as it was initially known, was born into a significant period in Irish history. The establishment of a new police service by the Provisional Government was one of the key foundation stones of the Irish Free State.

From its genesis at a meeting in the Gresham Hotel in February 2022, convened by Michael Collins, An Garda Síochána became one of the great successes of the early years of our state. Its tradition of maintaining law, order and security, combined with a close bond with the communities it serves, is a remarkable legacy left to us by those who built the State. It is a tradition that An Garda Síochána upholds every day.

In many ways it is remarkable – given the turbulent preceding decade, and the tragically high number of lives lost and families irreparably damaged – that from its early days An Garda Síochána was exclusively unarmed, apart from the regulation baton. This intentional emphasis on service, as opposed to force of arms, has become embedded in the culture of An Garda Síochána. That our police remain largely unarmed is a particular source of pride for our country.

Over its first hundred years, An Garda Síochána has faced a succession of challenges, from establishing the trust of the people following years of unrest and war, to the Emergency, the Troubles, the growth of organised crime, COVID-19 and all of the challenges of the many decades. On each occasion, individual Gardaí have risen to the challenge and kept us safe.

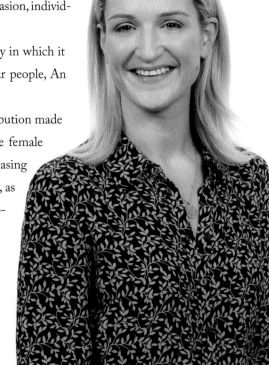

An effective policing service is one that reflects the society in which it operates, and it has been vital that, while always serving our people, An Garda Síochána has developed as the decades have passed.

I think it is particularly important that we note the contribution made by the women of An Garda Síochána since the first twelve female recruits joined in 1959. Over the intervening 60+ years, increasing numbers of women have chosen to join An Garda Síochána, as sworn members and as civilian staff, and women are now represented across the Garda organisation, including, increasingly, within the highest ranks.

It is crucial too that An Garda Síochána continues to

Helen McEntee, TD, Minister for Justice.

meet its commitment to increasing diversity and ensuring that everyone living within our country can see members of their communities – *our community* – serving them within the organisation. The contribution that will be made to policing by this broader representation of our society within Garda ranks is immense, with lasting positive impacts, especially in the pivotal Garda roles of community policing and human rights.

Alongside the increasingly sophisticated response to particular types of crime, there is, of course, truly no substitute for the visible Garda presence in local communities. My Department and the Government are committed to supporting An Garda Síochána as it continues to further develop and build on its ambitious reform programme, centred on effective community policing. It is fitting that this substantial policy reform coincides with An Garda Síochána's centenary, and I believe that we can enter the organisation's second hundred years with a great degree of optimism.

It is fitting too that the anniversary has fallen following what has been another remarkable contribution to Irish society by An Garda Síochána. A phenomenal effort was made and sustained across the Garda organisation to aid in combatting the spread of COVID-19. I commend all Gardaí for the special efforts made to support the most vulnerable in our communities throughout the pandemic, particularly our elderly and ill family members and neighbours and those in our communities suffering from domestic abuse. One hundred years later, An Garda Síochána is again serving local communities in exceptional times.

The centrepiece of this year's celebrations will be the commemoration of the events of 27 August 1922, when Commissioner Staines led 380 Civic Guards through the Palace Street gates into Dublin Castle following its evacuation by the British Army.

Dublin Castle has an important role in the history of the service, and today it is also home to the Garda Memorial Garden. This is where we remember the members of An Garda Síochána who made the ultimate sacrifice in the course of their duty. When we celebrate An Garda Síochána, we celebrate and remember them.

The centenary is an opportunity for us all to publicly commemorate the people and the events of the past hundred years that have shaped the Garda organisation, and to thank all those members of An Garda Síochána and staff, and their families, for their unending dedication. My very best wishes to them all.

IN MEMORY
OF THE MEMBERS
OF THE GARDA SÍOCHÁNA
WHO GAVE THEIR LIVES
IN THE SERVICE OF
THEIR COUNTRY
✝

PREFACE

In marking the centenary of An Garda Síochána, the organisation wanted to tell its story, of how it came to be and how it developed over the generations into a highly trusted national and security policing service.

In doing so, we wanted as much as possible to give insights and perspectives into this from current and retired Garda personnel who have lived through it. It was also important to get an external view from academics, historians and experts.

On the face of it, this sounds relatively straightforward. But when we stepped back and looked at the vast array of work An Garda Síochána has done, the issues it has faced, and how it has evolved into a modern policing and security service over a period of 100 years, it quickly became apparent that not everything that has been achieved and not every element of the work done could be covered. So tough choices had to be made.

Many different types of policing exist in this country and we have tried to include as many of these as possible – from rural policing to border policing to city policing to specialist policing – each one unique and with disparate challenges. But, due to space constraints, undoubtedly we have missed some aspects that deserved attention.

To make the book easy for the reader to navigate, it has been divided into three main sections: The First Generation, The Second Generation, and Modern Policing, and the centenary of An Garda Síochána is covered largely chronologically.

I hope that the choices we have made will enable readers to get a sense of what it means to work for this incredible organisation that does so much good every single day.

There have been times, though, when that has not always been the case. When standards have fallen well below public expectation. It is important that this is recognised and acknowledged, as is the fact that the vast majority of Gardaí who are serving or who have served the people of this country have done so diligently and professionally.

Opposite page: Memorial stone at Garda Headquarters in the Phoenix Park.

The driving force for this book has been Garda Stephen Moore. The author of two previous books on the organisation, Stephen has done extensive and exhaustive work in sourcing authors, conducting interviews, and compiling and checking submissions. Stephen has been ably assisted by Sergeant John Reynolds, PhD, an expert in Garda history and author of two books on the topic, and the Garda Director of Communications, Andrew McLindon.

We have been fortunate to have had great support and expertise from The O'Brien Press in getting this project from concept to print. I want to thank all involved for their patience, professionalism and help in delivering a quality book.

An Garda Síochána is a unique police service. It is unarmed. It is strongly community-focused. It has a dual mandate of both policing and national security. It is a reflection of the people it serves.

As the father of modern policing, Robert Peel, said:

The police are the public and the public are the police; the police being only members of the public who are paid to give full time attention to duties which are incumbent on every citizen in the interests of community welfare and existence.

This book is dedicated to all those Garda personnel who throughout the century have served this country and its people so well. From the first recruits of An Garda Síochána who earned the respect of communities by their actions and commitment to supporting them; to the twelve brave women who in 1959 joined an all-male police service; to those who gave their lives in the line of duty to protect others. And to all those who worked so tirelessly to keep people safe over the last 100 years and do so now and into the future.

John Twomey
Chair of The Guardians *Editorial Board*
Deputy Commissioner, An Garda Síochána (2015-2021)

The information in the book is correct as of 31 May 2022.

Significant Events in 100 Years of An Garda Síochána

Garda Tom Daly

1922	**9 February**	Committee meets at Gresham Hotel, Dublin. The Civic Guards are formed (renamed Garda Síochána na hÉireann in August 1923).
	21 February	First members of An Garda Síochána attested at Royal Dublin Society (RDS), Ballsbridge. First Commissioner, Michael Staines, appointed.
	24 April	An Garda Síochána leave the RDS to facilitate the Spring Show, and move to Artillery Barracks, Kildare.
	15 May	Majority of Garda recruits revolt over training issues – the 'Kildare Mutiny' begins.
	June	Irish Civil War breaks out, leading to some desertions from An Garda Síochána.
	11 July	End of 'Kildare Mutiny' – discipline restored.
	August	First Gardaí deployed, initially in the counties around Dublin.
	August	The Criminal Investigation Department (CID) occupies Oriel House. At this point, it is entirely separate from An Garda Síochána.
	17 August	As his last official duty, Commissioner Staines leads 400 Gardaí to take over policing duties from Dublin Castle.
	September	General Eoin O'Duffy appointed Garda Commissioner; roll-out of recruits accelerated.
	October	First unarmed Gardaí deployed in disaffected south – initially to Waterford city.
	November	First Gardaí deployed in Cork/Kerry, ending most active phase of Civil War.
	14 November	Garda Henry Phelan becomes the first Garda to be shot dead in the line of duty.
	December	Royal Irish Constabulary (RIC) Depot in Phoenix Park handed over to An Garda Síochána as new Headquarters.

1923		*Iris an Garda* – precursor to *The Garda Review* – first published.
	October	CID disbanded because of concern over methods; partially reabsorbed by Dublin Metropolitan Police (DMP).
1925		Amalgamation of DMP and An Garda Síochána.
		Detective Branch of An Garda Síochána ('Special Branch') founded. First deployment in Leitrim.
1927	**July**	Kevin O'Higgins, Minister for Justice, assassinated by Irish Republican Army (IRA). Public Safety Act enacted.
1929	**December**	The case of the Missing Postman, Stradbally, Co. Waterford – disappearance of Larry Griffin leads to biggest criminal investigation in the history of An Garda Síochána, with allegations of Garda brutality.
1932	**February**	Commissioner O'Duffy plots Army/Garda coup – rejected by outgoing Government.
	March	Commissioner O'Duffy orders mass destruction of all Garda records for first decade of force.
1933	**February**	Éamon de Valera calls snap election, which Fianna Fáil wins comfortably. De Valera fires Garda Commissioner O'Duffy immediately.
	February	Eamon (Ned) Broy becomes third Garda Commissioner.
	July	Former Garda Commissioner O'Duffy appointed leader of Blueshirts – country teeters on edge of renewed civil war. Unrest and violence throughout country. Gardaí under frequent attack.
	August	Fearing Garda mutiny, first of nearly 400 Fianna Fáil party members attested as detectives and made members of Special Detective Unit (SDU) – the 'Broy Harriers'.
1933-36		Progressive replacement of senior Gardaí by Government.
		Constant street battles between An Garda Síochána, IRA and Blueshirts.
1937		Commissioner Broy retires. Civil servant Michael Kinnane is appointed fourth Commissioner.
1939	**December**	IRA raids Magazine Fort, Phoenix Park, stealing most of Defence Forces' ammunition reserve. Massive Garda response.
	December	Emergency Powers Act, 1939 passed to maintain Irish neutrality during the Second World War. An Garda Síochána given extended powers of search and arrest focused on tackling the IRA.
1940		Local Security Force (LSF) founded – augments An Garda Síochána during the Emergency; 25,000 strong in total. An Taca Síochána formed to supplement An Garda Síochána.

1940		Three Gardaí on duty shot and killed by IRA.
1952		Commissioner Kinnane dies in service; replaced by civil servant Daniel Costigan.
1957		Government closes significant number of Garda stations, merges Districts and allows Garda numbers to drop to near 6,000.
1959		Twelve female recruits commence training at Depot, Phoenix Park, and then go into service.
1961		'Macushla Revolt' – young Gardaí agitate for better pay and conditions.
1964		Garda Training Depot opened in Templemore – all training facilities transferred from Dublin.
1968		Conroy Commission established to look into Garda pay and working conditions.
1969		Beginning of the 'Troubles'.
1970	3 April	Garda Richard (Dick) Fallon shot dead after an armed robbery – first Garda to be killed during the period of the 'Troubles'. Twelve further Gardaí would be killed before the signing of The Good Friday Agreement in 1998.
1972		Riots in Dublin in aftermath of 'Bloody Sunday' – British Embassy burned down.
1974	17 May	Dublin and Monaghan bombings – deadliest incident in Republic during Troubles.
1977		Emergency Response Unit founded.
1979	8 January	Whiddy Island disaster in Bantry Bay – massive Garda response.
	29 September	Pope John Paul II arrives in Ireland – visit is biggest policing operation in history of State.
1981	18 July	Ballsbridge Riots – hundreds of Gardaí injured following protest by supporters of the H-Block hunger-strikers.
1982		'Phone Tapping Scandal' sees retirement of a number of senior officers.
1985	December	Garda Training Committee *Report on Probationer Training* – 'Walsh Report' – published.
1989		Namibian independence – first deployment of Gardaí on UN duty.
		Garda College reopens following renovation – first 'Walsh Report' recruits on two-year training programme.
1993		Beginning of transformation of Garda response to sexual offences and child abuse following emergence of shocking incidents such as the 'Kilkenny Incest Case'.

1995 **18 May**	Death of Sergeant Paul Reid in Sarajevo – first Garda killed on overseas service.
1996	Criminal Assets Bureau founded following murders of Veronica Guerin and Detective Garda Jerry McCabe.
	BSE (Mad Cow Disease) outbreak – thousands of Gardaí sent to Border in one of the biggest security operations in decades.
1998 **1 May**	Unofficial Garda industrial action – the 'Blue Flu'.
1999	Garda's PULSE (Police Using Leading Systems Effectively) computer system goes online.
2001	Foot and Mouth outbreak on island. Thousands of Gardaí sent to Border.
2005	Garda Síochána Act sets up new oversight body – Garda Inspectorate.
2007	Garda Síochána Ombudsman Commission (GSOC) founded.
2009	Recession leads to Garda recruitment being frozen.
2011 **May**	Queen Elizabeth II and US President Barack Obama visit Ireland within a week – massive security operation.
2013	Significant lengthy operation by Limerick Gardaí, supported by national units and in conjunction with other agencies, ends major organised feud after imprisonment of over sixty gang members, and large-scale seizures of drugs and assets.
2014	First woman appointed as Garda Commissioner – Nóirín O'Sullivan.
	Over 20,000 applications for first Garda recruitment campaign in five years.
2016	Establishment of Policing Authority to oversee the policing performance of An Garda Síochána.
2017	Disclosures Tribunal opens to examine allegations of mistreatment of Garda whistleblowers.
2018	Appointment of first Commissioner to have served with another police service – Drew Harris, the former Deputy Chief Constable of the Police Service of Northern Ireland (PSNI).
	Launch of Government's policing reform programme, *A Policing Service for Our Future*, based on Commission on Future of Policing in Ireland report.
2019	An Garda Síochána introduces biggest changes to organisation's structure since its foundation.
	Garda numbers reach highest level since 2010 – 14,307.
2020	COVID-19 pandemic – a range of measures put in place including substantial redeployment of Gardaí, introduction of Emergency Roster, and nationwide checkpoints and high-visibility patrolling.
2022	An Garda Síochána, in conjunction with international partners, undertakes wide-reaching transnational operation against Kinahan organised crime cartel.

Gardaí serve the public at all major sporting and cultural events nationwide, ensuring the safety of all involved. The first Special Olympic World Summer Games held outside the USA will be remembered as an astonishing success. The 2003 Games held in Ireland saw some 177 towns, cities and villages host national delegations, bringing the profile of the Games to a new high. Some 7,000 athletes from 150 countries participated and it remains to this day the biggest sporting event ever held in Ireland. Over the course of the nine days of the Games, An Garda Síochána played a pivotal role in the smooth running of this truly memorable event.

A REFLECTION

Assistant Commissioner John O'Driscoll

On Sunday, 17 January 2022, I walked across the yard at Dublin Castle, from the Garda National Drugs and Organised Crime Bureau, to where, 100 years earlier, Michael Collins, Chairman of the Provisional Government of the Irish Free State, participated in the handing over of Dublin Castle. Later in the day, the event was marked by a commemoration ceremony. However, for me, as I entered the Upper Yard at Dublin Castle, it was a time for personal reflection.

Michael Collins's mother and my own mother were born in the same house, on the O'Brien family farm, at Sam's Cross, Clonakilty, Co. Cork. His grandfather – my great, great, grandfather – was also born in the house. As a child, I, like Michael Collins – my first cousin, twice removed – visited the house frequently.

Assistant Commissioner John O'Driscoll.

When both of us were children, Michael Collins and I enjoyed the company of Michael O'Brien in that house at Sam's Cross. For Collins, who knew him in the earlier years of his life, Michael O'Brien was a first cousin and near neighbour; for me, he was my grandfather, and I had the privilege of knowing him in the final decades of his life.

In this house, Michael Collins and I were educated about Ireland and its history. For me, the history lessons included reference to Michael Collins's role in that history and, in particular, to the event commemorated at Dublin Castle and also the forming of An Garda Síochána. More poignantly, I would hear details about the final day of Michael Collins's life and his visit to Sam's Cross only hours before he died.

My grandfather used to recall emotionally how, on 22 August 1922, Michael Collins and his entourage parked outside the O'Brien family home at Sam's Cross. He described Michael disembarking from an armoured car and asking him to go across the fields to the Collins family home, to ask Johnny, his brother, to join them at Sam's Cross. A short time later, the three men – Michael, his brother Johnny and my grandfather – entered the Four Alls Public House, located across the road, where, with Jerry Collins, the proprietor, they chatted for a while before Michael left to continue his journey.

As Michael again boarded the armoured car, my grandfather's sister, Mary, called out to him from a bedroom window, asking him to take care. He told her not to worry – that all would work out. Tragically, a short time later, Michael Collins died at Béal na mBláth.

As a young child I used to accompany my grandfather to the annual commemoration ceremony at Béal na mBláth. One year, while sitting beside and chatting to Hannah Collins – Michael's then only surviving sibling – I took her photograph with my first camera. In later years, I wondered about the accuracy of that recollection, but recently I came across the negative of the photograph.

* * *

I am writing this reflection on 9 February 2022. One hundred years ago, this evening, Michael Collins held a meeting that led to the establishment of An Garda Síochána.

THE FIRST GENERATION

Above: Garda Richard (Dick) Nolan B123, joined the Dublin Metropolitan Police in 1923 and retired from An Garda Síochána in 1953. He served as a points man in College Street Station.
Opposite top: An early Traffic vehicle from the 'B' Division with a mounted PA system, 1938.
Opposite bottom: A Galway City District patrol car, a Ford Cortina 1976, parked opposite Galway Cathedral.

30th July 1938

CHAPTER 1

—A NEW FORCE —————————————————————

Garda Stephen Moore
Garda Tom Daly

T he Anglo-Irish Treaty, signed on 6 December 1921 and ratified by Dáil Éireann on 7 January 1922, heralded a new dawn for the people of Ireland. The War of Independence was over. A new force to police the island and uphold the 'Rule of Law' was being planned. However, this new force was to face a monumental battle to win acceptance and respect from the citizens whom it wished to serve. To understand fully what obstacles lay ahead, it is necessary to examine the history and culture of policing in Ireland prior to 1922.

THE ORIGINS OF POLICING IN IRELAND

Prior to the Dublin Police Act, 1786, law and order in Ireland were kept by three groups: night watchmen, employed by town boroughs; parish constables, employed by civil parish rectors; and military units, formed either as local militia or garrisoned regiments of the regular army. Over the years, the concept of a formalised policing system evolved. Constables were appointed in the baronies and parishes of Ireland, their duties being military and civil as well as criminal.

By the eighteenth century, this system of locally controlled self-policing was in decline, having become corrupt and ineffective. A growth in agrarian protest and political agitation from the 1760s onwards motivated central government to attempt major reform. The Dublin Police, introduced to the city in 1786, was the first centrally organised police force in the British Isles. In 1787, the Baronial Police ('Old Barney's') replaced the watchmen in most towns and formed the rural counterparts of the Dublin Police.

The development of civil policing began formally under the stewardship of Robert Peel. As Chief Secretary to Ireland, he initiated a structured form of policing, with the establishment of the Peace Preservation Force (1814–22). This was a special force, formed to support the Baronial Police, and dealt with unrest in any area proclaimed to be in a state of disturbance. The local ratepayers had to pay for the force, which made it extremely unpopular with landlords. By 1822, the Peace Preservation Force was deployed in 16 counties.

*A Dublin
Metropolitan
Police Officer at
Nelson's Pillar in
Dublin.*

In 1829, Robert Peel, having returned to London, established the London Metropolitan Police, or 'Peelers' as they were commonly known. Meanwhile, his successor in Ireland, Henry Gaulbourne, had introduced the Constabulary of Ireland Act, 1822, which gave Ireland a regional constabulary structure, known as the County Constabulary. Many members of the Peace Preservation Force joined the new force.

However, by the time Thomas Drummond became Under-Secretary to Ireland in 1835, there was huge opposition to civil policing. Making police reform his priority, he looked to London as a model. In 1836, at the behest of Drummond, two new Acts of Parliament were enacted, which paved the way for a reorganisation of policing

(1) The Constabulary of Ireland Act, 1836 established a centralised Irish Constabulary, a uniformed centralised force under the control of a single Inspector-General, who was based in Dublin Castle. In 1842, a Central Depot was provided in the Phoenix Park (Garda Headquarters). The force won the 'Royal' honour for its part in suppressing the Fenian Rising of 1867 and was henceforth known as the Royal Irish Constabulary (RIC).

(2) An Act for improving the Police in the District of the Dublin Metropolis, 1836 paved

the way for the establishment of the Dublin Metropolitan Police (DMP). On 1 January 1838, the DMP paraded for duty for the first time – 800 men, dressed in navy-blue top hats and frock coats, similar to their counterparts in London. As in London, the reform was an immediate success, giving the city social stability and peace it had never known.

By 1836, when the County Constabulary was officially merged with the reorganised Irish Constabulary, the force had grown to around 5,000 men.

AN GARDA SÍOCHÁNA

With the conclusion of The War of Independence and the signing of the Anglo-Irish Treaty, it was clear that the RIC had no place in policing in the new Ireland. This was agreed by Michael Collins, Chairman of the Provisional Government of Ireland, and the Chief Secretary, Sir Hamar Greenwood, as early as August 1921. Collins sought advice on policing from numerous quarters, especially from two agents he had used throughout the war, David Neligan and Eamon Broy, both of whom had worked in the 'G Division' of the DMP.

The level of violence occurring throughout the island of Ireland during this period was of great concern to the Government. Collins was eager to have the new police force trained and ready. However, with negative feedback from the anti-treaty side in relation to any new police force, it was clear that the formation of the new force would have to be achieved delicately, if not secretly. On 9 January 1922, Eamon de Valera announced his resignation as President of Dáil Éireann. The split between pro-treaty and anti-treaty supporters was now in the public eye, and the Provisional Government was tasked with trying to prevent that split from developing into open war.

The first meeting of the newly established committee for policing occurred on Thursday, 9 February 1922, in the Gresham Hotel, Dublin. In attendance at this meeting were Michael Collins; General Richard Mulcahy, Minister for Defence; Eamonn Duggan, Minister for Home Affairs; Michael Staines TD; General Eoin O'Duffy; and Patrick Walsh, a former RIC District Inspector.

In the last week of February 1922, a report produced by Michael Staines and his committee was forwarded to the Provisional Government, and its suggestions were accepted without reservation. The report proposed a unified, unarmed force with a maximum strength of 4,300 men. They would be led by a Commissioner who would be responsible to the Government. The force would be non-political in its administration and composition. The name chosen for the new force was the Civic Guard. The name Garda Síochána na hÉireann (Guardians of the

Peace of Ireland) was incorporated in the new insignia and adopted in the Garda Síochána (Temporary provisions) Regulations, 1923. The new legislation passed in Dáil Éireann on 18 August 1923, and it gave retrospective sanction to the Civic Guard. From that moment onwards, the Civic Guard would be known as An Garda Síochána. Michael Staines was appointed the first Commissioner of the new police force.

MICHAEL STAINES

A native of Newport, Co. Mayo, Michael Joseph Staines (1885–1955) committed himself wholly to the national cause, initially in the Gaelic League, and as a founder member of Sinn Féin. He was present in the Rotunda in November 1913 to hear Eoin MacNeill's call to arms, and he was elected to the Volunteer National Executive.

In the retreat from the GPO in 1916, Staines was one of James Connolly's stretcher bearers. Following the Rising, he was one of the many interned at the Frongoch internment camp in Wales. His election as Commandant there admitted him to the secret councils of the revolutionary movement. In the reorganisation of the Volunteers, he was appointed Director of Equipment and Quartermaster General, his duties bringing him into close contact with Michael Collins.

Staines entered politics as an Alderman of Dublin Corporation. In the 1918 General Election, he was returned for the constituency of Dublin North Central, and he was present at the meeting of the first Dáil on 21 January 1919.

As the first Commissioner of the new force, Staines made temporary headquarters for the Civic Guard at the Victorian institution known as the Royal Dublin Society (RDS) in Dublin. The first recruits arrived on 21 February 1922. Many of them had served in the national movement between 1916 and 1921 and were recommended by the officers and clergymen in their home parishes.

Michael Staines leading the new Civic Guard into Dublin Castle to take policing powers from the British.

However, the new force was not long in existence when serious issues became apparent among the new recruits – issues that mainly involved their superior officers. This has commonly become known as the 'Kildare Mutiny'.

PRELUDE TO THE KILDARE MUTINY

On a vile morning, 24 April 1922, nearly a thousand drably dressed young men formed up and marched in column from the Royal Dublin Society (RDS) to a nearby train station. Having housed the newly raised national police force of Europe's youngest emergent state for two months, the RDS proceeded to evict them to host the annual Spring Show. A short train trip brought the men to Kildare, where they were allocated a small section of the old Artillery Barracks, recently vacated by crown forces. To neither their surprise nor their joy, their new billets had recently been used as stables, and their first evening was spent cleaning dung in the darkness. To complete their introduction, it was found that all their bedding had been thoroughly soaked during the train journey to Kildare. In the meantime, under the direction of Commissioner Michael Staines, the Officer Corps of An Garda Síochána slept on fresh linen in the old officers' mess in the barracks. It was an inauspicious start in Kildare for an already divided force.

From the outset, An Garda Síochána exhibited the same increasingly factional tendencies as the rapidly disintegrating country that had just achieved independence. Some had wanted the Royal Irish Constabulary (RIC) to continue, albeit rebranded, to police the country. The rejection of this idea had led to the foundation of An Garda Síochána, but who on the island could train a new police force for the unique policing conditions here? With no little difficulty, Michael Collins had recruited a small cadre of former or serving RIC officers of unimpeachable republican credentials to train the new force. The clandestine nature of their work for independence meant that few outside the Irish Republican Army (IRA) high command knew how much they had risked for Ireland, and they were resented from the beginning by the young men they trained, who chafed at discipline imposed by those they still perceived as enemies. The men agitated constantly at what they perceived to be the 'RIC ethos' creeping into the service – and even before they had left Dublin, a 'Protest Committee' had been formed to register their complaints.

There were other fissures, too. From his appointment, Commissioner Staines and many of the new HQ staff left the training of new recruits to the former RIC officers and failed to connect with the men they led. To make matters worse, one of the IRA's finest fighting officers during the armed struggle, Commandant Paddy Brennan, was appointed Assistant Commissioner, with responsibility for recruitment. He proceeded to seed the new force with his former subordinates in the IRA – in its first year, approximately a third of all recruits were former Clare IRA men – a discrete, strong faction within the new force, loyal first and foremost to their old Commanding Officer, loyalty to their Commissioner a poor second. At a time when families, communities, and counties were splitting into pro- and anti-treaty camps, the IRA Executive, led by the militants, recognised the risk to the anti-treaty side of a successful roll-out of a new police force, and they did their best to undermine it. Attacks took place on prospective recruits and their families, particularly in disaffected counties in the south, and there had been almost nightly sniping on the Garda accommodation in the RDS prior to the move to Kildare. Small numbers of anti-treaty men joined in the RDS and became active in subverting the morale of the trainees.

The Mutiny

While initially conceived as an unarmed force, in fact, by the time of the Kildare move, An Garda Síochána possessed over 400 rifles and well over a thousand revolvers, passed to them for self-protection from the stores of the disbanding RIC. From the time of their arrival in Kildare, recruits began to steal these guns in large numbers from the armoury. On the morning of 15 May 1922, seven of the eight companies of Gardaí in training went into open revolt, demanding the immediate removal of named training officers from Kildare. The Commissioner and his officers were unable to restore order. Assistant Commissioner Brennan could not be found, claiming later that he was unaware of what was going to happen.

Having passed a night surrounded in his accommodation, the Commissioner departed urgently for Dublin with his staff, first moving the non-mutinous company to Newbridge Barracks. The mutineers, flushed with power, 'appointed' Assistant Commissioner Brennan as their new Commissioner, and filled the other ranks from within. On 16 May, an army unit with an armoured car arrived at the camp to disarm the mutineers. Confronted by 300 armed and irate recruits, the army withdrew, much to the annoyance of the Provisional Government.

On 17 June, the anti-treaty fifth column felt it had achieved as much as it was going to and struck a final blow to An Garda Síochána by engineering an anti-treaty raid on the Garda armoury, taking any remaining weapons and ammunition. During the mutiny, one recruit was fatally shot in a drunken escapade and a local hotel was pillaged and looted by recruits. On 11 July 1922, the sheepish recruits agreed to return to duty in return for a commission of inquiry into their grievances.

Opening on 13 July 1922, the Commission of Inquiry collapsed in farce after only a few days as the Gardaí (who had requested it) stopped co-operating with it. Nonetheless, it made findings and recommendations – finding that the recruits were young men who should not be punished, that An Garda Síochána should be disbanded and re-formed (technically, it was), that senior staff be replaced, that henceforth the service should be fully unarmed (it took months to achieve this), and that management should consider publishing an educational periodical to remedy the defects in Garda training – thus leading to the birth of Ireland's oldest magazine, the *Garda Review*.

By accident more than design, the unarmed ethos of the modern An Garda Síochána stems from the Kildare Mutiny. Having received little or no training of any sort in their formative months, these untrained recruits were the originators of a century of service.

MICHAEL STAINES RESIGNS

With his leadership questioned, Staines saw no course open to him other than to tender his resignation, which he did in May 1922, on the basis that his membership of Dáil Éireann and Dublin Corporation were incompatible with his responsibilities as Commissioner of the Civic Guard. Five days earlier, he had led the Civic Guard through the gates of Dublin Castle for the official handover of policing powers by the British to the Free State. He remained until the groundwork for the new force was completed, his resignation being accepted with regret on 22 August 1922. On 9 September, his last day in office, Michael Staines defined the role of the new unarmed police force: 'The Garda Síochána will succeed, not by force of arms or numbers, but on their moral authority as servants of the people.'

Active Service Unit of the Civic Guard in Portarlington in August 1922.

GENERAL EOIN O'DUFFY

General Eoin O'Duffy succeeded Michael Staines as Commissioner of the Civic Guard, by which time the first shots of the Civil War had been fired. O'Duffy was a charismatic man who gave outstanding leadership to the new force during its first critical decade in existence. Alongside the Minister for Home Affairs, Kevin O'Higgins, he reconstructed the service, which would police by consent and adhere to its initial non-political stand. By the end of 1922, over 2,000 Gardaí had been allocated to 190 stations nationwide, and on 17 December 1922, members of the Civic Guard moved to their new headquarters at the Phoenix Park Depot.

On 20 November 1922, nearly two months after his appointment, O'Duffy made his first public address to the service, reinforcing the idea of a non-political police force, serving all the people of this island. He described the Civic Guard in the following words:

> They are prohibited from taking part in politics, or from associating with one more
> than another. They will serve whatever government the people of Ireland put into
> office, and as far as they can, they will protect the lives and property of all the people,
> irrespective of whether they support government in office for the time being or not.

O'Duffy wanted An Garda Síochána to adhere to a strategy of passive resistance when confronted by armed forces. He told his men:

> I trust that when you go to your stations you will not let down the Civic Guard and
> the people by abandonment of your post at the behest of any armed coward who
> would shirk from meeting you in combat on an equal footing. Far better the grave
> than dishonour. Don't be alarmed at the sound of a shot. You have heard it before,
> and you were not subdued because you had right on your side and gunmen had only
> might.

Fortunately for the Civic Guard, a directive from Liam Lynch, the Chief-of-Staff of the anti-treaty forces, was sent to all republicans, instructing them not to inflict physical injuries on members of the new unarmed force. They were to intimidate them, drive them from the countryside, destroy their barracks, commandeer their property, and remove their uniforms, but the guards themselves were not to be touched. Throughout the Civil War, this direction was well observed with a few exceptions. If the anti-treaty side had not taken this stance, many more unarmed young men would have been killed. As it was, by September 1923, almost 200 Civic Guard stations had been attacked with more than sixty destroyed. Almost 400 members had reported being physically beaten up, stripped of their uniforms, publicly humiliated, or robbed of their property.

However, O'Duffy's strategy of passive resistance advanced the general public's acceptance of the Civic Guard, with many young guards settled into their new stations and communities by the end of the Civil War. O'Duffy's love for Gaelic games and the Irish language was instilled in members of the service. On arrival to stations throughout the country, young guards involved themselves in local clubs and associations, thus accelerating further their acceptance by the communities they served. In 1925, the DMP amalgamated with An Garda Síochána, creating one police force to administer the rule of law.

READY TO FACE THE FUTURE

An Garda Síochána emerged from the first decade of its existence in good shape, well established and organised, and ready to face the future. Credit must be given to the excellent leadership of Commissioner Eoin O'Duffy. The new Government had aimed to produce a police force that would be widely accepted and respected by the people of Ireland. They had to erase the memory of the armed, and in most cases despised, RIC; in the main, this was achieved.

It had been a traumatic ten years, though. Six Gardaí, three Sergeants, one Superintendent and Kevin O'Higgins – by then the Minister for Justice – had given their lives in the service of the newly formed state. Many more members had been seriously assaulted. They had been burned out of their stations in different parts of the country and stripped of their uniforms. Discipline had been tough. There was little improvement in pay or conditions of employment, though, and they had even suffered a reduction of 10 shillings per week at one stage when the state coffers were low. Their stations and living accommodation could only be described as primitive in most cases. It is difficult for the present generation to imagine the enormous difficulties faced by the first members of An Garda Síochána.

Crowds line O'Connell Street in Dublin for the funeral of Minister for Justice, Kevin O'Higgins, in 1927.

For an unarmed police force, it must have been a daunting task to try to enforce the law and keep order in a fledgling country struggling with the myriad issues created by gaining independence, whilst also dealing with internal hostilities, and in a country where armed bands roamed. The new Gardaí took it on, persevered and succeeded in bringing the rule of law to an entire nation. They showed incredible courage and dedication, and a will to succeed. The first decade since the formation of An Garda Síochána would end on a high.

The Eucharistic Congress in Dublin in 1932 was a huge international success. It not only showcased the new-found state in a good light, but it highlighted the professionalism of the State's new police force in managing the policing of such a high-profile event. Dignitaries attended the Congress from all over the world and numerous tributes were paid to An Garda Síochána for the manner in which they had policed the event.

As we celebrate the centenary of An Garda Síochána, we pay tribute to all those gallant men who chose to join a new force. We especially salute those who sacrificed their lives in the course of their duties to ensure that An Garda Síochána would succeed, and that the rule of law would prevail. This was the foundation stone on which the democratic rule of this country was founded.

Below left: In this image of Gardaí escorting the Irish Sweep tickets in 1932, members of the Dublin Metropolitan Gardaí wear helmets in contrast to the Garda Síochána uniform caps introduced in 1922.
Below right: The Eucharistic Congress of 1932 highlighted the professionalism of the State's new police force.

CHAPTER 2

——THE FIRST GENERATION——
– A FAMILY IN SERVICE

Garda Stephen Moore
Retired Sergeant Martin Drew

THE FIRST GUARD

Garda Stephen Moore

Born on 12 September 1892, in Westport, Co. Mayo, Patrick Joseph (PJ) Kerrigan joined the Royal Irish Constabulary (RIC) in June 1913, with the constable number 67355. On the outbreak of the First World War, PJ resigned from the RIC and joined the Army, enlisting in the Irish Guards Regiment in February 1915 as Private number 6802. A short time later, he was promoted to the rank of Lance Corporal. Having been wounded, PJ was medically discharged from his regiment and awarded the Silver Wound Badge. He returned to Ireland and married Molly Finnegan, with whom he had four children.

PJ Kerrigan was the first member of Garda rank to join the Civic Guard.

The Kerrigans were close friends of Alderman Michael Staines TD, the first Commissioner of Ireland's new police force. It was at the behest of Staines that PJ Kerrigan made his way to the Royal Dublin Society (RDS) showgrounds on the first day of recruitment for the Civic Guard. PJ was the first member of Garda rank to join the Civic Guard, being assigned registration number 1. Five weeks later, he was promoted to the rank of Sergeant. Patrick McAvinia from Co. Cavan was allocated registration number 2, and James Charles Clarke from Co. Westmeath was allocated registration number 3. All three men had served in the RIC. Overall, between 1922 and 1932, a total of 180 former RIC members would join the new police force.

On 7 August 1922, PJ Kerrigan's Civic Guard career ended abruptly when he was dismissed from the service for allegedly striking a prisoner. His defence was that he had been called a 'Black and Tan' by the prisoner who went on to say that 'Michael Collins and Major Ennis had sold out the country'. Although PJ's appeal of the decision was unsuccessful, his policing career did not end there.

On 8 March 1923, PJ enlisted in the national Army. However, his first love was police work, and on 30 September 1924, he joined the Dublin Metropolitan Police (DMP), being allocated warrant card number 12521. After training, he served at Chancery Lane Station in the 'A' Division, wearing the number A117. He served briefly with the DMP band, playing the clarinet.

In April 1925, the DMP was subsumed into An Garda Síochána, becoming the Dublin Metropolitan Division (DMD), policing the Dublin Metropolitan Area (DMA). PJ thus found himself back in An Garda Síochána.

Sickness befell PJ Kerrigan soon after this, resulting in his absence from work and causing him to run up debts trying to look after his wife and children. His debtors notified his authorities, and he was charged with breaches of discipline. His pleas for leniency fell on deaf ears and, on 20 February 1926, he resigned voluntarily from An Garda Síochána.

Having no means of earning an income, PJ emigrated to Liverpool and later to the United States via Canada, leaving his Irish family behind. In the US, he went by the name Joseph Kerrigan. There he met and married Minnie Kleinberger with whom he had two children. He died in 1946 and is buried in Albany, NY.

PJ Kerrigan (1892–1946), the first registered Civic Guard of the Irish Free State, survived the Great War, the Irish War of Independence, and the Irish Civil War. He emigrated to Liverpool, Canada, and the United States, was employed in two armies and three police forces, married twice, and had two families. His own human faults and failings caused both families to be unaware of each other. However, through the research and persistence of retired Garda, author and historian Jim Herlihy, this was finally rectified, and PJ's two families were introduced to each other. PJ's son, James Francis Kerrigan, was a guest of honour at an event in Co. Cork to mark the seventy-fifth anniversary of An Garda Síochána.

A FAMILY IN SERVICE
Retired Sergeant Martin Drew

Duhallow in Co. Cork is the largest barony in Ireland's largest county. It lies on the borders of Kerry and Limerick – Sliabh Luachra country, where musicians have gained renown for a unique style of polka and slide. Poets Aogán Ó Rathaille and Eoghan Rua Ó Suilleabháin were born in the vicinity and wrote some of the finest verse ever written in the Irish language. In darker days, Co. Cork gained notoriety for its resistance to British rule; during the War of Independence, men like Tom Barry in West Cork and Sean Moylan in North Cork tormented crown forces.

During this period, the Kanturk battalion of Duhallow fought under the command of Moylan, attacking forces at Tureengarriffe where Divisional Commissioner Holmes of the RIC was killed, and later at Clonbanin, killing Brigadier General Cummings, the highest-ranking British officer to die in the conflict. While only the Flying Column, a group of about thirty men, was involved in the actual fighting, the rest of the battalion – about 750 men in all – took part in scouting, acting as lookouts, raiding for arms, trenching the roads, or otherwise disrupting communications.

In July 1921, a truce brought an end to hostilities with the British. The treaty that followed led to bitter division within the ranks of the IRA. Many of the most effective IRA commanders in the country opposed the treaty. Cork was no exception. Although Moylan made strident efforts to avoid a split, he threw in his lot with the anti-treaty side. Those who accepted the treaty left the IRA, as the country descended into civil war.

John Drew

Among those who left the Kanturk battalion were four brothers from the village of Boherbue: John, Edward, Stephen and Michael Drew. Early in May 1922, John, my grandfather, boarded the train to Dublin. However, an IRA unit at Charleville dragged him off the train and brought him to a house in the town for questioning. He managed to escape out a window and continue his journey.

On 8 May 1922, John Drew presented himself at the gates of the former Artillery Barracks in Kildare town. The barracks was now being used to train the new police force, the Civic Guard. Most of the new recruits (95 per cent) were former IRA members. Many carried with them two letters of recommendation – a letter from an officer of the IRA, and a letter from their parish priest. John Drew was no exception. He had a letter of reference from Daniel Vaughan, a former IRA captain from North Cork and now pro-treaty TD, and a letter from the Rev. Brick, parish priest of Boherbue. He was formally admitted into the Civic Guard and was given the registration number 1038.

Station party at Castleisland, Co. Kerry, in the early 1920s. Garda John Drew is seated front left. Also seated are (L to R): Garda Billy Burns, Sergeant James Bohan, Garda McLoughlin. Standing behind are: Garda James Tiernan (left) and Garda Pat Spillane.

Discontent Among the Rank and File

When John Drew joined the Civic Guard, he joined a police force that was closely modelled on its predecessor, the RIC, which had been disbanded. The man who perhaps had most influence on the formation of the fledgling force was its Deputy Commissioner, Patrick

Walsh, a former District Inspector in the RIC. The new recruits received training in firearms, and during the early days of the Civil War, its members were sent out to perform armed duties, guarding railway junctions and banks.

Garda Commissioner Michael Staines and his Deputy, Patrick Walsh, needed to provide a professional policing service to a country beset by a crimewave that attended the Civil War; murder and robbery were rife, and the new recruits would soon be going out into the community, having little if any experience in crime investigation. To overcome this difficulty, they recruited experienced former RIC men as officers of the new force – men who would be able to direct and guide the new recruits in their stations. This provoked outrage amongst certain quarters within the Civic Guard; some members felt that they were being obliged to take orders from men who, until recently, would happily have seen them dangling from the end of a rope. Some of the more educated, ambitious men – many of them former officers in the IRA – saw these ex-RIC men as a threat to their hopes of achieving high office.

As detailed in the previous chapter, the men mutinied.

THE DREW BROTHERS

Below left: Garda Edward Drew in 1922. Below right: Garda Michael Drew.

Bizarrely, during the period of the stand-off, both factions recruited men into the service – the mutineers in Kildare and Commissioner Staines in Ship Street Barracks in Dublin. One of those who joined in Kildare at the time was Edward Drew, a brother of John. He joined on 24 May 1922 and was given the number 1332. The following day, he was joined by Henry Phelan 1347, who was destined to become the first Garda to be murdered in the line of duty.

In September 1922, both brothers completed training. John was one of a party that opened a station at Wicklow Town, and Edward went to Kilrush, Co. Clare. In December 1922, their brother, Stephen Drew, joined and was given the number 2818. He was followed in February 1923 by his eldest brother, Michael Drew, who was given the number 3488. In December 1924, a fifth brother, Richard, joined the new force, which had by now been renamed An Garda Síochána. He was given the registration number 6350.

The Drew household was a large household, with eleven boys and two girls who survived into adulthood. John, Edward, Stephen and Michael had joined the new police force during the Civil War, and Boherbue remained largely anti-treaty. One night, anti-treaty forces demonstrated their disapproval of the brothers joining An Garda Síochána by firing shots through the front door of the house, narrowly missing 10-year-old Patrick who was sleeping in a room at the back of the house. On another occasion, a bomb was thrown into the byre at the rear of the house; little damage was done and the pony that was in the byre was uninjured. Perhaps the most serious incident came when Patrick and his twin brother, Joseph, were assaulted on the street by their older brothers' former Commanding Officer, Timothy O'Connor (Thade Con óg). O'Connor, a man occasionally possessed by a mercurial temper, is reputed to have carried a firearm while working on the farm.

Michael Drew senior, the father of the boys, was a powerfully built man with a fiery disposition; he was not going to ignore the attack on his sons. The following Sunday, after mass, he attacked O'Connor with a chisel, swinging him around like a rag doll; O'Connor fired three shots during the tussle before they were separated. Wiser counsels prevailed and, as nobody had been hurt, the incident went no further.

Being unarmed did not spare An Garda Síochána from acts of violence: nine Gardaí were to be murdered before the decade was over. Many stations of the new force were also attacked by armed men. These attacks resulted in the death of Sergeant James Woods in Scartaglen, Co. Kerry in December 1923; and on 26 November 1926, more than fourteen Garda stations were attacked throughout the country, resulting in the deaths of Garda Hugh Ward at Hollyfort, Tipperary, and Sergeant James Fitzsimons at St Luke's, Cork. During one of these attacks on Castleisland Station, armed men knocked a pipe out of John's mouth, taking a tooth with it.

As time passed, some of the bitterness of the Civil War was forgotten, and An Garda Síochána gradually gained acceptance in the communities that had been anti-treaty. This process accelerated when the anti-treaty Fianna Fáil Government took office and recruited new members into the service. The brothers were gradually able to return home without fear of retribution. Tom Drew, a younger brother, was assisted by Sean Moylan – by now a Government minister – in obtaining employment with the Office of Public Works. Even O'Connor and old Michael Drew had a rapprochement; after accidently knocking him down following a funeral, O'Connor gave Michael a lift home, and they established cordial relations.

CHALLENGING CONDITIONS

Life in An Garda Síochána was incredibly challenging. While initially members of the service received a generous salary, this was drastically cut in one of the harsh budgets of the

1920s and never recovered. Working conditions were also difficult. Over half of the 1,200 RIC stations which had been abandoned during hostilities were destroyed to prevent their reoccupation by crown forces. This policy deprived An Garda Síochána of the use of many custom-built police stations. When Gardaí were deployed to towns and villages around the country, they were often forced to occupy accommodation unfit for human habitation. Sadly, Richard Drew, stationed in Bookeen, Co. Galway, was one of the many Gardaí whose health suffered because of substandard accommodation. He contracted tuberculosis within a short time of his arrival there, and he was discharged as medically unfit in August 1926. He died in February the following year; he was only 21 years of age.

Nor was a long career destined for Stephen who transferred to Howth, on the outskirts of Dublin. Like many men of this generation, he struggled to adapt to the rigours of a disciplined force. Having incurred a fine for the breach of some disciplinary measure, he resigned in 1927. Stephen emigrated to New York where his younger brother, Denis, helped him to secure a position at Chase Manhattan Bank, a post he held until his retirement in 1967. He came home for a visit in 1962, for my parents' wedding, and posed for a photograph in my father's Garda uniform – a photograph that unfortunately no longer survives. He died in New York in 1976; he was 74 years old.

A FAMILY AFFAIR

After a short attachment to Wicklow, my grandfather, John, transferred to Castleisland in 1923, and later to Cahersiveen. On his marriage to a local girl, Kathleen O'Donoghue, he was obliged to transfer out of Cahersiveen to Beaufort, where he was to spend the rest of his career. Edward transferred to Waterford and took part in the search for Larry Griffin, the missing postman of Stradbally, and later to Dublin. He finished his career at Harcourt Terrace, guarding the Dáil. Michael served at Clonroche in Wexford, later transferring to Store Street in Dublin. One of his colleagues at Store Street was Garda George Mordaunt who transferred to Special Branch in 1942. On 24 October of the same year, during a raid for wanted men, George was shot dead in the laneway at the rear of Michael's home at Oak Road in Donnycarney.

All three brothers retired on the eve of their sixty-third birthdays. Michael retired in 1961 and died in 1984, aged 86 years. John retired in 1962 and died at 89 years of age in 1989; Edward retired in 1965 and died in 1992 at the ripe old age of 90. They were part of a generation who, although poorly educated, had a deep commitment to service. Morally courageous, with a firm resolve, they rid Irish society of the gun, and they helped to forge a democracy which, although far from perfect, gave the following generations a firm foundation to work towards the ideals for which they strove – a republic that cherished all of its children.

Above left: Edward Drew outside Dáil Éireann in 1933.
Above right: Clonroche, Co. Wexford, 1924. Garda Michael Drew is standing on the left.

Only John had family that followed him into the service. His son Patrick joined in 1958 and his grandson Martin (the author) joined in 1984. Two nephews and a grandniece also joined An Garda Síochána. Further afield, John's grandson, Sean, joined the West Midlands Police, and a grandnephew, Kevin, is a New York State trooper.

Below left: PC Sean Drew, West Midlands Police, in 1983.
Below right: Templemore, 1984 (L to R): PC Sean Drew, Garda Martin Drew, Garda Paddy Drew, Detective Sergeant Michael Drew.

CHAPTER 3

GENERAL EOIN O'DUFFY

Retired Inspector John Duffy

I t is no exaggeration to say that the second Commissioner of An Garda Síochána was one of the most controversial figures in modern Irish history. This chapter looks at his career, focusing mainly on his constructive years, his military career, and as the head of the national police force.

EARLY YEARS AND MILITARY CAREER

Eoin O'Duffy was born Owen Duffy on 28 January 1890 in the townland of Carrigaduff, Castleblaney, in Co. Monaghan. The son of a small farmer and the youngest of seven children, he attended Laragh National School and was an avid learner. As a Catholic, he was very aware of the influence of colonial rule and the dominance of Protestants in Ulster. He denounced the practice of segregation, most notably in education. After school, he worked in the county surveyor's office, where he rose to the position of Assistant to the Surveyor in the Clones Road District.

During this period and prior to joining the Irish Volunteers and his association with Michael Collins, O'Duffy had become a prominent member of the Monaghan GAA. This has been regarded by many as a catalyst to his advancement within the Irish Volunteers. After some time as part of the Irish Volunteer Army, O'Duffy was appointed Deputy Chief-of-Staff to General Richard Mulcahy. He was also a member of the Irish Republican Brotherhood's (IRB) Supreme Council, alongside Michael Collins, and had access to a powerful network of intelligence and influence. He rose to the rank of General and during his tenure he enforced strict discipline in the Army, which had a dramatic impact, especially on several feuding officers insisting on getting their own way.

Along with being a disciplinarian, O'Duffy was also a powerful organiser. With the backing of Collins, he excelled at his role and helped to develop a more organised army. With the tragic death of Michael Collins on 22 August 1922, O'Duffy's military role came to an end. His extensive army experience rendered O'Duffy an ideal candidate to take charge of Ireland's new police force, An Garda Síochána (The Civic Guard) in September 1922.

COMMISSIONER OF AN GARDA SÍOCHÁNA (11 SEPTEMBER 1922 – 22 FEBRUARY 1933)

As outlined in previous chapters, soon after the formation of the Irish State in 1922, matters took a turn for the worse when some members of the new police force, who were sympathetic to the anti-treaty element in the Civil War, forced the hand of Commissioner Michael Staines. This arose after certain members sought to terminate the services of some ex-members of the Royal Irish Constabulary (RIC), whom Collins regarded as necessary to bring their experience to bear on the newly formed Garda Síochána.

Garda Commissioner Eoin O'Duffy.

At this time, the Minister for Justice, Kevin O'Higgins, approached the Chief-of-Staff of the Army, Richard Mulcahy, with a request that he would consider releasing O'Duffy who was then the officer in charge of the South Western Command. O'Higgins wanted O'Duffy to replace Staines as Garda Commissioner. However, this was contrary to the recommendation of the O'Sheil-McAuliffe Commission, which had been established to inquire into the Kildare Mutiny. The Commission had recommended the appointment of Commandant Seán Ó Muirthile as the replacement for Michael Staines. Staines had voluntarily offered his resignation on the grounds that, as an elected public representative, it was not appropriate that he hold the position of Commissioner.

O'Higgins had known O'Duffy and appreciated his track record in the Army. He saw his ability to organise and enforce discipline, which he believed was imperative for the success of the new police force, a force which had already been torn apart by disloyalty and indiscipline during the Kildare Mutiny. O'Duffy went about his new task with vigour and determination, insisting on the highest standards from all recruits. Many of his early directives (General Orders) laid down standards that forbade the failure to pay debts or to indulge in the drinking of alcohol. He encouraged active participation by the membership in sport, including athletics, cycling, boxing and GAA games.

His reverence for the Church and its ministry was to play a central role in the life of a Garda recruit. A recruit could not absent himself without good reason from the weekly church parade from the Phoenix Park Depot to the church in Aughrim Street. O'Duffy arranged that three priests would be present to hear confessions at the depot on given Saturdays. In 1923, he arranged a ceremony on the Depot Square to consecrate the service to the Sacred Heart.

The General was determined to leave his mark on the new police force in the new Irish state and there can be little doubt that he achieved that objective.

The banner headline on the *Garda Review* of August 1926 read:

The Garda is a soldier of peace. His war against the criminal never comes to an end.

He can never be a quitter; he has to win or fail, to defeat or be defeated.

O'Duffy possessed exceptional energy in drafting plans to increase recruitment. When he took charge in September 1922, he had a force of some 1,689 men, with recruitment virtually at a standstill. By 1925, following the amalgamation of the Dublin Metropolitan Police (DMP) with An Garda Síochána, the strength of the service had risen to 7,646. The new Commissioner was his own man when deciding recruitment policy; although under pressure to accept recruits with previous military service, he decided that a military man was not always the best to fulfil a policing role.

Another issue that came to the fore following his appointment was that of whether or not to arm the new police force. At first, he issued General Order No. 1, which provided for the use of carrying firearms on duty, training in their use, and the safe custody of firearms. However, when such orders were reissued in 1923, this provision was dropped and O'Duffy became wedded to the principle enunciated by his predecessor Michael Staines based on 'moral authority' as the best means to achieve legal compliance.

POLICING, SPORT, RELIGION AND INTERNATIONAL TRAVEL

Eoin O'Duffy had an ambition that the new force should be known internationally, and the vehicles he used to achieve this were largely policing, sport and religion. One of his first trips abroad as Garda Commissioner was to attend a police conference in New York in 1923. Here, he was able to forge many new ties, among whom was Colonel Walter Scott, the Honorary Chairman of the New York Police. Scott later provided a bond for the striking of the 'Scott Medal', which remains the highest award for valour bestowed on a member of An Garda Síochána who has been seriously injured or killed in the line of duty. Another example of his ambition to make known the new force on the foreign stage was his attendance at a conference in Berlin in 1926, to discuss policing with representatives of many European states.

His involvement with the National Athletic and Cycling Association of which he served as President took the Commissioner to many events in Great Britain and Northern Ireland. As team manager at the Los Angeles Olympic Games in 1932 – where Ireland had a team of four athletes and four boxers – O'Duffy experienced all that Los Angeles had to offer. He attended many social events and was entertained by Louis B. Mayer of Metro-Goldwyn-Mayer Studios. On his return, he advanced proposals that Ireland would provide a vast national stadium in the Phoenix Park. Support for such a proposal fell on deaf ears.

During his years as Garda Commissioner, based as he was in the Phoenix Park, he took a keen interest in developing the sports grounds and pitches that were part of Garda Head-quarters. He established Coiste Siamsa, a body to be run by the membership for the promotion of sporting activity within An Garda Síochána. His commitment to the GAA was strengthened by his belief in its influence in reducing political bitterness in the aftermath of the Civil War. His attitude to anti-treaty republicans was balanced, and he attended central council meetings of the GAA comprising many anti-treaty republicans. Certainly, his involvement in sport and international travel gave him a platform that he relished.

In 1928 – prompted by Fr William Gleeson, Jesuit chaplain of the Gardiner Street police sodality – Commissioner O'Duffy, much to the displeasure of the authorities in the Department of Justice, organised a pilgrimage of 300 uniformed members. The pilgrimage extended over three weeks and was to the Eternal City of Rome, with stops in London, Paris, and Turin. This was followed in 1930 by a pilgrimage to Lourdes of some 344 members; on this occasion, they did not parade in uniform.

INFLUENCE, LEGACY AND DECLINE

The complexity of character and personality that constituted Commissioner Eoin O'Duffy have been and will continue to be examined by historians for years to come. His time as a military officer and later as Garda Commissioner are the high points of his career. In terms of influence, many aspects of his policies for the management of the early force are still relevant today. His absolute insistence on high standards for both Army and Garda officers still surfaces whenever issues arise in either force.

A legacy that can rightly be attributed to O'Duffy is that of his determination to involve the new force in competitive sports – a tradition that preceded O'Duffy's Commissionership in both the DMP and the RIC, but one that likely would not have survived had he not taken the initiatives that he did.

A man who felt the pain of family loss in the tragic deaths on duty of those first members whose funerals he attended, he went on to initiate the establishment of the Garda Benevolent Fund. Likewise, in 1928, with the onset of tuberculosis, he supported the Representative

Body of the time to establish what we now know as 'The Garda Medical Aid Society', with a grant of £5,000 from the then 'Reward Fund'.

General O'Duffy's influence and legacy are well documented in the historic record of An Garda Síochána, but like many careers the final chapter can contain a downside, and in the case of the late Commissioner, there was certainly a significant downside. Having served successfully for almost eleven years, he faced the prospect of a general election in 1932 being won by Fianna Fáil under the leadership of Éamon de Valera, against whom O'Duffy had a hidden bias politically and whom he regarded as a threat to Irish democracy. Having been the strong man of law and order for eleven years and having previously been instrumental in organising the national Army, O'Duffy felt under threat with Fianna Fáil coming to power, and he entertained the possibility of staging a coup d'état. This fortunately did not happen, but its very contemplation was very problematic for O'Duffy's continued tenure as Garda Commissioner.

Nonetheless, O'Duffy presided over the 1932 election and the organisation of the Eucharistic Congress, both hugely successful in a policing sense. Notwithstanding their success, it was clear that de Valera, who led the new Government, did not wish to have O'Duffy occupy the position of Garda Commissioner.

In February 1933, an investigation was launched into suspicious activity involving Colonel Michael Hogan and Detective Inspector Billy O'Connell, who were suspected of being involved in a conspiracy orchestrated by O'Duffy, aimed at preventing de Valera from taking power after the 1932 election. This investigation led to the arrest of Hogan and O'Connell, both of whom were charged with breaches of the Official Secrets Act. On 22 February 1933, three days after the arrest of O'Connell and Hogan, O'Duffy was summoned to de Valera's office. The Taoiseach bluntly told O'Duffy that he had made an irrevocable decision to remove him from his post. O'Duffy, shocked, mentioned his successful handling of the Eucharistic Congress and the general election, and he demanded to know what offence he had committed. De Valera told him that there was no charge but that owing to the duties the police would soon be called upon to perform, his position would become a difficult one. O'Duffy refused to accept an alternative position; his career as a public servant was over. In a single afternoon, O'Duffy had lost his job, his home, his driver, his personal staff and a public role that had meant everything to him for over a decade. In the event, the jury at the Green Street trial of Colonel Michael Hogan and D/Inspector Billy O'Connell returned verdicts of 'not guilty'. Hogan was permitted to resume his military career, while O'Connell was reduced to the rank of a uniformed Sergeant – years later, in 1955, he was restored to the rank of Inspector.

As Garda Commissioner, O'Duffy executed his plan of mixing sport, culture, and religion to encourage the general public's acceptance of a new police force. He instilled a belief in the new force, powered by a new moral order, and his leadership is largely responsible for the high level of acceptance initially attained by An Garda Síochána from the Irish public, an acceptance which has not waned to this day. A land that was savagely divided by the Civil War came together, and the rule of law was maintained by the first members of this new police force.

The former Commissioner would go on to become leader and a founding member of the political party Fine Gael. However, his slide into fascism with the establishment of 'The Blue-shirts' alienated him from the political party whose democratic beliefs stood fast. The demise of O'Duffy's influence within An Garda Síochána, and in Irish society as a whole, can now be seen as a blessing, especially as we have seen the results of fascism on many of our European neighbours. In the evening of his life, he admitted that he had made two great mistakes – 'I did not marry, and I entered politics.'

Eoin O'Duffy died on 30 November 1944, at the early age of 52. To outward appearances, he was a broken man, physically infirm, and half-forgotten by the generation in whose service he had spent himself in his constructive years.

CHAPTER 4

ORIEL HOUSE

Inspector Paul Maher

Recruits to An Garda Síochána always learn about the 'Oriel House men' around the time the Civic Guard was formed. Were they police or military, or were they a bit of both?

Oriel House is the red-brick building on the corner of Westland Row and Fenian Street in Dublin. It was here that Michael Collins established a team of Military Intelligence officers and Criminal Investigation Department (CID) officers. Within that team was a Protection Corps tasked with protection detail for government ministers and departments. For a time, 'Oriel House' also had offices at 88 Merrion Square. Originally it reported to the Department of Defence but from September 1922 it began to report instead to the Department of Home Affairs.

In deciding whether they were police or military, it is important to consider the intended role of the service in Oriel House and what functions the Provisional Government wanted them to perform. Also important is the context of policing in Ireland at this time and how

Oriel House.

the men of Oriel House – mostly Volunteer veterans of the War of Independence – saw their role in the absence of training, statutory authority and oversight.

In his book, *Defending Ireland: The Irish State and its Enemies*, Professor Eunan O'Halpin asserts that Oriel House was established to

… provide protection for key figures in the Independence movement, to monitor the covert intelligence of the British Military and civilian agencies, and to tackle armed crime in Dublin. Its activities subsequently expanded to include intelligence work against opponents of the Treaty and, notoriously, the suppression of the anti-treaty IRA in Dublin.

According to the Army Enquiry Committee Papers, from the moment it was established, Oriel House suffered from a lack of direction. As testified by Captain Martin Nolan, it was seen by some as a dumping ground. Others, such as Colonel Eamon (Ned) Broy, later Garda Commissioner, regarded it as a stop-gap for those awaiting appointment to positions not yet established by the Provisional Government. Major General Russell gave evidence about the recruits to Oriel House:

> The very nature of their work before the Truce had left them anything but normal.… If such a disease as shell shock existed in the IRA … the first place to look for it would be amongst those men.

Working in a vacuum created by the British leaving and the Free State taking charge, the delicate administration faced its toughest challenge with the Civil War. Republican Police were now inefficient, the depleted Dublin Metropolitan Police (DMP) was unarmed and incapable of meeting the threat posed by the Irregulars, and the unarmed Civic Guard, operating outside Dublin, was just getting started and was simply not yet up to the task.

WHO'S IN CHARGE?

After the death of Michael Collins in August 1922, General Mulcahy filled much of the leadership vacuum. The firing of Mulcahy for unilaterally deciding on a round-up of Irish Republican Army (IRA) leaders during the 'Army Mutiny' crisis of 1924 clarified the boundary between civil and military authority in the first two years of the Irish Free State, but the waters were muddied, and Oriel House operated in those waters.

The political situation regarding policing was difficult. According to Dr Brian McCarthy, on 14 April 1922, the day the Four Courts were occupied:

> Liam Mellows, secretary to the Army Executive, wrote to the Secretary of Dáil Éireann on behalf of the 'Irregulars' and proposed six conditions to prevent the Civil War. One of the conditions required the Provisional Government to disband the Civic Guard.

Irregulars felt no loyalty towards the new police force, which was trying to become established, trained and distributed throughout the Free State as rapidly as possible. The divided loyalties manifested themselves in incidents such as the occupation of the Four Courts, the Kildare Mutiny and in the difficulties faced in bedding down the courts. Oriel House, despite the lack of clarity as to its position and role, faced down some of those challenges. However, the men lacked training and discipline and were seen as secondary to Army Intelligence.

The leadership at Oriel House included War of Independence veterans who were

Top: Firearms Authorisation Card – Webley Revolver – Authorised by Superintendent Joe Kinsella, Criminal Investigation Department, Oriel House.
Above: Detective Thomas Storey, Oriel House.
(Both photographs: courtesy Garda Museum Oriel House Collection.)

used to getting things done under wartime conditions. According to Conor Brady:

> From August 1921 until November 1923 when they were disbanded, Oriel House
> and its Detectives became a feared institution, not only in Dublin but throughout the
> country. They were headed by Pat Moynihan one of Collins' most trusted agents, who
> had a vital role in his intelligence network.... Moynihan had three Lieutenants, Joe
> Kinsella, a 1916 veteran who had acted as arms and explosives distribution organiser
> during the war from his office at the Inchicore Rail Yard, Finion O'Driscoll, a tough
> intelligence officer from Cork, and Peter Ennis, who was subsequently to become head
> of the Garda Síochána's Special Branch.

Indeed, the politicians of the Provisional Government believed that Oriel House was a necessary entity and even justified its methods because of the effectiveness of the results, as they saw them. In a witness statement, Ernest Blythe recalled:

> Oriel House was a somewhat doubtful institution, and a good many suggestions were
> made that its methods were too like the worst we hear. However … Oriel House at
> the time was carrying on under war conditions, and if investigators were sometimes
> somewhat tough with prisoners, I should say that the circumstances were such that
> tough methods were not only excusable, but inevitable.
>
> I heard later on that Oriel House operated very successfully. I think that Mr Moynihan
> had some of the qualities of the detective of fiction and I heard of him following up
> very slight clues and effecting arrests, and locating arms dumps.

Not everyone shared Blythe's view that their methods were excusable and inevitable. On 5 November 1922, Maud Gonne McBride and Charlotte Despard, suffragette and pacifist, organised marches to protest at how the Provisional Government treated prisoners.

THE COURTS

During the War of Independence, the Sinn Féin courts, which ran parallel to the crown courts, had their decisions enforced by the Republican Police. Post-treaty, during the Oriel House era, internal relationships between pro- and anti-treaty cohorts were fraught, and the relationships between the Republican inheritors of British institutions and the agents within those institutions – such as the judiciary – must have been trying.

Captain Moynihan of Oriel House often brought himself to the attention of the national press. When he crossed swords with a Dublin magistrate, it only added to his standing and reputation in Oriel House. However, his bombastic behaviour towards the court was seen as a very poor example to his subordinates and he was reported to the Minister for Home Affairs.

The occupation and subsequent bombardment of the Four Courts may have been seen by some as the bombardment of the British legal system.

POLICE BUSINESS – INVESTIGATIONS BY ORIEL HOUSE

The recently acquired 'Division Letters Book', dating from 20 February 1922 to 31 May 1923, gives an insight into what was reported to Oriel House and what was investigated. The DMP reported serious crime incidents only, but after a few weeks they began to end their reports with, 'Report to Oriel House'.

Prisoners taken by Oriel House and Free State troops were brought to Wellington (later Griffith) Barracks, and Military Tribunal results were not disclosed to the DMP. The DMP also dealt with the activities of demobilised British troops who were out and getting drunk during curfew. Armed robberies were rife, as was an element of misinformation and propaganda. The Division Letters Book includes many reports of robberies where witnesses stated that the assailants told them: 'We are from Oriel House'.

The report of one investigation into a robbery at Winstanley's, near Christchurch details the arrest and charge of William Donoghue by 46G of Oriel House. Parallel to such investigations were Military Tribunals that were administered by the Free State Army, suggesting that the prosecution of crime and the trial of offenders did not follow any specific formula.

On 11 December, a factory at 37 Kevin Street Lower was raided by a party of armed men. The Managing Director, Reuben Segal of Dufferin Avenue, reported to Oriel House officers that 150 CID badges had been stolen.

An incident of personation occurred on 27 December 1922 when two men announced themselves as Oriel House men at 48 Newmarket. Staff raised the alarm and the DMP took them into custody, whereupon both men admitted that they were looking for drink. Oriel House brought them to the Magistrates Court where they were remanded in custody to be dealt with by the Military courts.

CONTEMPT OF COURT.

Mr. Johnson said that he would like the Minister to inform the House whether his attention had been drawn to a case reported in the newspapers the other day concerning the conduct of the Director of this Department towards the police magistrate (Mr. Lupton), which showed a distinct want of understanding of his position as the head of the C.I.D.

He committed the grossest contempt of court, which was by no means a good example to the members of his force He (Mr. Johnson) thought that it was desirable that they should know whether the Minister had taken due notice of the conduct of Captain Moynihan in court, and let him understand that the duty of a police officer, whether of a disciplinary department or any other, was to give assistance in the administration of justice, and to treat a magistrate or judge in charge of a court with respect.

It was necessary for the re-assurance of the public that they should know that the Minister frowned upon the conduct of the head of that Department in that instance, and that there should be no encouragement to officers of the C.I.D. or other forces to flout magistrates.

Irish Independent article, 1922. Exact date unknown.

CID badge. (Garda Museum Collection)

DISCIPLINE IN ORIEL HOUSE

In an anxious week for Oriel House, some were found the worse for wear by an officer of the Free State Army, as noted in an army report dated 27 December 1922. On an engagement with Oriel House men earlier that week, detectives had been drunk and carrying firearms, with their Commanding Officer barely managing to prevent shootings between both parties.

Military Archive files contain later complaints relating to discipline. For example, on 17 January 1923, Detective Polton showed firearms to female attendants at the Theatre Royal. In April, a raid at 45 Lower Gardiner Street resulted in missing property being reported to Captain Moynihan by the owner, a former officer in the Irish Volunteers.

SERIOUS INCIDENTS

The following catalogue of incidents involving injury to Oriel House men was ascertained from records at the Garda Museum:

- On 25 August 1922, Criminal Investigation Department (CID) Motor Driver John J. Murray was wounded in the leg at Dean's Grange; he died later of his wounds.
- On 27 August 1922, a bomb was thrown at a party of CID men at the Canal Bridge, Drumcondra. It failed to hit the men but exploded outside a provision store and injured two women.
- On 17 September 1922, Oriel House was stormed, and CID officer Anthony Deane was shot dead.
- On 31 October 1922, there was attack on Oriel House by Dublin IRA Battalion V, involving explosives.
- On 22 December 1922, CID Assistant Inspector Matt Daly was wounded at Ellis Quay, Dublin; he died on 29 December 1922.
- On 22 December 1922, while patrolling the Arran Quay area with the CID and Free State troops, CID Assistant Inspector Matt Daly was ambushed and shot. He died later of his wounds. Meanwhile, Constable Weldon of the Bridewell DMP station was kept out of the way at gunpoint by one of the assailants.
- In the summer of 1923, the Civil War ended. However, on 19 October 1923, Thomas Fitzgerald, CID Motor Driver, was shot dead at Ashtown, Co. Dublin following an armed robbery of £40 from Rathbornes' candle factory at Castleknock by three dispatch riders of the National Army.

ATROCITIES

Free State Intelligence officers and Oriel House have borne the shame of many atrocities of the Civil War. The murder of Noel Lemass, brother of Civic Guard instructor and later Taoiseach Seán Lemass, is one of the most notorious incidents. Another was Colonel Charlie Dalton's arrest of three young republicans who were subsequently murdered in Clondalkin. Commissioner Michael Staines of the Civic Guard stated at an inquest that the Civic Guard had no connection with Oriel House or Free State Intelligence.

Most of the criticism contained in the records of the Bureau of Military History is of Oriel House and CID. Yet the pro-treaty Government allowed them the freedom to operate in any manner they deemed appropriate. Frank Sherwin, an anti-treaty Volunteer, said that the Army Intelligence Units were a law unto themselves, often drunk and trigger happy and that 'Wellington Barracks was the worst'.

DISBANDMENT OF ORIEL HOUSE

The Oriel House units were quickly disbanded soon after the Civil War, with many personnel going into the DMP and An Garda Síochána.

When Collins established Oriel House, he had a minimum of two men from each county allocated to the unit to maintain an element of familiarity throughout the State. If IRA Brigade officers were less than supportive of the Civic Guard, then Oriel House men were tasked to nominate and vouch for recruits. In his book, *Policing Independent Ireland 1922–1982*, Sergeant Greg Allen notes that this recruitment drive was supported by Oriel House, with Captain Ennis of Oriel House distributing Civic Guard recruitment forms to each IRA brigade officer.

CHAPTER 5

EAMON BROY

Áine Broy

My father, Colonel Eamon (Ned) Broy, was born in Rathangan, Co. Kildare, on 22 November 1887, three years prior to Michael Collins and five years after Éamon de Valera. Like those gentlemen, he would go on to play a key role in the fight for Irish freedom. The son of a farmer, Patrick Broy, and his wife Mary (née Berry), who hailed from Clonbrock, Co. Offaly, Ned had three siblings – Michael, John, and Margaret – all of whom lived well into old age.

A STRONG SENSE OF IRISH NATIONALISM

Having been taught French and German by local teacher Joseph Byrne, Ned developed a love of languages at a young age. This remained with him throughout his life, and often assisted him in different chosen careers. He was also greatly influenced by Sam Hanks, a Quaker who ran the local flour mill in Rathangan. With a library of books, many of them concerning Irish nationalism, Hanks had concluded that violence and not speechmaking would be necessary for Irish patriots to succeed. This idea was consumed by the young Ned, and the two practised rifle-shooting together and discussed the future of a free Ireland. At Tom Guinan's local forge, Ned heard stories from the older residents of Rathangan. Their accounts of the Irish Rebellion of 1798 and the Irish struggle instilled in him a strong sense of nationalism.

By 1909, Broy was in Dublin attending Gaelic League classes. His Irish-language teacher was Sinéad Flanagan whom he described as 'a beautiful dainty little lady'. He often recalled that all the men in the class were mad about her until a tall, thin, bespectacled man whisked her off and married her. That man was Éamon de Valera.

Broy attended Skerry's College in Dublin and, in 1911, joined the Dublin Metropolitan Police (DMP). He was a keen athlete, and the great athletic facilities owned by the DMP encouraged him to join. At this time, he achieved his matriculation in French, English, history and geography, and also attended night classes in motor engineering, mechanics and typewriting. His typewriting skills would play a vital role in his career in the DMP, and in his relationship with Michael Collins and the Irish Republican Army (IRA).

After his initial six-month training in the DMP Depot at Kevin Street, Broy started work in the 'E Division'. In 1917, he was appointed to the 'G Division' and moved into his new station at Great Brunswick Street (modern-day Pearse Street). The 'G Division' was the political section of the DMP, and Broy had access to the most confidential files held within the British Intelligence Services operating in Ireland at the time. He soon began making carbon copies, which he passed on through intermediaries to Collins.

MEETING MICHAEL COLLINS

My father did not meet Michael Collins until early 1919. He later described their first meeting:

> I was deeply intrigued to meet him and on looking up the police record, I discovered he was a Cork man, a six-footer, very intelligent, young and powerful. There was no photograph of him at the time. From the moment I saw Michael at the door, before he had time to walk across the room and shake hands – I knew he was the man. He was very handsome, obviously full of energy, and with a mind as quick as lightning. We talked from 8 p.m. to midnight.

Broy described Michael Collins as 'very handsome, obviously full of energy, and with a mind as quick as lightning'.

Both men agreed that the use of force was essential to securing independence from the British, and that the Royal Irish Constabulary (RIC) should be targeted, especially in rural stations.

On one occasion during the War of Independence, a detective from the DMP became aware that the Dáil was meeting in the Mansion House. He advised the 'G Division', telling them to bring a military party, as Collins and several other wanted men would be in attendance. Broy telephoned Éamon de Valera with this information – de Valera was not a wanted man at this time. Fearing that the operator might inform the authorities, Broy put his knowledge of languages to good use. To avoid speaking in English and having his conversation overheard, and conscious that the operator might also be able to understand Irish, he decided to converse in French.

The military proceeded to surround the Dáil, but Collins and the other wanted men were long gone.

SMUGGLING COLLINS INTO GREAT BRUNSWICK STREET

By spring 1919, Broy recognised that to understand the workings of the 'G Division' fully, it would be beneficial for Collins to visit the records office in Great Brunswick Street and read the record books for himself. On 7 April 1919, Broy smuggled Collins and an accomplice, Sean Nunan, into the station. The plan required Collins to telephone the station at midnight using the codename 'Field'; Broy's codename was 'Long'. A report earlier in the day about shootings in nearby Store Street nearly halted their plan. Also working that night was Inspector Daniel Barrett, a renowned busybody who would have been quick to report a light in an office. Despite the obstacles, when Collins rang at midnight and said, 'Field here, is that Long?' Broy replied, 'Yes … bring a candle.' This meant that the coast was clear, and they could proceed.

A copy of the station's master key had earlier been made, and when Collins and Nunan arrived at the station, Broy let them in, gave them the key and showed them the way to the records office. He also showed them a way out in case anything was to happen. Just as he was doing this, a stone came through the station window. Collins and Nunan hid in a dark passage as Broy went to investigate. A policeman was arresting a drunken soldier who had thrown the stone. When things calmed down again, Broy returned to Collins and Nunan and they pressed on. Collins laughed when asked if he had brought *'G Division' CID* the candle, saying that he had thought it a joke, so Broy went and got some candles and *of the DMP, at* matches. He then locked Collins and Nunan into the records room, allowing them to *Dublin Castle, 23* conduct their investigations.
February 1922.

At the unveiling of the plaque at Pearse Street Garda Station, in the middle Áine Broy, and on both sides members of the Collins family, Assistant Commissioner John O'Driscoll and former Justice Minister Nore Owen.

The two men stayed until approximately 5 a.m. Collins wanted to know the exact degree of British knowledge regarding the Volunteers. He also wanted to use the Police Model, with improvements and modifications for Volunteer purposes. One hundred years to the day, on 7 April 2020, I had the great honour to unveil a plaque at the door where my father smuggled Collins and Nunan into the station. The bravery they all had shown was astonishing, risking their lives for Irish freedom.

Michael Collins and Eamon Broy became good friends and met frequently at Tommy Gay's house on Haddon Road in Clontarf, where they also met other DMP informers.

Prison and London

Ned Broy was arrested in February 1921 and imprisoned at Arbour Hill Military Prison. He was charged with high treason, which carried a death sentence on conviction, and spent five and a half months in solitary confinement, most of it wearing the same old raincoat. Collins took the time to go to Callaghan's on Dame Street, where the DMP uniforms were made; he got my father's measurements and had a new suit made for him, which he presented to my father in prison. This was a powerful gesture by Collins at a time when so much was going on. The truce of July 1921 saved my father's life, and Collins made sure of his release.

After his release from prison, Broy was asked by Collins to accompany him as secretary to the London treaty negotiations in October 1921. He stayed at 15 Cadogan Gardens with Collins and members of 'The Squad'. His room was next to Collins's room on the third floor. Each day, both men would attend mass at 8 a.m. at Brompton Oratory, which was nearby.

Garda Commissioner Eamon Broy.

POST-TREATY CAREER

Although Broy supported the treaty side, he was not actively involved in the Civil War. Collins appointed him adjutant of the first Irish Air Corps, which gave him the title Colonel. He joined An Garda Síochána in 1925 with the rank of Chief Superintendent. In 1933, when Fianna Fáil replaced Cuman na nGaedheal in Government, de Valera appointed him Commissioner, replacing General Eoin O'Duffy.

Serving as Commissioner until his retirement in June 1938, Broy navigated the perilous waters of an ever-changing political landscape in a fledgling state recovering from bloody civil war. Always, he tried to adhere to the non-political ethos upon which the service was founded. He represented An Garda Síochána at conferences across Europe, where his knowledge of languages enabled him to communicate easily with his peers from other jurisdictions.

LEGACY

It was only after reading his witness statements held at the Military Archives that I fully appreciated my father's bravery and dedication. In August 1959, I first accompanied him to Glasnevin Cemetery to commemorate Michael Collins and Arthur Griffith. I have attended every commemoration since, but sadly without the company of my father since his passing in January 1972.

In recent years, it has been acknowledged that Eamon Broy played a pivotal role during the War of Independence. He was a courageous republican and a proud Irishman. As Commissioner of An Garda Síochána, he helped a new police force to earn the trust and acceptance of a nation. He continued the work of previous commissioners and maintained the non-political ethos of the service. This was hard at times, and loyalties were tested, but by the time of his retirement An Garda Síochána had taken a further foothold in the Irish psyche.

CHAPTER 6

PROGRESS AND GOODWILL

Retired Inspector Phelim Patrick (Pat) McGee

From the 1920s to the 1960s, the organisation and its personnel underwent significant change and growth, including increased Garda numbers, the outbreak of the Second World War, and the introduction of new ways of policing.

EARLY YEARS

Following Michael Staines' resignation as the first Commissioner of An Garda Síochána in August 1922, he was succeeded by Eoin O'Duffy, who took command of a force of 1,689 men – the recruiting of female members was still some 37 years away. With recruiting virtually at a standstill, the new Commissioner, with a small HQ staff, worked long hours with great urgency to establish the new police force. Through their efforts, a tentative establishment scheme was presented to the Department of Home Affairs, providing for a complement of

Garda training, 1938.

5,520. By February 1924, with the service close to establishment strength, there were on file 6,000 applications from hopeful candidates, bringing to 30,000 the number of applications that had been examined since O'Duffy's appointment as Commissioner. The amalgamation in 1925 of An Garda Síochána and the Dublin Metropolitan Police (DMP) provided for a maximum establishment nationally of 7,646 men.

Candidates sat an examination in arithmetic and dictation and in the ability to write 'a sensible letter'. O'Duffy welcomed a Home Affairs proposal to give responsibility for the entrance examination to the Civil Service Commission. However, he did criticise the set standard which compared to third class in primary school, deeming it unrealistic as the service made its way through the 1920s into the 1930s. In a letter to the Department of Justice, dated 28 February 1931, the Commissioner outlined: 'the day of the dull, unintelligent policeman is gone.'

ARCHAIC RESTRICTIONS

The Garda Code (1928) brought together in one volume all the instructions that had been issued as routine orders and circulars since 1922. In the introduction, 'discipline and obedience' were defined as 'that which makes a man responsive to authority and enables him to persevere in the accomplishment of his purpose'.

The lives of the first generation of guards, on and off duty, were restricted to an extraordinary extent. The Code provided for every conceivable contingency in the local management of the service. Many of its archaic rules were adapted word for word from the Royal Irish Constabulary (RIC) Code. Good order in barracks was copper-fastened in 65 separate regulations.

Garda on duty, 1938.

The men worked seven days a week: reveille (wake-up call) at 7.45 a.m., morning parade at 9 a.m., followed by a study programme of police duties. This class lasted for an hour but was not counted in the return of duties performed. The day ended with a roll-call at 11 p.m. When men were not on patrol, they were required to parade in the dayroom. Leave of absence of any kind, including annual leave, was 'a privilege and not a right'.

In later years, Commissioner Kinnane made efforts to address the difficulty of outmoded regulations. In doing so, he had to move cautiously to maintain the delicate balance between his ambition for a less stringent regime and the needs of a disciplined force. He also needed to avoid upsetting more conservative officers. At the time, his initiatives were welcomed by the *Garda Review* as 'the first step in a new deal ... from now on our members can feel assured that their welfare will be a major consideration in the administration of the force'.

CHANGING TIMES

Following the general election in 1932, the new administration replaced Eoin O'Duffy as Garda Commissioner with Eamon Broy. History has shown that the administration skills of Eoin O'Duffy played no small part in laying the foundation stones of a modern police force that has served the country well up to and including the present day.

As Commissioner from 1933 to 1938, Eamon Broy made a significant contribution to morale by fostering Garda sports. His friend, David Neligan, recalled: 'he had only one love, athletics'. In acknowledgement of his lifelong commitment, Broy was elected President of the National Cycling and Athletic Association (NACA) and later, in 1935, he was appointed President of the Olympic Council of Ireland. Leaving his mark as a catalyst in the process of healing the wounds of civil war, he made way for Michael J. Kinnane, who brought to the office of Commissioner the insights of many years of experience as Assistant Secretary in the Department of Justice, having watched over the development of the service since its formation in 1922.

THE EMERGENCY

The outbreak in 1939 of the Second World War saw An Garda Síochána play a major role in dealing with any threat arising from that conflict. In the spring of 1940, as the German armies beset the Low Countries and swept across France, the part-time soldiers of the Volunteer Reserve left the towns and villages to join the war effort, leaving Ireland without a home guard. In a radio broadcast, the Taoiseach, Éamon de Valera, called for the organisation of a Local Security Force (LSF).

Commissioner Michael Kinnane delegated his most experienced officer, Deputy Commissioner W.R.E. Murphy, to organise the LSF. Putting all other work aside, Murphy responded to the challenge with great zeal. On 4 June, he circulated instructions to all members of the service, followed on 24 June by further instructions on the separation of military and auxiliary police functions, and on 26 June and 13 July on the particular duties of the LSF.

An Garda Síochána was a foundation stone to the success of this project. The then leader of Fine Gael, W.T. Cosgrave, said at the time that the guards were 'good servants of the State,

Top left: Men training for the Local Security Force (LSF), 1940.
Top right: A member of the LSF receives a message, 1940.
Above: Female members of the LSF.

capable at a moment's notice of either stopping traffic to let children cross or defending the State with their lives if necessary'. Men of all ages volunteered in their tens of thousands, including old republicans who had never crossed the threshold of a Garda station. Local Sergeants instructed the volunteers in basic police duties, with citizens living in the vicinity of stations rostered for station or cordon duties or as messengers.

Superintendents became directly involved in organising a new army reserve, the Local Defence Force (LDF). On 1 January 1941, the task of overseeing the LDF was transferred to the Army, with a Garda seconded as an administrative officer in each LDF area. The LSF remained until the end of the Emergency in 1946.

AN TACA SÍOCHÁNA

It was deemed necessary at this time to recruit a special reserve force to supplement the existing strength of An Garda Síochána. Established under the Emergency Powers (Temporary

Special Police Force) Order, 1939, it was known as 'An Taca Síochána'. Consisting of up to a maximum of 400 men, it proved to be a major success. Members of An Taca Síochána had the power of arrest and wore Garda uniforms. After a short period, they were appointed permanent members of An Garda Síochána. In later years, some of them moved steadily through the ranks, including Edmund Garvey who became Commissioner in September 1975.

In Dáil Éireann, on 27 September 1939, the Minister for Justice, Gerald Boland, outlined the function and cost of An Taca Síochána:

> The Commissioner ... has selected from a list of candidates for An Garda Síochána the names of approximately 400 men who seem to him to have the best prima facie qualifications. These men have been invited to attend at Garda Headquarters where they are at present being tested as to suitability. Those who pass the test, up to a maximum of 400, will be recruited as temporary Gardaí under the title of the Taca Síochána. They will be paid at a rate of £3 a week, will wear Garda uniform, will serve under Garda Officers, and will, in practice, be indistinguishable from ordinary Gardaí. It is intended to assign them to Garda stations where they will perform ordinary police duties. It is not intended to appoint any Sergeants, Inspectors, or higher officers in the temporary force.

DISBANDMENT OF THE LSF

When the war ended, the services of the Local Security Force were no longer required. The following extract from the *Garda Review*, August 1945, paid tribute to its members:

> The official disbandment of the Local Security Force (LSF) after five years brought to an end an Emergency Service that added a new and bright page to the short but, nevertheless, storied history of An Garda Síochána. When the first call came, in June 1940, it met with a whole-hearted countrywide response. The manner in which these lay police learned their spare time calling and carried out their duties was one of the outstanding features of the force. More significant still was the success that resulted and that brought about a complete fusion between An Garda Síochána and the people with such a degree of co-operation that probably had never been known before in the history of our country.
>
> It reflected the credibility not only of the members of the force themselves, but also its organisers, from Deputy Commissioner W.R.E. Murphy down to the N.C.O.s whose work the building of this force was. We cannot allow the opportunity to pass without

extending to the former members of the LSF on behalf of An Garda Síochána our sincere thanks for their magnificent co-operation and goodwill. They have the satisfaction of knowing that they have served their country and they can always be proud of giving that service.

ECONOMIC CONSTRAINTS

As a result of the difficult economic situation in the country, recruiting for An Garda Síochána was discontinued in 1948. Commissioner Kinnane was alarmed at this measure, the results of which were felt most in Dublin. Of the 785 stations, half were operating on reduced strengths of a Sergeant and three guards, an economy measure dating from 1930, when 370 stations had been reduced from four guards to three.

The Commissioner had foreseen this and, towards the end of the following year, the officer in charge of the Dublin Metropolitan Division (DMD), Deputy Commissioner Murphy, protested to him at the 'grave damage to the system of beat and patrol duty by the depletion of manpower'. Outside the DMD, a parallel situation was developing.

In response to the concerns raised by Deputy Commissioner Murphy, the Government appointed an interdepartmental committee of inquiry, with the Minister for Justice himself, Séan MacEoin, taking the chair. Among those appointed to the committee was a future Garda Commissioner, Daniel Costigan. The committee was restricted by terms of reference having 'an over-riding emphasis on the obligation to save money'.

As recruiting numbers continued to fall, the committee presented an urgent interim report recommending the immediate induction of 300 recruits, with particular reference to the needs of the DMD. In its final report, in 1951, a chapter was devoted to non-police duties carried out for other Government departments.

With the confidence and authority conferred by a distinguished career in the civil service, Michael Kinnane took initiatives on matters that others may have hesitated to address. When he died in office in 1951, the *Garda Review* mourned the passing of a Commissioner who had dedicated himself to welfare in the service: 'By his own personal qualities and ability he won for himself ... an affectionate regard in the hearts of all our members.'

A NEW COMMISSIONER

His experience on the interdepartmental committee made Daniel Costigan an obvious choice to succeed Michael Kinnane, particularly if the policy of modernisation of the service was to continue. Noted as a brilliant administrator, Costigan had to contend with the difficulties precipitated by the retirement of the generation recruited in the 1920s.

The resumption of recruiting in 1952 coincided with Costigan's arrival at Garda Headquarters. After a lapse of five years, 1,126 applicants responded to the announcement, of whom only 303 passed the qualifying examination, set to a new higher standard, and 174 were called for training. The new Commissioner prepared to preside over the formation of a new force as the departure of the first generation of guards began in earnest. Costigan discarded the old procedures for learning police duties. The Police Duty Manual was replaced with a programme of lectures – a modest beginning to a radical process that evolved down the years to culminate in the Garda College at Templemore. The lectures 'contained everything a Garda needed to know to enable him to deal with everyday police problems'.

With some senior officers not responsive to change, it was not easy to bring about changes to how the service was organised and administered. But much was achieved, in increased mobility with patrol cars and motorcycles, and in the extension of the radio service. A radical plan for the reorganisation of the DMD was drafted and would be implemented in the early 1960s. On Costigan's initiative, changes to the uniform were made, women (Ban Garda) members were sanctioned and recruited, a driving school was established, and selected members were sent on training courses abroad.

Station party at Clontarf Station, 1952.

Gardaí on the march, Garda HQ Phoenix Park, 1953.

CHAPTER 7

WOMEN IN AN GARDA SÍOCHÁNA

Retired Chief Superintendent Lorraine Wheatley
Garda Stephen Moore

I n February 2022, An Garda Síochána commemorated the hundredth anniversary of its foundation; however, you will not see any female names amongst early lists of new recruits. It was not until 9 July 1959 that the first females joined the service. As an organisation, An Garda Síochána has come a long way since those twelve women entered through the iron gates of the Phoenix Park to begin their training, under the guidance of Sergeant Doreen Prissick of the Liverpool Police Force.

The first twelve female members, appointed on 9 July 1959 were:

- 00001W – Mary Browne, Galway
- 00002W – Angela Burke, Dublin
- 00003W – Elizabeth Noeleen Cooke, Cavan
- 00004W – Elizabeth (Josephine) Dwyer, Sligo
- 00005W – Kathleen McFadden, Donegal
- 00006W – Sarah McGuiness, Longford
- 00007W – Helena Hayden, Kildare
- 00008W – Bridget Sharkey, Donegal
- 00009W – Margaret Tierney, Galway
- 00010W – Mary B. Wymbs, Leitrim
- 00011W – Deirdre Killeen, Dublin
- 00012W – Mary O'Donnell, Limerick

THE HISTORY OF WOMEN IN AN GARDA SÍOCHÁNA

The journey towards the formation of a police force that included women began as far back as 1917, when four women were employed by the Dublin Metropolitan Police (DMP) to patrol the streets between 7 p.m. and midnight. Although not official members of that force, every morning they would provide Commissioner Sir Walter Edgeworth-Johnstone with a report on the 'moral state of the streets'. When recruiting suitable personnel, Johnstone said, 'What we want is a woman of fair education, strong common sense and robust health. A woman of this kind, if there is such, may belong to any class.' They had to be able to read well, write legibly and have a knowledge of arithmetic, spelling and composition. By 1919, Commissioner Johnstone believed that the experiment in employing women had been a success and requested the Treasury to sanction the employment of two additional women.

The first female recruits arrive at the Garda Depot in 1959.

During the establishment of the Irish Free State in 1922, the female assistants remained in place, but they were not replaced as they retired. Therefore, by 1955, only one female continued to patrol the streets of Dublin – Elizabeth Watters, who was then aged 73. During the period 1955–56, four further women police assistants were appointed.

STEPS TO APPOINT WOMEN POLICE OFFICERS

The Joint Committee of Women's Societies and Social Workers was identified in 1956 by civil servants in the Department of Justice as the main source of agitation for the appointment of women police officers. Having first raised the matter in 1936, the Joint Committee never stopped pressing it. During the 1950s, its members made the recruitment of female police officers a matter of national debate. This was achieved in part by gaining the support of local authorities. In November 1953, Garda Commissioner Daniel Costigan informed the Minister for Justice, Gerald Boland, that he was 'convinced of the present need for women police in Dublin; and their probable assignment to other centres as the need grows'. Though the proposal was rejected by Minister Boland and his successor, James Everett, two senior civil servants (Thomas Coyne and F.C. Connolly) agreed to collaborate in supporting recruitment of women into An Garda Síochána.

The Cabinet minutes of 27 September 1957 authorised the Minister for Justice, Oscar Traynor, to take the necessary steps for the appointment of women to An Garda Síochána. Approval to admit women was outlined in a memo, dated 21 February 1958, from Peter Berry, Secretary of the Department of Justice, to Commissioner Daniel Costigan. It stated: 'that provision has been made in the Garda Síochána estimates for the coming year for 400 recruits (388 men and twelve women)'. The preliminary announcement for female candidates was posted in the national newspapers, and posters were also displayed outside all Garda stations. There were 178 applicants, of whom forty-one were interviewed and twelve selected.

In a Dáil debate before their appointment, political leaders expressed firm views on what type of women should be allowed to join An Garda Síochána. Most agreed that women should be able to join the service as there were 'many police duties, mainly in connection with matters affecting children and young women, where it is desirable that policewomen should be employed'. However, one TD suggested: 'While recruits should not be actually horse faced, they should not be too good looking. They should be just plain women and not targets for marriage.' Another TD believed that the part of the country the women came

Passing-out parade of the first female Gardaí. They are led by their instructor, Sergeant Doreen Prissick of Liverpool City Police.

from could make a difference: 'The commanding personalities of the women of the West and North West should form the nucleus of this force'.

The assistance of the Home Office in London was sought by Commissioner Costigan to obtain the services of a suitably qualified female police Sergeant to act as instructor for the new female Gardaí. Sergeant Doreen Prissick of Liverpool City Police was nominated and acted as instructor, supervisor and counsellor to the new female recruits for the 22-week training course. On completion of training, the twelve female recruits – known as 'Ban Gardaí' – were allocated to College (Pearse Street) and Store Street stations.

THE PIONEERS

Stephen Moore

Of the first twelve female members who joined An Garda Síochána in 1959, seven are no longer with us. These pioneers forged a path which would eventually lead to equal status for both women and men within An Garda Síochána.

I had the great pleasure some years back to interview one of the first twelve female members of An Garda Síochána, or one of the 'twelve apostles', as they would be christened. Margaret (née Tierney), known as Peig, sadly passed away in July 2015 just a short time after we spoke.

I started by asking Margaret why she had wanted to join An Garda Síochána? She replied:

> It was something new. I had already passed the civil service entrance exam, and I
> thought I would try for the guards. I had three months before I could join the civil
> service so I said I would give the guards three months to see if I liked it, and if I
> didn't, I would join the civil service instead.

We went on to discuss the training she received in the Depot:

> I remember being handed a boiler suit to wear on a
> beautiful summer's day, because our uniforms would
> take at least a month to make. When we did our drills
> at the Depot, people would line up along the railings
> to stare at us. We reckoned more people came to see
> us than went to look at the monkeys in Dublin Zoo.

Margaret explained to me that the original twelve were split after training, with six sent to College Station (Pearse Street) and six to Store Street Station. When I asked her if she had felt accepted on arrival at Pearse Street, she replied:

The first female members of An Garda Síochána. Standing (L to R): Angela Burke, Mary Browne, Helena Hayden, Bridget Sharkey, Mary Bríd Wymbs, Sarah McGuinness, Mary O'Donnell. Seated (L to R): Deirdre Killeen, Margaret (Peig) Tierney, Kathleen McFadden, Noeleen Cooke, Elizabeth (Josephine) Dwyer.

Absolutely, it was a big step, but everyone was very nice to us – the guards and the officers. We stood on our own as members of the force. We did the exact same duties as the males: we did station duty, beat duty and traffic duty. We worked 10 a.m. to 6 p.m. each day, but we were always available for calls at night if needed, and we were needed. The only thing that wasn't the same as the men was that we had to live outside of the station, and we were on less pay than them – equal pay came in sometime later.

Margaret was promoted to the rank of Sergeant in 1960 and was soon transferred to Limerick:

I went to see the Superintendent in the Castle, and he told me that I had to transfer to Limerick. I didn't want to go to Limerick – it had an awful name at the time – but I was told I had to, to make room for new girls coming in. I brought four girls with me to Limerick, and they became the first serving Ban Gardaí outside of Dublin.

Margaret married Sergeant Michael Brown in 1965 and had to leave her job as a member of An Garda Síochána:

At the time, [women] couldn't be married and work in the civil service or any public job. I received six months' salary for every year worked. To get the gratuity you had to work a minimum of six years.

I finished by asking Margaret if she had enjoyed her time as a member of An Garda Síochána. Her reply was enthusiastic: 'Every single bit of it.'

Sergeant Margaret Tierney and Sergeant Michael Brown at the time of their engagement.

GAINING AN EQUAL FOOTING

Initially, women were a minority grouping in An Garda Síochána. They played a separate and different role within the service. Following the recruitment of the pioneers, the intake of women to the service was limited. In the 1970s, this began to change – a changing role for women in Irish society was reflected in the changing role of women in policing.

Prior to the enactment of the Anti-Discrimination (Pay) Act, 1974, female Gardaí found themselves often in lower-paid and less powerful work situations than their male colleagues. After the 1974 Act, female Gardaí were more integrated into mainstream policing. All 'women only' units were disbanded. Of the first twelve female members, six – including Sergeant Margaret Tierney – had to resign because of 'the Marriage Bar'. With its removal, women could pursue a career in An Garda Síochána as well as a family life. An Garda Síochána was brought under the remit of the Employment Equality Act, 1977 by EC Directive, S.I. 331 of 1985. While ten women were recruited in 1975, this number had risen to forty-six in 1978. In 1983, the first all-female class was recruited.

INCREASED OPPORTUNITIES FOR WOMEN

In 1987, The Walsh Report on Garda Training resulted in the introduction of new and extended systems of recruit training. From the 1990s, the number of women in the organisation steadily increased. To help address the challenges faced by women trying to balance work and family life, the NOW (New Opportunities for Women) programme, funded by the EU, was instigated by retired Chief Superintendent Mary Fitzgerald. This was an important initiative that involved a small group who would provide

A female Garda on patrol at the IFSC in Dublin.

leadership, training, support, and a forum to address concerns, and it resulted in the development of an informal support network and the introduction of job sharing, leave entitlements and other work/life balance options. A further report on Garda training, the Keating Report, published in 1997, introduced another revised system of training; it stated that by 2000 there would be a minimum of 25 per cent females in each new intake of recruits. A major recruitment drive was undertaken at this time.

Over the years, leave entitlements have evolved and improved to enable members to excel in their chosen career within An Garda Síochána and in their family lives. In 2002, the organisation introduced a new and more practical operational uniform for both males and females.

FIRSTS FOR WOMEN

In 1960, the first promotions for women occurred when Sarah McGuiness, Margaret Tierney, and Helena (Len) Hayden reached the rank of Sergeant. It would take another 21 years for further advancement; this came in 1981 when Sarah McGuiness and Phyllis Nolan were promoted to the rank of Inspector. The first female Superintendent was appointed in 1989 and this honour fell to Phyllis Nolan. Catherine Clancy became the first female to be officially appointed a detective in 1980, when she joined the investigation section of the Garda Technical Bureau. She was also the first female Chief Superintendent on appointment

Commissioner Drew Harris with Deputy Commissioner Anne Marie McMahon (left) and Assistant Commissioner Orla McPartlin.

in 1994 and attained another first when she was promoted to the rank of Assistant Commissioner in 2003. The first official female driver was Margaret Nolan; and she and Breda Tobin were the first females to serve as part of a UN mission when they took part in the 1989 UN Mission to Namibia.

Nóirín O'Sullivan became the first female Deputy Commissioner on her promotion in 2011, and on 25 November 2014, history was once again made when the Government appointed her as the first female Commissioner to head the service since the establishment of An Garda Síochána in 1922.

MY OWN STORY – LORRAINE WHEATLEY

Although women had been joining the service since 1959, by the time I joined in May 1985, the organisation had recruited just under 400 women. Becoming a Garda allowed me to fulfil my ambition of working closely with many different communities in our society. I quite fancied myself as a bit of a detective as well. The registration numbers for females in my intake started at 00388. In the 1990s, arising out of the NOW programme, the separate registration numbers for women would be discontinued and the 'ban' in front of 'Garda' would be dropped. When I started training, there were sixty people in the May 1985 intake, including eighteen women.

The training centre, now called the Garda College, was a great experience, where lifelong friendships were formed. Like the women of 1959, our course was for a period of 22 weeks, and training seemed to have remained relatively unchanged since their time. It was a long hot summer and I remember that most of us celebrated our twenty-first birthdays during our training. The only day off was Sunday, and those lucky enough to have cars and who lived within two hours or so of the centre made a mad dash home after mass. We had to return before the eleven o'clock curfew.

Whilst training, we lived three to a room. Our main concern was to ensure we passed our room and parade inspections, and we became masters at polishing floors. The other biggest challenge was to run up the Devil's Bit, which eventually we all managed. The March class passed out in August, and then we had the Training Centre to ourselves.

There was great anticipation on station-allocation day. We were scattered to the four corners of Ireland, but most of us were allocated to Store Street or Pearse Street stations in

Retired Chief Superintendent Lorraine Wheatley at the opening of the new Kevin Street Garda Station in 2018.

Dublin. We passed out on a foggy day in October. Afterwards, I, along with three of my classmates, went to unit B in Store Street. Recruitment was limited for the next number of years, so we were the 'junior man (woman)' for a long time, which meant working on a post on most days. As posts go, the GPO was considered a better option than the sorting office.

We were assigned to the flexi-units; getting on to regular units was a priority. Ban Gardaí were still few and far between, with generally only one on each unit. We were not treated differently from our male colleagues, but we did spend a lot of time dealing with children and sexual crimes. Joyriders were prevalent in the 'C' District, and drugs had crept into society by the time I arrived at Store Street.

In 1987, a lighter-coloured blue uniform was introduced for all members; the officers would wear white shirts. It would be the 1990s before women were issued with batons and trousers.

From 1997 to 2007, I was assigned to the Finance and Procurement Department in Garda Headquarters, formally known as the Barrack Masters. Here, I worked on some great projects, including the introduction of the euro, planning for the millennium, the introduction of new financial management systems, the operational uniform, and the introduction of body armour. From 2007 to 2020, I served in several great stations – Terenure, Donnybrook, Westmeath, Blanchardstown, and my last years of service were spent as the Chief Superintendent in the recently built Kevin Street Station in Dublin's Liberties. Like most of my colleagues, the visits of Queen Elizabeth II in 2011 and Pope Francis in August 2018 were among events that I will never forget.

The job has certainly changed since I joined; women are now working in all areas and are represented at all levels of the organisation. We have embraced diversity and have built on the work carried out twenty-five years ago under the NOW programme. During my service, I worked with fantastic colleagues and great communities. I experienced highs and lows, difficult cases, and challenges; however, it was lovely to spend my career playing a role in keeping people safe.

CONCLUSION

An Garda Síochána as an organisation has come a long way since its formation in February 1922. The recruitment of the first twelve females some 37 years later was a milestone in the history of the service; the standards set by those pioneers have played no small part in this. We have become a more diverse organisation, which reflects the society we serve.

Today, female representation within all ranks of An Garda Síochána is strong. Women perform duties across the whole range of operational units and bureaus. Every single day, the women of An Garda Síochána make a positive difference to individuals and their communities. There are currently 3,980 females, making up 27 per cent of total Garda numbers; this is above the European average for female representation within police services. In addition, 26 per cent of the Garda Reserve are female, and 76 per cent of Garda Staff.

In 2019, Garda Commissioner Drew Harris established a Woman's Network to support and encourage women in the advancement of their careers. The Network is chaired by Chief Superintendent Margaret Nugent. This network recognised the need to encourage more women to join An Garda Síochána, and the need to continue to give female Gardaí the encouragement and support to apply for specialist units, detective duties, and promotion, and so to increase female representation across An Garda Síochána.

Inspector Antoinette Cunningham, the first female General Secretary of the Association of Garda Sergeants and Inspectors.

Also in 2019, Inspector Antoinette Cunningham became the General Secretary of the Association of Garda Sergeants and Inspectors (AGSI), the first woman to hold this position in AGSI's 43-year history. She said:

> My vision and goals for AGSI remain strong. I am extremely passionate about welfare, rights, equality and transformation, all of which remain not only as challenges but as opportunities ahead, and my loyalty and commitment to AGSI and the Garda Organisation is as strong today as it was three decades ago when I joined the force.

Since 1959, women have made a crucial contribution to the development and success of the organisation. In doing so, we have not only helped protect the communities we served, but we have also inspired many more women to follow in our footsteps. An Garda Síochána is reaching a stage where gender is no longer a consideration in relation to appointment, allocation, or promotion. We certainly have gone beyond the roles that were assigned solely to women when they were first introduced into the service. The organisation continues to grow and evolve. The number of women in senior ranks continues to grow. One of the standout moments of this author's career was marching in the 1916 Centenary Parade. In 2022, at similar events commemorating An Garda Síochána, many proud female members were ready to march with dignity behind the flag of our organisation.

Rest in Peace Margaret Tierney, and all the pioneers who are no longer with us.

Currently there are 3,980 female members of An Garda Síochána and 72 per cent of Garda Staff are female. Thirty-eight female Gardaí work in the most senior roles in the organisation, with two female Deputy Commissioners, three female Assistant Commissioners, two female Executive Directors and an acting Executive Director, part of the Senior Management Team. Pictured before the St Patrick's Day parade 2022 in Dublin city are (L to R): Chief Superintendent Brian Woods, Chief Superintendent Margaret Nugent, Assistant Commissioner Anne Marie Cagney, Deputy Commissioner Shawna Coxon, Deputy Commissioner Anne Marie McMahon, Superintendent Helen Deely.

CHAPTER 8

JIM 'LUGS' BRANIGAN (1910–86)

Garda Stephen Moore

The name 'Lugs' Branigan resonates through the modern history of An Garda Síochána. It seems that everybody met the man or worked with the man, or at the very least knows a story about the man. In a modern police service, a place for Lugs Branigan would be hard to find, however he lived in very different times in a very different city.

Born on 6 January 1910 in the South Dublin Union in Dublin's James's Street, Jim Branigan was the eldest child of John Alick Branigan, a South Dublin Union official, and his wife, Ellen. The family lived in the Union complex.

As a small child, Jim witnessed the shooting of a British soldier by Irish rebels during the 1916 rebellion. It's difficult to imagine the effect this had on such a young boy; maybe it was to play a role in his future chosen career path. Jim left school at 14 years of age and joined the Great Southern Railways as an apprentice fitter. By all accounts, he was a quiet, unassuming young man. It has been documented that his shy personality led to his being bullied and occasionally beaten up while trying to finish his apprenticeship. In June 1931, when his apprenticeship was complete, Jim joined An Garda Síochána.

Having joined the service, Jim decided to dedicate any spare time to fitness and training. On entering the Depot, he was a tall, slim man, and only just made the grade on his chest measurements; he was determined to make himself stronger. A non-smoker who did not take a drink, he became a keen weightlifter, rower and boxer.

Throughout the 1930s, Jim Branigan fought in various inter-police boxing contests. He fought at cruiser weight, light heavyweight and heavyweight, and in 1936, he won the Leinster heavyweight title. He was by no means a skilled boxer or one of Ireland's greatest, but what he did have was courage – and plenty of it! During a boxing tournament in Germany in 1938, while fighting for the Irish international boxing team, Jim came up against a world-class boxer from the German team; he was knocked down nine times during the bout but on each occasion, he dusted himself off and continued boxing. His courage won an ovation from the local German crowd. Jim retired from boxing in 1939, but he remained in the sport which he loved and became a well-respected boxing referee.

In 1936, Jim was stationed in Kevin Street Garda Station in Dublin. He soon became well known on the streets by all who crossed his path, being quick in dispensing 'rough justice' on those he felt warranted it. By his own admission, rather than charging petty offenders, he gave them 'a bit of a going over' and sent them on their way. In the 1940s, a Dublin criminal dubbed him 'Lugs' because of his large ears, and this nickname stuck. However, Jim hated the name and anyone foolhardy enough to use it to his face would soon regret it. He seldom used a baton, but instead he would wear a pair of black leather gloves whenever he sensed trouble. His mere presence, especially when he donned the gloves, was often sufficient to calm tense situations.

Jim 'Lugs' Branigan was popularly regarded as the man who tamed Dublin's 'Teddy Boys', and he was well liked by law-abiding citizens on and around Kevin Street. He would often

Jim 'Lugs' Branigan – a legend.

act as an unofficial social worker, speaking up for young offenders in court, and even trying to fix them up with employment. He believed in second chances. A big dislike for Jim was domestic abuse and violence. He regularly got involved when it was not required of him and, indeed, he probably was not supposed to become involved. He saved many marriages by handing out stern warnings to husbands to 'change their ways or else'. Many criminals had a grudging respect for him, and he was often on good terms with their families.

Jim became a detective in July 1958. One of his roles was as an assigned bodyguard to visiting celebrities in Dublin, which led to his looking after Elizabeth Taylor, Cliff Richard and George Best, among others. In December 1963, he was promoted to Sergeant, in which role he was to take charge of a mini riot squad, which consisted of himself, a driver and two other members in a mobile. They soon became known as 'Branno 7', and would target anywhere in the city where trouble was expected. According to George Power, a former driver with 'Branno 7':

> We would drive around the city, paying particular notice to known trouble spots. It was on nights, and we would target the rowdy pubs. It was rough justice but every gurrier in the city knew 'Lugs' and trouble would stop whenever he appeared.

Jim kept himself extremely fit; he was still weightlifting and sparring with young boxers well into his sixties. He remained on active duty with the riot squad until his retirement on 6 January 1973. On his retirement, he received numerous tributes and gifts from the people of Dublin. One of these gifts was a canteen of cutlery and a set of Waterford glass which were sent to him by a group of Dublin prostitutes, who always saw him as a protector and father-like figure.

Jim carried numerous scars from his time in An Garda Síochána. He felt that his outspokenness and honesty held him back from further promotions within the service. Most of his retirement was spent in Summerhill, Co. Meath, where he grew crops and bred budgerigars for competition. Jim 'Lugs' Branigan died on 22 May 1986. He died a legend.

CHAPTER 9

POLICING IN CORK

Retired Sergeant Tim Bowe

In September 1922, three officers of the Civic Guard travelled from Dublin by boat to Cork to prepare for the arrival of the first contingent of the Civic Guard. The officers were Superintendents Eamon O'Duffy, Eamon P. Cullen and George O'Dwyer. On Wednesday, 8 November 1922, a party of eighty Civic Guards in uniform, accompanied by a few Inspectors, boarded the passenger cargo steamer SS *Bandon* at Sir John Rogerson's Quay in Dublin. They were unable to travel by train because anti-treaty forces had blown up rail bridges at Mallow and other areas. The next day, they sailed up Cork harbour to Albert Quay close to Cork City Hall, where they were greeted by Superintendent Eamon O'Duffy, Superintendent Eamon P. Cullen and Inspector Peter Fahy. The following morning, the *Cork Examiner* reported that a further contingent of Civic Guards had departed from Dublin bound for Cork on the steamer, *Lady Carlow*.

The first station party at Cobh, known as the 'Pioneers'. Front row (L to R): Sergeant James Phelan, Garda Pat Nally, Garda David Scannell. Back row (L to R): Garda John Noonan, Garda Thomas Kelly, Garda Michael Cullen, Garda, Pat Foley. (Photo courtesy Retired Garda Michael McNamara)

The first civic guards were billeted in the old Cork School of Music premises within yards of the Union Quay Royal Irish Constabulary (RIC) barracks which had been destroyed by fire on 14 August 1922. The Cork School of Music premises acted as an administrative base and parade centre for the new force. The Cork Civic Patrol (CCP), which had successfully provided an unarmed police force, ceased operation and many of its volunteers joined the Civic Guard.

Following the arrival of the second contingent of Civic Guards on 10 November, the service was divided into sections, with officers and guards dispatched to establish new barracks at Bandon, Cobh, Midleton, Kinsale and Youghal. Sergeant James J. Phelan, together with Guard Pat Nally and five others, travelled by paddle steamer down the harbour to open a barracks next to the Commodore Hotel in Cobh.

BARRACKS AT MOORE'S HOTEL

The first Cork City barracks was at No. 4 Morrison's Island (Moore's Hotel). James Quinlan was Sergeant in charge until 1925. Six men took up duty in civilian attire and became the first Detective Branch under Detective Inspector Jer Sullivan. Within a short period, Inspector Peter Fahy was promoted to Superintendent and appointed District Officer (Cork South). Superintendent Eamon P. Cullen was promoted to Chief Superintendent with an appointment as Divisional Officer Cork East Riding. In 1924, he was promoted to Assistant Garda Commissioner and transferred to Garda HQ. He became Deputy Garda Commissioner in 1936.

During 1924, Sergeant Patrick Carroll (BL) was appointed to Court Records at Cork Courthouse. Within five years, he had risen to Chief Superintendent and returned to Union Quay Station where he served as Garda Divisional Officer from 1929 to 1934. He gained further promotion and served as Garda Commissioner from 1967 to 1968.

Garda William Barrett opened the Garda Barracks in Blarney on 24 May 1923. In September 1924, Gardaí James Banim, Thomas Bane and Michael Maher established the barracks in Ballincollig. On 31 March 1926, a new Garda barracks was opened near Blackrock Castle with Sergeant Francis Crowe in charge. By this time, the fire-damaged Union Quay Barracks had been restored to its former glory.

MOVE TO UNION QUAY

On 1 April 1926, Gardaí moved from Moore's Hotel Barracks to occupy Union Quay Station. At the official opening, fifty of the station party, wearing their new metropolitan uniforms, paraded for a photograph in front of their impressive Garda Divisional HQ. Sergeant James Phelan, one of the first men to join the service, holds the record as the first Sergeant in charge at Union Quay Station and the longest-serving Sergeant in charge in the country (1925–63).

BRIDEWELL GARDA STATION

Shortly after the RIC vacated the old Bridewell Barracks in April 1922, the building was burned down. A few years later, construction began on a new building, which was completed in 1932. The *Cork Examiner* on 13 June 1933 gave an account of Gardaí taking possession of the first Garda station built by the Irish State:

> The Cork Civic Guard authorities took over possession of their new Bridewell situated at the junction of Kyrl's Quay and Cornmarket Street yesterday. Possession was formally given to Chief Superintendent Patrick Carroll who was accompanied by Superintendent T. McNeill, Inspector J.F. Ryan and Station Sergeant Edward Ryan. In all 36 men will be housed in the new Bridewell which has married quarters for Sergeant Ryan.

Gardaí outside Union Quay Station, April 1926. Front row (L to R): Sergeant Dan O'Brien, D/Sergeant Jim Moore, Sergeant John Henehan, Sergeant Joe Beirne, Superintendent Edmond Mansfield (Cork South), Superintendent James Carbury (Discipline Superintendent Cork City), Superintendent George Butler (Cork North), Inspector Pat Creane, Sergeant David Flynn (I/C Barrack Street), Sergeant Pat Mitchell (Court Records), Sergeant Jim Phelan (I/C Union Quay Station). Second row (L to R): Garda Tom Kane, Garda James Murnane, Garda L. Reidy, Garda Tom Kelly, Garda David Grady, Garda Marcus O'Shea, Garda John Dolan, Garda E. Tobin, Garda John Casserley, Garda Con O'Leary, Sergeant George Styles. Third row (L to R): Garda Peter Clinton, Garda Michael Hickey, Garda William Buckley, Garda Dan Harty, Garda John Kelly, Garda John Kearney, Garda William Monahan, Garda John Cooke, Garda Joe Kennedy, Garda Michael O'Dea. Fourth row (L to R): Garda Patrick Gonigle, Garda Peter Mulderrig, Garda Jim Kennedy, Garda Matt Fottrell, Garda Andy Turley, Garda Malachy Egan, Garda Tom Breen, Garda James Bones, Garda Michael Duke. Fifth row (L to R): Garda William O'Keeffe, Garda Michael Mullaly, Garda Thomas Duffy, Garda Matt Browne, Garda Con Buckley, Garda Peter Deane, Garda Declan O'Callaghan, Garda William O'Keeffe, Garda John Hughes.

FIRST FEMALE GARDAÍ – 1961

History was created at the Bridewell on 8 May 1961 when Sergeant Helena Hayden, accompanied by five female Gardaí, arrived in Cork. The five new recruits were Mary T. McKenna, Margaret Lohan, Mary V. Molloy, Brigid A. Lee and Mary B. O'Riordan. The marriage ban resulted in all six being forced to resign.

Shortly after the ban was revoked, Garda Sally O'Keeffe created history by continuing to serve in An Garda Síochána after marriage.

CORK JLO SCHEME

A Juvenile Liaison Officers (JLO) scheme was established in September 1963 to deal with young offenders. Sergeant Terry Kelly, based at the Bridewell, was responsible for its inauguration and implementation, and remained in charge of its operation up to his promotion to Inspector in 1978.

TRIBUNAL – 1967

On 30 May 1967, Liam O'Mahony died while in custody at the Bridewell. He had been arrested while drunk the previous evening. Subsequently there were allegations that he might have been beaten. An 11-day judicial inquiry in August 1967 ruled that he had sustained fractures to his ribs as a result of falling off a stool in the Long Valley Bar.

In 1970, the Bridewell was refurbished, cell accommodation increased, and four Station-House-Officers (SHOs) were appointed to oversee the treatment of persons in custody.

BANDON – WEST CORK DIVISION

On Saturday, 11 November 1922, Superintendent Eamon O'Duffy, along with three Sergeants and fifteen Gardaí, took up quarters in the old RIC barracks at South Main Street, Bandon. This was the Divisional HQ for Cork West until 1991. The *Southern Star* reported their arrival in a vehicle that resembled a jeep, in the rear section of which were men in smart dark uniforms. Locals were surprised that unarmed guards were expected to enforce law and order in an area that was a hotbed of armed atrocities.

Two days later, Superintendent O'Duffy sent six men, including Garda Jim Bowen, to open a station in the Old Soldiers' Home in Kinsale (now part of AIB). On Monday, 25 February 1923, members of the Civic Guard opened stations in Bantry and Skibbereen. A Garda barracks was opened in Macroom on 6 April 1923.

BEATS, RIVERS, BRIDGES AND GARDA CORDONS

During the first 25 years, beat and cycle patrols were the 'eyes and ears' of the service, helping in the prevention and detection of crime. The rivers Bandon, Blackwater and Lee with their many bridges were used by Gardaí after major crimes to curtail the movements of criminals. This cordon system resulted in many police successes.

In the 1940s, patrol cars were issued to Garda districts and in the 1950s the first Garda motorcycle was allocated. Around this period, a two-way radio system was fitted in patrol cars, and a radio communications room became the nerve centre at Union Quay Divisional HQ. By 1973, a fleet of brightly coloured Traffic Corps cars assisted with policing the roads throughout the county. Ten years later, a special mobile taskforce was established, and today Cork has a highly trained Armed Support Unit.

PRESIDENT DE VALERA'S OFFICIAL VISIT TO CORK – 1963

Prior to the arrival of President Éamon de Valera in Cork on St Patrick's Day, 1963, to unveil a memorial in St Finbarr's Cemetery, plainclothes Gardaí performed night duty inside the cemetery entrance gate. Two men carrying a primed bomb approached the cemetery but, on seeing a light inside the gatekeeper's lodge, made a detour, climbing over the cemetery wall and making their way up the long pathway to reach the memorial. As they laid the bomb near the plinth, it exploded, killing one of them and causing serious injury to the other. Only slight damage was done to the plinth where 12 hours later President de Valera performed the unveiling ceremony in the presence of 5,000 spectators.

CONROY COMMISSION – 1970

The Conroy Commission report resulted in a four-unit, 28-day roster system, with Gardaí enjoying seven rest days and overtime payments. While this brought extra Gardaí, it also resulted in a gradual reduction of Gardaí for Cork city beat patrols. In 1976, a 'Beat Tolerance' was agreed between Garda Representatives and Garda management, which ensured a daily Garda presence on seven designated city streets. Today, CCTV cameras have replaced the beat patrol officers, while community policing units are bridging the gap to ensure visibility of Gardaí on the ground.

FIRST FEMALE CLERICAL OFFICERS

During the 1950 and 1960s, selected Gardaí were employed as clerks in district and divisional offices. In 1970, close to twenty-five male Gardaí were designated clerks, working from 9 a.m. to 5 p.m., Monday to Friday. After the Conroy Commission, female civil servants were gradually allocated to Garda stations. In September 1971, Marie O'Callaghan created history when she reported for duty at the Divisional Office, Union Quay Station. Today, the office staff have completely changed, with civil servants – both male and female – performing most of the administrative roles.

CORK GARDAÍ DRAFTED FOR MAJOR EVENTS

Even though Cork is situated in the southwest, it was the first port of call by Garda authorities whenever reinforcements were required for policing major events, such as the State visits of US Presidents J.F. Kennedy in June 1963 and Ronald Reagan in June 1984. Twenty years later, US President George Bush got an unfriendly welcome when he arrived at Shannon Airport to attend an EU–US summit; Cork Gardaí spent two weeks at Shannon on security duties. In May 2011, Gardaí from Cork were again employed when US President Barack Obama made a State visit to his ancestral home in Moneygall, Co. Offaly.

Protection of British Prime Minister Edward Heath, while attending peace talks in September 1973, resulted in 150 Gardaí making the long trip to Dublin. They departed from Cork on Sunday morning, and 40 hours later returned home.

In September 1979, a special train from Cork transported 300 Gardaí to perform security duties in Galway where Pope John Paul II celebrated a youth mass attended by 250,000 people. Gardaí remained in situ for many hours, and it was 6.00 a.m. on Monday when the train carrying exhausted Gardaí arrived back in Cork.

Two years later, a contingent of 150 Cork Gardaí was bussed to Dublin to assist with policing a protest march organised by supporters of H-Block hunger strikers. While forming a protective frontline barrier near the British Embassy, many Gardaí were seriously injured after they were targeted by missiles.

CORK MAJOR EMERGENCY PLAN
WHIDDY OIL TANKER DISASTER – 1979

Superintendent Seamus McMahon was District Officer in Bantry when, at 1.00 a.m. on Monday, 8 January 1979, he was woken by an explosion on a French oil tanker at the Whiddy oil terminal. Fleets of ambulances with medical personnel and helicopters responded instantly when he initiated the Major Emergency Plan. Garda personnel with multi-agency teams worked day and night as bodies were brought to Cork University Hospital where the difficult tasks of identification, post-mortem examinations and arranging inquests began. A tribunal of inquiry under Judge Declan Costello acknowledged that the Major Emergency Plan had worked efficiently.

BUTTEVANT RAIL DISASTER – 1980

At 12.45 p.m. on Bank Holiday Monday, 1 August 1980, the Dublin–Cork express train carrying 230 passengers crashed at Buttevant rail station, killing eighteen people and seriously injuring seventy others. Sergeant Batt Kirby drove immediately to the accident scene to assist Sergeant Kevin Edwards and Mallow Gardaí with the rescue-and-recovery operation.

AIR INDIA DISASTER – 1985

At 8.13 a.m. on Sunday, 23 June 1985, an Air India Boeing 747 jumbo jet disappeared from radar after a bomb exploded. The plane crashed into the Atlantic Ocean approximately 100 miles off the Cork coastline, resulting in the loss of 329 lives. Gardaí initiated the Major Emergency Plan, and helicopters, ambulances, Gardaí, naval and military search-and-rescue teams helped to recover bodies. Over the following months, Gardaí assisted with the idenb tification of bodies, post-mortem examinations and arranging inquests. A memorial garden and sundial to the memory of the victims can be seen at Ahakista on Sheep's Head Peninsula near Bantry. On the twentieth anniversary, in 2005, the Canadian Mounted Police presented a plaque to An Garda Síochána in Cork in recognition of their efforts.

SEARCH-AND-RESCUE MISSIONS
MISSING 11-YEAR-OLD ROBERT HOLOHAN

Following the disappearance of 11-year-old Robert Holohan from his home near Midleton on 4 January 2005, Gardaí, with assistance from over 700 people, coordinated daily searches in areas throughout east Cork. After eight days, the child's body was discovered in an isolated ditch 12 miles from his home. A local youth was arrested, charged and convicted.

'TIT BONHOMME' – FISHING TRAWLER TRAGEDY

At 5.45 a.m. on Saturday, 12 January 2012, a distress call was received from the *Tit Bonhomme*, a fishing trawler sinking in stormy seas at the entrance to Glandore Harbour. As Gardaí mounted a massive search for the skipper, Michael Hayes, and four crew members, the Garda Divisional Officer realised that his own brother was among those missing. Despite his grief, Chief Superintendent Tom Hayes led his divisional team and search crews that included the Irish Coastguard, Naval Service, Civil Defence and hundreds of volunteers. The search continued for 26 days until all five bodies had been recovered and brought home.

FURTHER MAJOR PUBLIC EVENTS
CUTTY SARK – TALL SHIPS RACE

Cork Gardaí received international praise for policing and security arrangements during the Cutty Sark – Tall Ships race in July 1991. The arrival of a fleet of 100 fully rigged sailing ships during a week-long maritime extravaganza attracted 100,000 visitors daily to Cork.

TOUR DE FRANCE – CYCLE RACE, JULY 1998

The largest traffic-policing operation in Cork for over a hundred years was for the prestigious Tour de France cycle race. The second stage, from Enniscorthy to Cork, on Monday, 13 July 1998, witnessed 200 top-class riders in action. Some 700 Gardaí were employed, closing public roads and policing the race as it passed through the county, with tens of thousands lining the route. The months of pre-planning and co-operation with French officials and race organisers afforded An Garda Síochána international expertise.

PROTECTION FOR A QUEEN

The State visit of Queen Elizabeth II and the Duke of Edinburgh captured the hearts of the Irish nation. Their final official engagement on Friday, 20 May 2011, was a visit to the English Market on Grand Parade, Cork. After days of unprecedented tight security, Gardaí were faced with policing over 30,000 spectators. As soon as her tour of the food aisles was completed, the Queen took Gardaí by surprise when she did a walkabout along Grand Parade, talking to excited schoolchildren who were pressed against steel barriers. It was the highlight of her state visit, which ended when her flight departed from Cork Airport.

PATROLLING THE SOUTHWEST COASTLINE

Over the past thirty years, Cork Gardaí have been involved with the Irish Naval Service, Customs and Revenue Officers in many arrests and seizures of drugs on yachts off the southwest coast, including *Dances with Waves* in 2008 when €750m-worth of cocaine was seized, making it the largest Irish anti-smuggling operation to date.

In October 1971, six large suitcases containing firearms and ammunitions which had arrived on the Cunard *QE2* liner were seized by Gardaí and customs officers at Cobh. Detective Inspector James McMahon and Sergeant Tom Nestor later travelled to New York to give evidence in a conspiracy charge to export arms. Over a decade later, in September 1984, Inspector Eric Ryan and Garda Liam Hayes, accompanied by Irish Navy officers, intercepted the *Marita Ann* fishing trawler inside Irish territorial waters. The trawler contained seven tons of firearms and ammunitions which had come from Boston, destined for the Irish Republican Army (IRA). Martin Ferris served a 10-year prison sentence for his part in the affair.

CROSS-BORDER INVOLVEMENT

On 2 December 1983, while engaged in house-to-house searches in Carrigtwohill for kidnapped senior business executive Don Tidey, Garda John Dennehy and I were held captive at gunpoint by INLA leader Dominic McGlinchey and his gang. The terrorist, who was wanted on warrant by the Royal Ulster Constabulary (RUC) for murder, was staying at the home of a local IRA sympathiser. On 17 March 1984, Dominic McGlinchey was captured during a shoot-out with armed Gardaí in Co. Clare; he was handed over to the RUC. Having been released from prison, he was shot dead during an internal feud in Drogheda in 1994.

After a £27 million robbery in December 2004 from the Northern Ireland Cash Centre in Belfast, the Police Service of Northern Ireland (PSNI) sought cross-border assistance from An Garda Síochána. Two months later, at the home of a businessman near Farran, Co. Cork, Gardaí seized almost £3 million in cash. A man was subsequently convicted of money-laundering charges.

NEW GARDA DIVISIONAL HQ STATIONS

During 1991, two impressive new divisional HQ stations were opened, one at Anglesea Street in Cork city, and the other in Bandon. Five years later, the Garda divisional boundaries were redrawn, with Cork divided into three Garda divisions, namely: Cork City with HQ at Anglesea Street, Cork North with HQ at Fermoy, and Cork West with HQ in Bandon.

Since then, modern Garda stations have been constructed at Ballincollig, Bantry, Blarney, Carrigaline, Carrigtwohill, Clonakilty, Cobh, Douglas, Glanmire and Macroom.

CONCLUSION

Cork city and county have changed in many ways since the arrival of An Garda Síochána in 1922. Not only has daily life changed – with the arrival of motor cars to our roads, motorways and modern technology – but the population has also increased by 50 per cent. Policing in Cork has had to evolve and adapt to meet these changes. No doubt, there will be further changes and challenges in the years ahead. However, we can be sure that the strong foundations laid down by the first members in 1922, and the sacrifices that were made in the intervening hundred years, will ensure that a proud heritage and legacy will be passed on to future members of An Garda Síochána in Cork.

THE SECOND GENERATION

INTRODUCTION

Garda Stephen Moore

Recruitment in An Garda Síochána had been slow and intermittent since the original recruits signed up with the formation of the service in 1922. This was about to change. When those members started to retire en masse after their terms of service had expired, it became apparent that major recruitment would be needed to keep Garda numbers steady. The 1950s saw recruitment for new members begin once again, and in 1959 the first female recruits were attested. In 1960, the Minister for Justice, Charles J. Haughey, stated that Garda recruitment would increase to 600 or 700 per year, to keep the service at its current strength of 6,400.

The second generation of recruits were different from their predecessors. They were better educated, and they had no personal experiences from either the War of Independence or the Civil War. Society was changing, and this coincided with a new era for An Garda Síochána. Attempts to modernise the police service would see training move from Garda Headquarters to a new Training Centre in Templemore. Economically, Ireland was changing too, and a new government, led by Taoiseach Seán Lemass, heralded unforeseen industrial growth and foreign direct investment for the country.

The Garda Band was established shortly after the foundation of An Garda Síochána. In 1938, The Garda Band amalgamated with the Dublin Metropolitan Garda Band. The band was disbanded in 1965 but was re-established in 1972 to celebrate the fiftieth anniversary of An Garda Síochána. Besides providing music for official Garda functions, the band undertakes a strongly community-oriented programme each year. In 2022, the band was busier than ever, providing music for all the different events to celebrate the centenary of An Garda Síochána.

In recent years, An Garda Síochána has enhanced its armed-response capability with the introduction of a specialist section – Specialist Tactics and Operations Command (STOC) – and an expansion of Armed Support Units across the country.

CHAPTER 10

— NEW GENERATION — NEW CHALLENGES

Retired Inspector Tim Doyle

Jack Marrinan as a Garda recruit.

In 1952, 100 new members were enrolled in An Garda Síochána. The following year, a class of 240 began training. Such was the attractiveness of a Garda career that the intake included young men from both New York and Great Britain. Clare-born Sean Ó Mearnain was another new recruit. He soon became known as Jack Marrinan. Being of medium size, Jack was not selected for a city-centre station where tall men were needed for point duty. Instead, he was eventually allocated to Rathfarnham, then a country station in the Wicklow division; much new housing would soon transform it into a Dublin suburb.

Jack Marrinan was ambitious. However, although he passed the Sergeants' exam, he was passed over at the promotion interview. He also sought appointment as a crime detective but again faced disappointment. In the meantime, an appeal from the parish priest in Rathfarnham to Archbishop John Charles McQuaid led to his obtaining permission to attend night classes in Trinity College Dublin, despite the hierarchy's ban on Roman Catholics attending. He graduated with degrees in arts and commerce. Marrinan would again encounter McQuaid in circumstances of great significance for the service and the development of policing in Ireland.

RISE TO PROMINENCE

On 4 November 1961, an event took place that set Jack Marrinan apart from all others of his rank. An unauthorised

The Macushla Ballroom in the 1970s.

meeting of Gardaí was taking place in Dublin's north inner city. Gathered in the Macushla Ballroom, almost 1,000 predominantly young Gardaí were rebelling against stifling bureaucracy and draconian disciplinary regulations within the service. Marrinan climbed onto the stage, addressed the gathering, and took charge; a committee was formed, and a set of demands formulated. The ferment had erupted when Gardaí with under five years' service were excluded from an earlier pay award and further penalised when those in 'living-in' stations suffered a £1 per week pay cut for bed and board. A decade of transplanting young men from their rural homes to 'live in' in city stations on low pay blew up in the face of the Garda authorities, and their overseers in the Department of Justice.

Within days, Jack and ten other Gardaí seen as ringleaders were sacked. However, to the consternation of Garda authorities, An Taoiseach Seán Lemass and Justice Minister Charles Haughey, Marrinan led the insurgents on a countrywide campaign. It took the intervention of Archbishop John Charles McQuaid to bring them back into the fold. The shrewd Archbishop had spotted what the Garda authorities had missed – Marrinan and his supporters were the cream of the second-wave crop, not the troublesome malcontents that Garda Commissioner Daniel Costigan had believed them to be. Within a week, all the Gardaí were reinstated.

Three months later, Jack refused promotion to the rank of Sergeant. Shortly thereafter, he was unanimously elected General Secretary of the newly reconstituted Garda Representative body (GRB). He sought as his assistant a fellow Clare man, Michael Conway, who had organised the Garda Group Assurance Scheme, having run the Garda Medical Aid Society during the 1950s. Both men remained close throughout their careers.

Marrinan took over the monthly *Garda Review* where his hard-hitting editorials influenced both other media and politicians. He also retained the expertise of economist Garret FitzGerald, legal advisor Michael O'Kennedy and talented young journalist Conor Brady. In 1963, the GRB successfully negotiated its first independent pay award. A second pay claim was conceded in 1966.

THE CONROY COMMISSION

In September 1968, the GRB seized the initiative and forced then Minister for Justice Mícheál Ó Móráin to appoint a commission under Judge J.C. Conroy. The terms of reference were 'To examine, make recommendations and report on the remuneration and conditions of service of An Garda Síochána'. The Conroy Commission was the first such commission since the foundation of An Garda Síochána.

The 250-page Conroy Commission report, published at the end of January 1970, made 52 recommendations on virtually every aspect of Garda service: accommodation, allowances, development of managerial and leadership skills, discipline, education, hours of duty, (including new rosters and night-duty payments), pensions, recruitment, representation, training, uniforms, welfare, and widows. It also introduced two new terms to the Garda vocabulary – rest days and overtime – as well as outlining relevant payment conditions. The final paragraph highlighted the unsatisfactory nature of the relationship between the Department of Justice, which had oversight of the service, and the senior Garda officers. Implementation of the recommendations formed the agenda for much of the rest of Marrinan's working life.

One lasting effect of the Conroy Commission was to hitch the wagon of the GRB and its successor, the Garda Representative Association (GRA), to the cause of professionalisation of the service. Marrinan and his cohort knew that the unique relationship between An Garda Síochána and the public was precious and needed to be nurtured and developed. Thus, many improvements in the police service first saw the light of day in GRA/GRB circles. Two sentences stand out in the hundreds of pages written about the Conroy Commission. Jack Marrinan submitted that the sight of a uniformed member on public duty was the greatest deterrent to criminal activity. Judge Conroy wrote: 'The main functions of a Garda are vested in them by virtue of their office and not by directives of higher authority.'

However, policing was about to become even more challenging.

THE NORTHERN IRELAND CONFLICT

Two months after the publication of the Conroy report came the savage murder of Garda Richard Fallon in a republican bank raid in Dublin, thus opening the bloodiest chapter in the service's history. According to the *Garda Review*:

> The murder of Dick Fallon introduced fears in every Garda spouse and family that when a loved one went on duty there was now a worry about him or her ever coming home.

Top: Garda Michael Reynolds was shot dead while pursuing bank raiders on 11 September 1975 Above: Garda Michael Clerkin died when a booby-trap bomb exploded in 1976.

Conflict in Northern Ireland had crossed the border and would remain an intractable problem for many years to come, absorbing manpower and resources and diverting attention from other problems, important but less immediate.

In June 1972, Inspector Sam Donegan was killed by a booby-trap bomb on the Cavan/Fermanagh border. Aged 60, with 37 years' service, he was looking forward to his retirement. He left a wife and six children. Garda Michael Reynolds was off-duty, driving his private car, with his wife and two-year-old daughter as passengers, when he came across the aftermath of a bank raid. He pursued the fleeing perpetrators and was shot dead in a public park on 11 September 1975. Between May 1974 and October 1976, booby-trap bombs came south with a vengeance. In Dublin, thirty-three innocent people lost their lives with ten times as many injured. In March 1976, the Dublin-to-Cork mail train was held up at Sallins, Co. Kildare. Following a Garda investigation, five individuals were charged. *The Irish Times* published a series of articles claiming that brutal interrogation methods were employed by Gardaí, coining the phrase 'the Heavy Gang'.

At 8 a.m. on Monday 27 August 1979, a lone Garda in the midlands stopped a car at a checkpoint. Following a short conversation, the two male occupants, who could not give a satisfactory account of their movements, were arrested by Garda Seamus Lohan, and detained. Three hours later, 80 miles away, in Co. Sligo, a booby-trap bomb exploded in a boat, killing 79-year-old Lord Mountbatten along with four others, including his 14-year-old grandson and a 15-year-old local boy. The bomb had been placed the previous night. The arrested men were charged with those murders.

In July 1976, the British Ambassador and a female civil servant died at Sandyford in Dublin when a bomb exploded under their car. Liam Cosgrave's Government moved to introduce legislation allowing terrorists to be detained for seven days. On the evening of the vote, Laois Gardaí received information that Irish Republican Army (IRA) members were gathering at a vacant farm near Portarlington. A booby-trap bomb took the life of Garda Michael Clerkin, Detective Tom Peters was permanently blinded, and the other Gardaí were injured, some badly.

Over the first five years of the 1980s, eight more Garda colleagues died as a result of the conflict: Detective John Morley, Garda Henry Byrne, and Detective Seamus Quaid in 1980;

Garda Pat Reynolds in 1982 and Sergeant Pat McLoughlin in 1983; Recruit Garda Gary Sheehan in 1983; Detective Frank Hand in 1984 and Sergeant Paddy Morrissey in 1985. During Frank Hand's vicious murder, his colleague Detective Mick Dowd was also shot but survived.

The bleakness of those days is hard to imagine now. The pain of the bereaved relatives, the sombre funerals and the serried ranks of blue uniforms remain seared in the memory of the survivors. In retirement, Jack Marrinan spoke of attending those farewells to slain comrades, and of being with the parents of Recruit Garda Gary Sheehan, shot dead during the search for kidnapped Don Tidey, and of not having words to console them – the very worst day in his life was how he described it.

INCREASED POWERS OF INVESTIGATION

In public and in private, Jack Marrinan and his GRA colleagues lambasted successive governments, urging them to fast-track new investigative powers for serious crime. 'Our men and women put their lives on the line for the people we protect from dangerous criminals – you need to give us the powers to do our jobs' was the unrelenting message that he put across in the media. Successive Garda Commissioners were happy to have the most effective communicator in the service do their plain speaking for them.

In the mid-1970s, Marrinan wrote:

> The relationship between the Department of Justice and the
> Garda Commissioner deprives the latter of a good deal of per-
> sonal responsibility and initiative that one would expect from a
> man of his eminence. I worry about our authorities rushing to
> employ extra Gardaí and packing them off to the Border, armed
> with 18 weeks' training without any clear long-term plan. These
> members do not have the structured apprenticeship of being
> allocated in small numbers to stations up and down the country,
> arriving at intervals of two or three years that gave the previous
> cohorts time to settle in. Too many members spending time on
> posts and roadblocks have no chance of on-the-job satisfaction or
> getting inside their profession.

Top: Garda Patrick Reynolds was shot dead in 1982.
Above: Garda Frank Hand was murdered in 1984.

CONCLUSION

As we celebrate the hundredth anniversary of the foundation of the service, it would be a mistake to read the story of the second generation of An Garda Síochána simply in terms of the exceptional men and women who came through to mould and adapt and develop the service to what it is today. The emergence of leaders like Jack Marrinan is best understood as an indication of the calibre of the post Second World War intake. The second generation's most remarkable achievement was that they withstood the most serious sustained assault on the integrity of the State, displaying courage, fortitude and commitment, while dealing with the daily challenges that face police services everywhere. Of course, they left work to do, but they left An Garda Síochána in much better shape than they found it.

CHAPTER 11

POLICING THE TROUBLES

Sheelagh Brady, Former Garda Sergeant

In the aftermath of the Emergency in Ireland, An Garda Síochána faced opportunity and challenges. Crime rates were low, and threats from armed or subversive groups had largely dissipated. New intakes entered, joined by the first females to the service, and increased technology added to the arsenal of policing techniques used (fingerprint advances, photography, ballistics, and radio). In his 1974 book, *Guardians of the Peace*, Conor Brady described this era of policing as 'a policeman's paradise'. The period, however, was juxtaposed with new challenges for the service. By the end of the 1940s, the members who had initially joined were approaching retirement, and the number of Gardaí dropped. The illusion of paradise was short-lived. The 1950s and 1960s saw politicians and senior management faced with low morale, distrust, and feelings of unappreciation within the rank and file. This combination of low crime with high rates of retirement, compounded by low morale, was to have a significant impact on policing in Ireland. Members who had experience of policing the Emergency were leaving, and those who had cut their teeth during the 1950s and 1960s had little or no experience of policing national security threats or serious organised crime (SOC), resulting in an ill-prepared service for the challenges that lay ahead.

POLICING CONTEXT

Against the backdrop of the Troubles, it was often alleged that the Republic was a haven for republican paramilitaries. However, the reality is more nuanced. In the 1970s, police co-operation between An Garda Síochána and the British authorities was conducted discreetly, as was policing the border more generally. Discretion became a key part to how An Garda Síochána policed not alone the border, but Ireland as a whole. Many members of An Garda Síochána were transferred throughout the country to areas where the Irish Republican

Army (IRA) was reportedly active, gaining exposure to policing paramilitaries. Having been trained and worked thus far in a low-crime environment, the majority of these Gardaí had little or no prior experience of policing crime. All that was to change.

The rapidly increasing crime rate made the period from the late 1960s onwards exceptional. Between 1965 and 1970, the crime rate nearly doubled, and it continued to rise until its peak in 1983. The increases cannot be solely explained by the rise in politically motivated criminal activity, however. The same era witnessed an emergence of organised criminals, often co-operating with paramilitaries when it suited. By the 1970s, crimes such as kidnap, Offences Against the State, seizing of vehicles, explosives and firearms, and armed robberies were increasingly common. An Garda Síochána had to adapt their activities to such crimes, with increased manpower allocated to protection duties. The legacy of this existed well into the 2000s, when it was still common throughout the country to have armed Gardaí and/or military providing protection duties in respect of cash escorts or the movement of explosives, for example.

This rise in crime was not unique to Ireland. Similar trends were also experienced between the 1960s and the 1980s in other industrialised societies. Factors such as urbanisation, internal migration and a rise in prosperity are often used to explain such trends. Opportunity-based crime, such as property crimes (larceny, car theft, and burglary) rose. In Ireland, drugs reportedly had a more significant impact on the crime profile than any other influence, including the Troubles. The growth in the drugs problem resulted, in turn, in another significant challenge for policing. Drug markets became more organised and structured, reinforced through the use of lethal weapons. With the murder of journalist Veronica Guerin, the demands on An Garda Síochána increased again.

While there may not be a direct correlation between these increases and the conflict in Northern Ireland, some factors relating to the Troubles may have influenced a facilitative environment for the rise – for example, a greater availability of weapons, the paramilitaries' need for funding, and the diversion of Government attention from crime prevention to security.

LEGISLATIVE RESPONSES

In response to this changing context, the Government increased Garda numbers and enacted legislation, including, in 1972, the Prisons Act, in response to riots by republican prisoners in Mountjoy Prison. During the debates on this Act, the Minister for Justice also announced the re-enactment of the Special Criminal Court. Shortly afterwards, the Offences Against the State Act was amended, making membership of the IRA an offence again. Section 30 of the Act provided for the arrest, search and detention of people suspected of being involved in offences against the State. However, while this section was widely used, it did not translate into a high rate of charges and subsequent prosecution. This may reflect a position where Gardaí wanted to deter rather than prosecute.

Some specific incidents influenced legislative change. For example, on foot of the killing of the British Ambassador and an explosion near the Special Criminal Court in 1976, a state of emergency was declared, which led to the passing of the Emergency Powers Act, 1976. This allowed Gardaí to detain people on suspicion of offences against the State, for seven days, on the direction of a Chief Superintendent. Moreover, the Criminal Law (Jurisdiction) Act, 1976 allowed prosecutions in the Republic for offences committed in Northern Ireland. After the Omagh bombing, the Act was amended again to curtail the right to silence, and Garda powers of detention for purposes of interrogation were expanded.

While these legislative measures may have been deemed useful and necessary, they were not without issue. A person could be detained on the word of a Chief Superintendent, questioned, and then brought before a non-jury trial. This led to calls from human rights and civil liberty organisations for it to be abolished.

However, the existence of the Court has been ratified by the Dáil and all governments since, and has seen numerous significant convictions for terrorism and serious organised crime offences handed down.

INCIDENTS OF NOTE

Within the context discussed above, some specific incidents occurred, which – alone or combined – significantly impacted policing during the Troubles.

In 1972, two bombs in Dublin on 1 December killed two and injured 127. Only weeks later, two more people were killed in an explosion in Belturbet, Co. Cavan, followed by another death in an explosion in Dublin, a month later. In 1974, three explosions took place on the same day in Dublin and one in Monaghan, killing thirty-three and one unborn child.

The following year, a person was killed in an explosion at Dublin Airport, and a further two were killed a month later, in an explosion in Dundalk. There were many other explosions in the Republic that did not kill people. For example, in October 1972, Connolly Station in Dublin was bombed. A month later, a cinema in Dublin was bombed, and forty people were injured. Smaller explosions also took place throughout the country, in the

Gardaí and soldiers prepare to search a forest area at Ardmoneen, Co. Cavan, on 20 December 1983 following the kidnapping of businessman Don Tidey.

form of car bombs, letter bombs, and incendiary devices. External reports found that An Garda Síochána was ill-equipped to respond to some of these incidents.

There were also several high-profile kidnappings, including the abduction of Lord and Lady Donoughmore in 1974, the abduction of Dutch businessman Tiede Herrema in 1975, the kidnapping of Don Tidey in 1983, and the kidnapping of Jennifer Guinness in 1986.

Serving Gardaí had not experienced incidents of this nature before. This, together with the increased threat to their safety, had a significant impact on policing. Garda Richard Fallon was the first member to be killed since 1942. His death in 1970 sent shockwaves through the service. The public also increasingly recognised the risk members faced going out on duty. This was reinforced by further deaths of members throughout the 1970s and 1980s. Indeed, deaths continued up until 1996, with the killing of Detective Garda Jerry McCabe bringing the number of officers killed during the Troubles to twelve.

The risk to members of An Garda Síochána could also be seen in the number of assaults reported against Gardaí, which continued to rise from 1973 to 1981. Attacks were also targeted at those outside the service. For example, in 1982, a bomb was placed on the car of Dr James Donovan, the head of the Forensic Science Laboratory. Moreover, four members of the Royal Ulster Constabulary (RUC) were killed during the two decades whilst visiting the Republic. The British Ambassador, Christopher Ewart Biggs, and a British civil servant were killed in 1976, and in 1979 Lord Mountbatten and four others were killed, demonstrating the level of risk throughout the country. These incidents, especially the latter, resulted in a call for Gardaí to be armed; this was resisted by the organisation and the members who regarded it as an unsatisfactory response to a highly complex problem. In many ways, their resistance reconnected policing in Ireland with the people and with politicians.

Two public order events are also worth highlighting in this regard. One of these was the burning of the British Embassy in Dublin in 1972, which is dealt with below by retired Chief Superintendent Paul Smyth who was on duty at the time. Nearly ten years later, approximately 14,000 took to the streets of Dublin, protesting about the treatment of the hunger strikers in the Maze Prison. A riot reportedly broke out, with Gardaí pulling batons when attacked with stones and petrol bombs.

Aerial view of South Leinster Street in Dublin following the 1974 Dublin and Monaghan bombings.

POLICING RESPONSE

Many of the internal policing documents applicable in the early years of the Troubles dated back to the 1940s and 1960s. A new Crime Investigation Techniques manual was not introduced until 1979, to replace one from 1946. The Code of Practice, first published in 1965, was also outdated. Despite a lack of experience, resources, and expertise, An Garda Síochána responded, developing new skills to police national security threats, while at the same time responding to serious organised crime, drugs, and other increasing crime trends. These skills provide the foundations that underpin policing and investigations in Ireland today. However, they took time to develop and embed, and investigation processes were not always consistent.

This was also the era of the so-called 'heavy gang'. No lack of training or experience excuses reports of heavy-handedness and serious allegations of police brutality and excessive use of force, but in an era where the threat posed was perceived to warrant the enactment of powers that removed certain rights of suspects, it is not surprising that some within the service may have believed that such tactics were worth it.

There is now greater oversight of the actions of An Garda Síochána, and this is likely to increase with the Policing, Security and Community Safety Bill, which includes provisions to enhance the independent oversight of national security infrastructure. This is largely influenced by the Commission on the Future of Policing in Ireland (COFPI) report, which recommended that An Garda Síochána should retain its national security function, but with a dedicated budget, direct recruitment of specialist expertise, and working in conjunction with new and strengthened governmental security bodies.

This reflects a growing recognition that co-operation and coordination are now essential given the complexity of crime and terrorism.

Unlike during the Troubles, cross-border co-operation is less discreet, as seen recently in joint investigations in cases relating to human and drug trafficking.

CONCLUSION

The Troubles have left a significant legacy on policing in Ireland today, especially in the context of national security. An Garda Síochána had to develop skills and responses to the threats associated with the Troubles, which were influenced also by an increase in SOC cases and developing drug gangs. In time, the organisation changed from prioritising the security of the State to more community-based policing needs. One thing that remained consistent throughout the Troubles, though, was that An Garda Síochána maintained its identity as an unarmed police service. For all the positive and negative actions associated with the organisation since its inception, the unarmed nature of the majority of members who have worn the uniform recognises the value of preserving that tradition, valuing the relationships it facilitates with the public.

This strong relationship with the community is one of the reasons why An Garda Síochána's unique position as both the national police and security service works so well. It enables information gathered locally by Gardaí to be quickly shared through the organisation, and avoids the 'turf wars' between state agencies that has hindered action against terrorist groups in some jurisdictions.

The work performed by Gardaí locally and nationally, along with the co-operation of the RUC and Police Service of Northern Ireland (PSNI), was vital to degrading the capabilities of terrorist organisations. This work continues to this day in tackling terrorismt intent on undermining peace.

The views expressed by the author are her own.

THE BURNING OF THE BRITISH EMBASSY
Retired Chief Superintendent Paul Smyth

For decades, the British Embassy in Dublin was located in a terraced Georgian house, at 39 Merrion Square. The building symbolised the relationship of confidence and trust that existed between the people of Ireland and the United Kingdom. On 30 January 1972, that relationship changed after members of the British Army shot and killed thirteen unarmed civil rights marchers in Derry. The shootings on that Bloody Sunday led to protest marches and disturbances occurring spontaneously throughout the country. The British Embassy was an obvious flashpoint but with all resources required locally, Garda Headquarters were unable to ferry surplus resources from the country to Dublin.

The British Embassy was guarded 24 hours a day. As a young Sergeant on that Bloody Sunday evening, I inspected the Gardaí on duty outside. Each day, my duty hours started at six o'clock in the morning and lasted until well past midnight. The following morning, I watched as the haze slowly lifted on Merrion Square. The spectre of black bushes, scrawny shrubs and tall thin trees created a foreboding feeling. A small group of onlookers stood nearby.

As the days passed, the number of protesters outside the embassy increased. When hostility seemed inevitable, Garda reinforcements arrived. We formed a semicircle, three rows deep, at the steps outside the embassy door. As the crowd drew closer, those in the front line began to kick out viciously at us. Quick to understand the danger we were in, we fell back, tightly locking arms together, and then quickly sprang forward. The oncoming protesters were trapped by the crowds building up behind them and were unable to retreat. For the remaining days of the protest, stewards from the crowd ensured that a healthy distance was maintained between the two front lines.

At one stage, we heard that a large parade was on its way to the embassy. The local Superintendent arrived with reinforcements. Well-spaced lines of Gardaí were formed across the roadway in front of the embassy, facing Holles Street. Eventually, the protesters came into view, some carrying black coffins. A band played music. The protestors negotiated with the Superintendent who allowed a small number through to place the coffins at the door of the embassy. The coffin-carriers then returned to the main body of protestors and the Gardaí immediately formed a semicircle in front of the embassy. The crowds poured onto the street in front of them.

Stewards in the crowd, which by this time amounted to several thousand, created a long, narrow human corridor in front of the embassy door. A can of petrol and bottles, which were initially concealed from our view, were positioned near the railings of the park at the far end of the corridor. A man ran up through the human corridor, carrying a bottle of petrol plugged with a piece of burning cloth. He tossed it in over our heads and it landed on the top step, beside the coffins. When the bottle hit the ground, the petrol ignited. This action was repeated over and over again but the embassy door remained intact.

The real trouble started when the crowd moved back, allowing a lorry to drive up and stop near the kerb in front of us. Having been ordered by a Sergeant to move his lorry, the driver parked on the opposite side of the street. A number of men climbed onto the back of it and began to address the crowd with a loudhailer. I was standing in the front line of Gardaí slightly to the right of the embassy. Garda Inspector Johnny Robinson stood in front of us near Chief Superintendent Eamon Doherty, who was in the middle of the roadway.

Suddenly, a man with his face covered appeared from behind the lorry. He had a plastic shopping bag in his hand, and he swung it a couple of times and lobbed it over our heads. It landed on the top of the steps in front of the embassy door. A speaker jumped from the back of the lorry and ran towards the Chief Superintendent, saying, 'Get your men out of there; there's a bomb in that bag.' The Chief Superintendent consulted with the Inspector, who ordered us to run.

The assembled Gardaí scattered in all directions. I rushed back towards the steps intending to throw the bag into the basement, to minimise the damage the bomb could cause. But when I reached the first step, I saw a light inside the basement window. Fearing that there were people there, and that if I threw the bomb down, it could kill them, I turned and ran across the road, sheltering behind a lamp post just as the bomb exploded, blowing open the embassy door. The impact felt like a rabbit punch to the back of my neck.

When the smoke settled, we returned to our positions in front of the embassy which was still standing. The human corridor was again formed in the crowd. Petrol bombs were repeatedly thrown over our heads. Torrential rain poured down. The broken embassy door provided a target for the bombers. A few protestors climbed along balconies from adjacent houses onto the embassy balcony. They broke windows and threw in burning cloths. As the crowd chanted 'Burn, burn, burn', the petrol bombers became more active and reckless, moving the can of petrol to the front of the human corridor to enable them to throw petrol bombs into the hallway. This narrowed the distance between the two front lines. I was standing immediately in front of the can of petrol.

A petrol bomber ran forward, knocking over the can and spilling the petrol onto the road and over the legs of my trousers. As he threw his petrol bomb, the ignited cloth fell from it and landed on the ground beside me, igniting the petrol there and on my trousers. Luckily for me, the flames were smothered under my greatcoat, which was saturated by the heavy rain that had fallen. Later that night when I arrived home, my wife was anxiously waiting for me, having watched TV coverage of the events. To reassure her, I tried to downplay what had happened but when we were going to bed, she could see my badly singed legs.

The petrol bombing continued until the embassy was a burned-out shell. The British Government had pressurised the Irish Government to call out the Irish Army to support the Gardaí in protecting their embassy. To prevent the use of lethal force the Government had refused and it was left to the unarmed Gardaí to achieve the unachievable.

The Irish Government's decision is understandable. Memories of the 1916 Rising, the War of Independence and the Irish Civil War were still very much alive. The President of Ireland and many other politicians of the time had fought in these wars and learned the lesson that violence begets violence. The destruction of the British Embassy was a diplomatic embarrassment. However, while the bricks and mortar of the British Embassy were sacrificed, no lives were lost. Common sense trumped symbolism.

Retired Chief Superintendent Paul Smyth at the location of the former British Embassy on Merrion Square in Dublin.

CHAPTER 12

A BORDER BEAT

Retired Garda Pat O'Donoghue

Although classified as a border town, Dundalk in Co. Louth was policed in the same way as any other major provincial town in Ireland until 1970. The quarter century between the mid-1940s and 1970 was, on the whole, a quiet time for policing in Ireland. As the 1970s began, this peace was shattered by the re-emergence of violent conflict in Northern Ireland. Incidents along the border brought the conflict further south.

The evening of 21 September 1972 was a defining moment in the policing history of Dundalk, with far-reaching consequences for Gardaí and the security of the State. At around 6 p.m. a political protest rally took place at the Market Square with about a hundred people in attendance. At the end of the rally, a man with a loudspeaker called on the crowd to line up in military formation and march to the Garda station at the Crescent. On their way, they ripped up paving stones for ammunition and hijacked a lorry to block the road. Groups of local youths willingly joined the mob. By the time they reached the Garda station, their numbers had doubled. They proceeded to attack the station with stones and petrol bombs.

Sergeant Hugh Shreenan, his wife and two-year-old daughter lived in the married quarters. He was there with his family and a small number of Gardaí when the attack took place. In no time, the rioters had broken all the front windows of the Garda station, and a patrol car and private members' cars had been overturned and burned. When the mob proceeded to break in the front door of the station, the occupants of the building were saved by the quick thinking and bravery of Detective Garda Denis Daly who managed to get his hands on an official machine gun, faced the mob, and fired volleys of shots over their heads. The sound of gunfire scattered the crowd from the front of the station.

Phone calls for assistance had earlier been made to outlying Garda stations and the local Army barracks. Troops from the 27th Battalion in full riot gear were first to arrive on the scene. Confronted by the rioters, who pelted them with stones and paving slabs, the troops eventually had to fire CS gas to gain control. At the same time, a fire engine trying to make its way to the Garda station also came under attack, with its windows and equipment being smashed. Fire-brigade assistance was summoned from Drogheda and Carrickmacross. As the rioters made their way back to the town centre, the Army ringed the Garda barracks for fear of further attacks.

On the way to the town centre, the mob ran riot, breaking traffic lights and shop windows, and looting premises. By then, extra Gardaí had arrived on the scene from nearby stations and faced the rioters at Market Square. The sight of the Gardaí approaching with their batons drawn was enough to make the rioters disperse. Eventually, with the town saturated with Gardaí, law and order were restored.

Since the foundation of the State, this was the first time a Garda station had been attacked in such a manner, with such devastating consequences for the town and the Gardaí protecting it. It heralded the emergence of a very dangerous era. Yet nobody was prepared for the no-warning car-bomb blast at Kay's Tavern, Crowe Street, Dundalk, on 19 December 1975, in which two civilians – Jack Rooney and Hugh Watters – were killed. The bombing of Kay's Tavern and the murder of Seamus Ludlow the following year underlined both the vulnerability of Dundalk and the surrounding district to retaliatory violence from loyalists, and the extra demands this threat placed on policing in a border district.

With the spillover of the northern conflict, those 20–30 years were to be a severely testing time, and Dundalk Garda District would be tested more than most. In the course of the Troubles, three members of An Garda Síochána from the district were murdered on duty; over twenty Scott Medals were awarded to Gardaí for facing down gunfire and other acts of bravery; and, unfortunately, two other members were accidentally killed on duty.

DIPLOMATIC HEADACHES

While every tour of duty a Garda performs is unique and unpredictable, no member could have expected the extraordinary events of the night of Wednesday, 5 May 1976, when Garda Colm Murray went on checkpoint duty at the Flagstaff Road near Omeath in Co. Louth, close to the border. At 10 p.m. a Triumph car approached the checkpoint from the north. On shining a torch on the front passenger, Garda Murray saw him place a submachine gun at his feet and try to conceal it with a large map.

The driver and his passenger, both dressed in civilian clothes, produced British Army identification; they said that they must have taken a wrong turning on their return to Bessbrook Military Barracks. On receiving the assistance of an Army corporal from the nearby sentry post, Garda Murray informed the two British soldiers that as they were in the Irish Republic, he would be detaining them. He also took possession of their weapons – a submachine gun, two automatic pistols and about a hundred rounds of ammunition. The men were arrested under the Offences against the State Act and were escorted to Dundalk Garda Station.

At 2.15 a.m., two more cars approached the checkpoint, as if in convoy. The six occupants, also in civilian clothes, identified themselves as British soldiers; between them, they were armed with three submachine guns, two automatic pistols and a sawn-off pump-action shotgun, with about 200 rounds of ammunition. They also carried a night-sight, two-way radios, and maps. On questioning, it emerged that they were a British Army SAS unit searching for their comrades who had been arrested earlier. Garda Murray arrested them and demanded that they hand over their weapons, which they did only when Irish Army personnel made their presence felt. The men were taken to Dundalk Garda Station under Garda/Army escort, where they were interviewed at length.

The incident created a diplomatic headache for the Government. If the soldiers were charged, it would affect diplomatic relations with Britain, but neither could they appear to be released without charge. The authorities had to act quickly to avert trouble, and the soldiers were charged under the Firearms Act with possession of unlicensed firearms, and possession of firearms with intent to endanger life. They were later released on bail of £40,000 put up by the British Embassy.

In March 1977, the eight soldiers went on trial and were subsequently fined £100 each for possession of firearms and ammunition without firearms certificates. The incident was recorded as a map-reading error, and an apology was received from the British Government.

CAPTAIN ROBERT NAIRAC

Another event that highlights the complexities of border policing occurred in May 1977, just north of the Louth border. Captain Robert Nairac, a British Army officer, was kidnapped and taken across the border to Ravensdale where he was interrogated before being killed. Because it was a cross-border incident, the main Garda investigation was coordinated from Dundalk Garda Station. This investigation led to a conviction being secured in the Special Criminal Court in Dublin in November 1977 for the murder of Captain Nairac.

AMBUSH AT CARLINGFORD LOUGH

On 27 August 1979, a British Army patrol was driving past an entrance to Narrow Water Castle, at the head of Carlingford Lough, when a massive explosion took place, resulting in the killing of six soldiers and serious injury of the remainder. Assuming they were under attack from the southern side of the border, the soldiers began firing across the water towards the Omeath area in the Republic. Two civilians who were in Omeath – William Hudson and his cousin, Barry Hudson – went down to the shore to see what was happening. Tragically, they came under fire from the British Army; William Hudson was shot dead, and Barry Hudson was seriously wounded. In the meantime, the ambushed soldiers had radioed for help. When it arrived, an incident-command point was set up beside a stone gateway on the opposite side of the road from where the initial explosion had occurred. No sooner had this happened than another massive explosion took place, destroying the wall and killing another twelve soldiers. The ambush appeared to have been meticulously planned.

As a result of these incidents, eighteen British soldiers on the northern side of the border lost their lives and one civilian lost his life on the southern side. A major cross-border investigation, based in Dundalk, got under way. Several people were arrested in relation to the bombing but, due to lack of evidence, were later released. On the same day, Lord Mountbatten, a member of the British royal family, was killed by a bomb blast at Mullaghmore, Co. Sligo.

Three days later, on 30 August 1979, Dundalk witnessed one of the most violent nights of its history. The European Cup tie between Dundalk and the Belfast team Linfield was to be played at Oriel Park. Arrangements had been made for strict security. As the game progressed, Oriel Park became like a war zone, with Linfield supporters throwing stones, burning flags, and tearing down fences. By this stage, an extra 300 Garda reinforcements had arrived from Dublin and outlying areas, strengthening the Garda position.

By the end of the night, over a hundred people had been treated for injuries, including fifty Gardaí. While not all Linfield supporters had taken part in the riotous behaviour, it was nevertheless clear that the political violence of the day had also infected sport. At the end of a troubled decade, this background of violence represented a heavy burden on policing in Dundalk.

THE TROUBLED 1980S

Moving through to the 1980s, dealing with this exceptional violence continued alongside the standard policing of a major provincial town. The border stations of Omeath, Dromad and Hackballscross were still heavily manned with uniformed Gardaí. The 36 official border crossings had regular checkpoints, which were mostly manned by unarmed uniformed Gardaí backed up by armed units from the local 27th Battalion from Aiken Barracks in Dundalk. Shooting incidents against Gardaí continued along the border. On 21 July 1983, gunfire ripped through the driver's side of a Garda patrol car, over the head of the driver and out through the rear window, as they followed a suspicious vehicle at Omeath.

SERGEANT PATRICK MORRISSEY

For the Gardaí in the District, the most tragic incident of the decade occurred on 27 June 1985. As Sergeant Patrick Morrissey was about to enter Ardee Courthouse, he was told of an armed raid that had just taken place at the local employment exchange; shots had been fired at Gardaí arriving at the scene. Sergeant Morrissey flagged down the patrol car and went with Garda Peter Long and Garda Brendan Flynn in pursuit of the gunmen. They set up a checkpoint in Tallanstown village, intending to intercept the getaway car. Two men riding a motorcycle approached the checkpoint and failed to stop. Recognising the men as the raiders, the Gardaí gave chase in the patrol car. At Rathbrist Cross, the motorcycle crashed into a car, seriously injuring the female driver and her three-year-old daughter. While Garda Long and Garda Flynn attended to the injured family, Sergeant Morrissey, alone and on foot, followed the suspects who had run up an avenue leading to a private house. As he caught up with them, a shot was fired and he fell to the ground, seriously wounded. One of the gunmen stood over him and, at point-blank range, shot him dead before running away. Following a search, the two gunmen were arrested and taken into custody. Both were convicted by the Special Criminal Court in Dublin in December 1985 and were sentenced to death. This sentence was later commuted to 40 years' penal servitude. Sergeant Patrick Morrissey was posthumously awarded the Gold Scott Medal.

Sergeant Patrick Morrissey who was shot dead while pursuing armed raiders.

COURT APPEARANCE IN DUNDALK

Dundalk experienced another riotous day on 14 August 1986. Peter Robinson, then deputy leader of the Democratic Unionist Party, and a future First Minister in the Northern Ireland Assembly, had been remanded to appear at Dundalk District Court, charged with unlawful assembly and assault at Clontibret, Co. Monaghan.

Approximately 800 extra Gardaí were drafted into the Dundalk area for the day. The court case ended with the case being further adjourned. Gardaí in riot gear directed Mr Robinson's supporters back to their cars. As the cavalcade of supporters was leaving town, some had their windscreens smashed by flying missiles, and more trouble flared. Again, a baton charge was required, and it took the full numerical strength of the Gardaí on duty to restore order.

AN INLA FEUD

On 25 April 1987, Mary McGlinchey was bathing her two sons on a Saturday evening at her home in Dundalk, when two gunmen broke in the back door, ran up the stairs and fatally shot her in front of her children. It is generally believed that this vicious killing was part of an Irish National Liberation Army (INLA) internal feud. Mary had been married to Dominic McGlinchey and both were self-declared members of the INLA, very heavily involved in its structure and activities. Dominic McGlinchey, who was serving a sentence in Portlaoise Prison at the time, was eventually released in 1993, but the following year he was shot dead in front of his son at a phone box on the outskirts of Drogheda. Despite major investigations, both crimes remain unsolved.

THE MURDER OF SENIOR RUC OFFICERS

Before the end of the 1980s, another very serious cross-border incident took place, which gained international headlines and led to one of the biggest enquiries in the State.

On 20 March 1989, Chief Superintendent Harry Breen and Superintendent Bob Buchanan of the Royal Ulster Constabulary (RUC) attended a cross-border security conference at Dundalk Garda Station. On their return, shortly after crossing the border, they drove into an armed ambush and were shot dead by four masked and armed men wearing battle fatigues. The shooting was later claimed by the South Armagh Brigade of the Provisional Irish Republican Army (IRA). Questions were asked regarding how such a well-planned and successfully executed ambush could have been arranged in such a short span of time. An allegation that a mole in Dundalk Garda Station was passing information to the IRA was hotly disputed by all Garda and civilian staff working in the station at the time.

Investigations into the shootings were carried out, both north and south of the border, but these were inconclusive. Eventually, the Irish Government commissioned Judge Peter Corry, a retired Canadian Supreme Court judge, to carry out an independent investigation and to report his findings. Based on Judge Corry's findings, the Government set up a tribunal, which was to be a full judicial enquiry into all matters surrounding the killings.

In July 2006, Judge Peter Smithwick began his investigation, and on 7 June 2011, the public hearings began in Dublin. Two and a half years later, on 3 December 2013, Judge Smithwick's findings were published. While he had been unable to find direct evidence of collusion, he believed that on the 'balance of probability' there had been collusion between Gardaí from Dundalk Station and the Provisional IRA in the murder of the two senior policemen.

There is no doubt that this finding cast a shadow and a doubt over all personnel working in the station at the time. The conclusions of the Smithwick Tribunal were accepted by An Garda Síochána, but while respected, they were not totally accepted by the members of An Garda Síochána who worked out of Dundalk Station during those perilous times.

CEASEFIRE

Entering the 1990s, paramilitary activity appeared to be easing, and ceasefire talks were beginning in Northern Ireland. However, without warning, on the evening of 18 July 1991, a further atrocity took place. Tom Oliver, a highly respected farmer who lived on the Cooley Peninsula, was abducted as he went to tend to his stock. The following day, his body was found near Belleeks in Co. Armagh; he had been shot many times. Although the murder elicited sympathy and support nationally for the Oliver family, nobody has been made accountable for it; the investigation is ongoing.

On 31 August 1994, a unilateral ceasefire was declared by the Provisional IRA. This resulted in a scaling-down of Garda resources along the border. However, in 1996, a new crisis arrived, requiring all 36 border crossings to be manned again. Bovine Spongiform Encephalopathy (BSE) or 'Mad Cow Disease' had been found in animals in Britain, and for the protection of Irish meat products, the border had to be sealed. The operation was expensive for the State, but the results were successful.

THE 'DISAPPEARED'

Even after the 1994 ceasefire, the years of violence cast their shadow. Families of the 'disappeared' continued to campaign to have the remains of their loved ones returned. Eventually, in 1999, an Independent Commission for the Location of Victims' Remains was established. With its help, the bodies of two of the disappeared were found in north Co. Louth.

On the morning of 28 May 1999, Gardaí at Dundalk Garda Station received information that a coffin with a body in it lay at a corner of Faughart Cemetery, a few miles north of Dundalk. The information also said that the coffin was above ground and contained the body of Eamonn Molloy. This was the first of the disappeared to be returned to his family.

The following day, in response to further information received, a search party of Gardaí was sent to Templetown Beach, Carlingford, to dig for the remains of Jean McConville, a widowed mother of ten young children, who had been abducted from her home in Belfast on 7 December 1972. However, by July 1999, there had been no breakthrough in the search, and the dig was called off. The following year, a search of a different area of the beach was equally unsuccessful.

On 26 August 2003, a man out walking his dog came across human remains at the nearby Shelling Hill Beach; these remains were proven to be those of Jean McConville. It appears that the remains eventually became exposed due to the tide and the shifting of the sands. The beach had held its secret for over thirty years but now brought closure to this part of Jean McConville's story.

THE VISIT OF BILL CLINTON

A massive security operation was put in place when US President Bill Clinton visited Dundalk with his family on 12 December 2000, receiving a very warm welcome from the townspeople. The event put Dundalk on the world stage again but far more positively this time, and from a policing point of view it was a major success.

FOOT-AND-MOUTH DISEASE

On 21 February 2001, foot-and-mouth disease was found in animals in Great Britain. The following day, checkpoints were set up and our border with Northern Ireland was cordoned off, thus putting into action what became one of the biggest security operations ever undertaken by the State. Again, in north County Louth, with its 29 miles of border, very strict security measures were required; the 36 crossings were funnelled into 19 static checkpoints, with every vehicle that passed through being checked. The whole operation was very successful, aided by the goodwill and co-operation of the general public.

FURTHER GARDA TRAGEDY

While the years of violence seemed to have passed with the arrival of the new century, more Garda tragedy was yet to follow. On Friday evening, 25 January 2013, Detective Garda Adrian Donohoe and Detective Garda Joe Ryan were on cash-escort duty. At 9.30 p.m. the Garda car entered the car park of Lordship Credit Union with another car which they had accompanied from a different credit union. Suddenly a car crossed the road and blocked the entrance to the credit union. As Detective Garda Donohoe got out of the car to investigate, a masked raider came from behind and shot him; he died almost instantly. Detective Garda Ryan, who was the driver, was held at gunpoint by three masked and armed raiders. Two raiders then broke into the car belonging to the credit union staff and made off with €7,000 in cash and assorted cheques, leaving a much larger sum behind them. The five-man gang fled the scene, taking with them the keys of the patrol car. Detective Garda Adrian Donohue was posthumously awarded the Gold Scott Medal. One person has been convicted of the capital murder of Detective Garda Donohue and the investigation into his murder is continuing.

Sadly, within three years, another tragedy occurred that was to rock the local Garda service yet again. On Sunday evening, 11 October 2015, following a complaint of domestic abuse, Garda Tony Golden went in the Garda patrol car with the victim and her father to a housing estate in Omeath. The purpose of the visit was to protect the victim while she retrieved her belongings, as she was moving away from her abusive partner. On Garda Golden's advice, the victim's father stayed in the patrol car for his own safety. As Garda Golden and the woman entered the house, the male occupant challenged them and shot Garda Golden five times. He then shot his partner several times before turning the gun on himself and taking his own life. Local Garda Gary O'Callaghan was first to respond and provided assistance, but it was too late for Garda Golden. Miraculously, the young woman survived. Garda Tony Golden was posthumously awarded the Gold Scott Medal.

CONCLUSION

Policing methods have changed extensively since the days when Gardaí policed their districts on foot or on bicycles, and with little or no means of communication outside their barracks. The contrast with modern policing which makes full use of forensic science and IT is stark, indeed. Nevertheless, Gardaí have successfully policed the Dundalk area throughout – a task that became considerably more difficult from the 1970s.

Before Irish independence, the Louth–Armagh county boundary was no more significant in terms of policing than the Louth–Meath boundary. With independence came the partition of Ireland, and the Louth–Armagh boundary became an international border, which has been in place throughout the existence of An Garda Síochána. Border patrolling is a unique policing experience. In peaceful times, a border presents its own challenges, but in troubled times it takes on a totally different dimension. Experienced Gardaí have referred to the border as being a multicultural area to police, where Gardaí encounter a northern culture, a southern culture, and a distinct border culture located uncomfortably between them.

The great unpredictability of daily policing in Dundalk Garda District made unusual demands on those who served in the area, and often prompted truly courageous responses. A significant number of members who served in Dundalk have been awarded the Scott Medal for bravery, and – including Garda John Lally and Detective Garda Desmond Dixon who died accidentally – five Gardaí within the district have lost their lives in the course of duty. Although Dundalk Garda District has often been a challenging and even dangerous area, I found it a rewarding place in which to serve the public, and I have many good memories, along with the sad ones.

CHAPTER 13

THE TECHNICAL ——— BUREAU: THE BEGINNING AND THE EARLY YEARS

Retired Inspector Edwin S. Handcock

'There is a definite "cut" or "stamp" on these boys, you can see it in their manner and even in their gait,' wrote Captain Dennis O'Kelly following a visit to the Technical Bureau in 1958. He continued:

> A few weeks' test and a Garda is or is not retained in this branch. Many young men voluntarily withdraw and return to ordinary duties, why? The work is very often, by its nature, repulsive and it is no eight-hour-a-day task. Meals, sleep, home, wife and kiddies – all must wait. Day-light and darkness are of no account.

Having served for 27 very enjoyable years in the Bureau, I can say that Captain O'Kelly gave a surprisingly accurate description of our duties, but I strongly disagree with his 'repulsive' comment – it could be a bit gruesome at times, but that was all part of the job.

So, why did I join the Technical Bureau? My interest in crime detection began during my grammar-school days when I read *The Adventures of Sherlock Holmes*; I was soon hooked on crime-scene detection, and my future career was decided. Having joined An Garda Síochána in 1965, I subsequently enrolled in a correspondence course with the Institute of Applied Science in Chicago,

The Ballistics Section of the Garda Technical Bureau. Edwin Handcock is fourth from right.

and in 1973 was awarded a Diploma in Scientific Crime Detection. I followed my dream and joined the Ballistics Section of the Technical Bureau in 1974.

ESTABLISHMENT OF THE BUREAU

The first reference to the establishment of a technical unit is contained in 'The Garda Síochána Establishment Scheme' 1930 booklet in which Commissioner Eoin O'Duffy outlined the necessity of forming such a unit. He stressed the need for members with qualifications in areas such as photography, topography, making of models, fingerprints, expert examination of handwriting, and identification of guns through examination of bullets fired from them.

Detective Sergeant George Lawlor, who was stationed in Galway at this time, also studied with the Institute of Applied Science in Chicago and was awarded a Diploma in Finger-prints, Police Photography, Firearms Identification, Criminal and Civil Investigation, Modus Operandi, Identification of Handwriting and Typewriting. In 1932, he responded to a HQ circular requesting constructive ideas in any area of police work. Lawlor submitted a 3,000-word essay which received high praise from Assistant Commissioner Eamonn Cullen who wrote of it: 'There is scarcely a point with which one may disagree and that says a good deal.'

The Garda Technical Bureau was established on 7 October 1934. Deputy Commissioner W.R.E. Murphy – better known as Liam Ó Murchadha – was the driving force behind its formation. On 9 July 1934, he issued a circular in which he requested details of any member possessing special interest, ability or training in the following subjects: Chemistry, Physics, Pathology, Wireless Telegraphy, Handwriting, Ballistics, Photography, Use of Microscope, Engineering (Civil, Mechanical or Electrical), Making of Models, Languages or any subject which might prove useful in the detection of crime or presentation of cases in court. When the Technical Bureau was established three months later, it had five sections – Investigation, Fingerprints, Photography, Mapping and Ballistics; it later included the Dublin Criminal Register.

Based in Garda HQ, the Firearms Section had originally been established in 1932 for the examination and testing of firearms and ammunition. It was renamed the Ballistics Section when it became part of the Technical Bureau, with responsibility for the examination of firearms and ammunition, the restoration of erased identification numbers, examination of glass fragments, tool and instrument marks, and microscopic photography in relation to their examination. The Ballistics Section also serviced and repaired revolvers issued to the Detective Branch.

Superintendent Patrick Sheridan was the first officer in charge of the Bureau. He had studied criminology under the renowned Swedish criminologist, Dr Henry Soderman,

co-author of *Modern Criminal Investigation*. Sheridan was an expert on shoe marks, tyre marks and tool marks, and he wrote extensively on these subjects in various police and forensic journals. Two months after the formation of the Bureau, he published an excellent article about tracks and marks, which appeared in a 'Technical Supplement' in the December 1934 edition of the *Garda Review*. Although written 87 years ago, much of the advice and instruction contained in it are still relevant to crime-scene examination today.

At work in the Ballistics Section.

DETECTIVE SERGEANT GEORGE LAWLOR

Detective Sergeant George Lawlor joined the Investigation Section of the Bureau, being promoted to Inspector in 1935 and Detective Superintendent in charge in 1949; he died in 1961 while still serving. He was fortunate to have been admitted into An Garda Síochána as he was half an inch below regulation height; by his own admission, he passed by standing on tiptoe while being measured. Prior to joining the service, he was an active member of the Irish Volunteers from 1918. Having been interned in Ballykinlar Internment Camp for 13 months, he was released in December 1921 and joined An Garda Síochána in 1923. He became a legend in the world of scientific crime detection and contributed extensively to various professional journals.

SUPERINTENDENT DAN STAPLETON

Superintendent Dan Stapleton was another larger-than-life personality to join the Bureau. Having qualified as a chemist in 1912, he opened a medical hall – as pharmacies were then known – in Kilkenny. As a lieutenant in the First Battalion Kilkenny Brigade Irish Volunteers, he made explosives, serviced weapons and refurbished ammunition. A keen sportsman, he won three All-Ireland hurling medals with the Kilkenny team. He joined the Free State Army and was promoted to Commandant. Working with a colleague, he designed a device which enabled the firing of blank cartridges in Lewis machine guns. In 1934, while still serving in the Army, he was appointed as Technical Advisor to the Ballistics Section.

In 1936, at the age of 50, he left the Army and was seconded to the Ballistics Section with the rank of Superintendent; because of his age, special legislation had to be enacted. During his 17 years in the Bureau, he gained an international reputation. Details on the results of using the 'Moulage Process' – a method he developed for the identification of glass fragments – were published in 1940 in the British Home Office *Scientific Aids to Criminal Investigation*.

The newly established Technical Bureau was located in the old Royal Hospital Infirmary building at Military Road, St John's Road, Kilmainham. This rambling old building, designed by Thomas Burgh and built circa 1730, may have looked forlorn from the outside, but it served the Bureau well until it was moved in 1979 to a new four-storey building at Garda Headquarters in the Phoenix Park.

Presenting forensic evidence.

SOME EARLY INTERESTING CASES
THE MURDER OF MARY 'MOLL' MCCARTHY

Superintendent Dan Stapleton played a key role in the infamous case of 38-year-old Harry Gleeson, who was executed for the murder of Mary 'Moll' McCarthy, in New Inn, in November 1940.

Harry Gleeson, who had played hurling with Rockwell Rovers and was a good fiddle player, worked on the farm of his uncle, John Caesar, in the townland of Marlhill, New Inn. On the morning of Thursday, 21 November, having finished the milking, Harry was out in the fields when, on climbing a fence, he saw the dead body of a woman, with a small black dog sitting on her chest, growling. He reported the finding first to his uncle and then to the Gardaí in New Inn. It was the body of Moll McCarthy, a single woman, aged 38, the mother of seven children; she had been shot twice. Gleeson was the only suspect. He was arrested and charged with murder.

Dan Stapleton recovered two Eley Hawk cartridges and wadding from the scene. He also examined the American-made single-barrel 12-gauge shotgun alleged to have been used, and pellets removed from the body; the gun belonged to Harry's uncle, John Caesar. At the trial, Stapleton gave evidence of the position where the murderer could have stood when he fired, and the range of shot. The first shot, which hit the victim's neck, was fired from a range of 5 or 6 feet; the one that blew away part of her face was discharged from a close range of approximately 6 inches, and fired downwards, almost perpendicular. Following a ten-day trial, Harry Gleeson was convicted of murder and executed on 23 April 1941.

In 2013, the Attorney General ordered a review of the case. The review, conducted by Shane Murphy SC, highlighted profoundly serious inconsistencies in the medical evidence, and suppression of evidence. On 19 December 2015, Harry Gleeson was awarded the first posthumous pardon in the history of the State; it was signed by President Michael D. Higgins.

A VIOLENT RAMPAGE IN GOREY

Captain O'Kelly's use of the word 'repulsive' could apply to a grim case that inspired the ingenuity of Detective Garda Eamonn O'Fiachain of the Ballistics Section. On the afternoon of Tuesday, 14 November 1961, in the Garden City area of Gorey, a local man went on a violent rampage. He threw stones through the windscreen of a car, assaulted and knocked a neighbour down on the road, and then assaulted a Christian Brother. When members of An Garda Síochána arrived, they learned that there was a dead woman in a nearby house.

When they entered the kitchen, the Gardaí saw the body of 65-year-old Mrs Charlotte Doyle, lying on the kitchen floor with large areas of her skull and face missing. Pieces of bone, brain matter and blood were on the floor, with splattering on the walls, window and furniture. A large black cast-iron skillet cooking pot was on the floor beside the remains. The victim's pet cat was dead in the kitchen; its head had also been crushed.

On leaving the house, the Gardaí discovered a man asleep on the lawn of a house nearby. There was blood on his face, and blood and what appeared to be brain matter on his clothes; his hands and upper garments bore traces of a black substance, resembling 'Pot Black'. He was brought to Gorey Garda Station. When his clothes were being examined by Dr McGrath, the State Pathologist, a small triangular piece of bone was found embedded in a hole in the leather sole of one of his shoes; it appeared to be a piece of human skull.

Detective Garda O'Fiachain brought all the pieces of bone from the scene to Dr McGrath and asked him to rebuild the skull so that he could compare the piece of bone from the shoe with the rebuilt skull. Dr McGrath replied that this was a job for a Ballistics man as they had the expertise in rebuilding fragments of glass and the like. He gave O'Fiachain two skulls to assist him; one belonged to a Royal Irish Constabulary (RIC) officer who had been shot in the head during the War of Independence. O'Fiachain also bought a second-hand book on anatomy from a book stall on Dublin's quays.

In the Ballistics Laboratory in John's Road, O'Fiachain carefully boiled the dead woman's skull in a pot of water over a gas ring, gradually removing all the tissue, leaving him with approximately fifty pieces of bone. He then rebuilt the skull by gluing all the pieces of bone together. The piece of bone from the suspect's shoe fitted successfully into the rebuilt skull.

The case never came to court as the suspect was deemed medically unfit to stand trial. Nevertheless, it is a classic example of one of the varied functions performed by the Ballistics Section prior to the establishment of the Forensic Science Laboratory in 1975/76.

NURSE MAMIE CADDEN

Detective Sergeant George Lawlor was involved in the case of the notorious Nurse Mamie Cadden, in 1956. This was one of the Technical Bureau's most famous early cases and brought international recognition to both the Bureau and George Lawlor in relation to applying science to crime-scene investigation.

At 6 a.m., on 18 April 1956, a milkman discovered the body of 33-year-old Helen O'Reilly, lying on the footpath beside steps leading to the basement of 15 Hume Street, Dublin. She was naked from the waist down, with her skirt pulled up around her head, and partly covered by her black coat. A nylon stocking and head scarf were tied loosely around her neck. She had clearly been dragged by the legs along the footpath for a short distance. A parcel on the steps contained her shoes and her handbag with her bank book and other items.

There was only ever one suspect. Mamie Cadden was a qualified midwife who had become a back-street abortionist. She practised her trade in a flat at 17 Hume Street, a few yards away from where the body was found. The post-mortem established that the cause of death was heart failure due to an air embolism, resulting from an instrument, syringe or tube being inserted through the neck of the womb to inject gas or liquid. A strong smell of disinfectant emanated from the womb.

Nurse Cadden kept a diary in which she recorded details of her appointments. Lawlor, who interviewed her at length, discovered that she recorded her clients by reference to some item of their clothing, never by name. The entry for Tuesday, 17 April 1956, had been altered to read '2 p.m. Blue Coat'. Detective Garda Michael Horgan of the Photographic Section, Technical Bureau, was able to prove, with the aid of filters, that the original entry was '8 p.m. Black Coat'. The victim was wearing a black coat.

Dr Maurice Hickey, the State Pathologist, microscopically examined the clothing of the deceased and other evidence from the scene. On the victim's black coat, he found:

- Grey but dyed blond hairs that were similar to those on Cadden's hairbrushes
- Grey/brown rabbit hairs similar to those in Cadden's rabbit-fur cape
- Red wool fibres similar to Cadden's red dressing gown, and
- Over 80 coconut fibres similar to those on the mats from the scene.

A rabbit hair, similar to those of the fur cape, was stuck on a cigarette butt adhering to the heel of one of the shoes found in the parcel on the steps. In describing his findings, 'similar' was as far as Hickey could go at the time.

The Mapping Section made a scale model of the murder scene, which became a court exhibit. (Many years later, I rescued it from the basement of the courthouse and put it on display.)

Following a 10-day trial, which began on 22 October 1956, Mamie Cadden was convicted of murder and sentenced to be hanged. Her sentence was subsequently commuted to penal servitude for life. In 1958, she was declared insane and was transferred to the Central Criminal Lunatic Asylum (as it was then called) in Dundrum, where she died peacefully the following year.

CONCLUSION

The Bureau was a happy place to work, and the camaraderie was superb. On joining the Bureau, one piece of excellent advice I received was from Detective Superintendent Dan Murphy who recommended that when examining a murder scene, 'You cannot get there quick enough, you cannot stay long enough, and you cannot go back often enough.'

In May 1976, I was thrown into the proverbial deep end and sent on my first solo unsupervised murder case to examine the scene at a flat in Dublin's Seán MacDermott Street. Following a row, Patrick Hyland had been murdered by his roommate, Sean MacEoin, a carpenter. MacEoin killed Hyland by repeatedly hitting him over the head with a hammer. The following morning, having tried unsuccessfully to burn the body in the fireplace, he made use of his carpenter's tool bag to dismember it. He then disposed of body parts in the River Liffey and in litter bins along the quays. He was duly tried and convicted of murder.

Time never stands still. Some sections of the Technical Bureau are to be merged into Forensic Science Ireland. As the old Bureau as I knew it drifts away into the mists of time, I hope that history will treat it, the founder members, their achievements and their contributions to scientific crime investigation, with the respect they deserve.

CHAPTER 14

THE JFK VISIT

Retired Sergeant Fachtna O'Donovan

'The three happiest days I've ever spent in my life' is how US President John Fitzgerald Kennedy described his homecoming visit to Ireland in June 1963. His sister Eunice, who accompanied him, recalled that he was 'very happy there, he never stopped laughing'. Following his return to Washington, Kennedy wrote glowing letters of thanks to President Éamon de Valera, Taoiseach Seán Lemass, and Minister for External Affairs, Frank Aiken. He also wrote to Garda Commissioner Daniel Costigan, thanking the service for the handling of the visit. This letter, however, did not come into the public domain, as the Commissioner was prohibited by a senior official in the Department of Justice from circulating its contents.

PLANNING FOR THE VISIT

The whistle-stop tour of the country involved significant logistical planning for An Garda Síochána. Commissioner Costigan reported to the Department of Justice that 'while any attempt on the life of the President is most unlikely, we cannot overlook the possibility of some lunatic, fanatical communist, Puerto Rican, or other such like person, coming here to assassinate the President'. State papers from 1963 reveal that three separate threats were received before the visit, including that a sniper would assassinate him on his way from Dublin Airport, that a bomb would be placed on board an aircraft at Shannon Airport, and that a bag of flour would be dropped on his head. Security measures included Gardaí travelling ahead of the motorcade, armed with rifles, Thomson guns and revolvers, and the use of binoculars to check all roofs along the route from Dublin Airport. Visiting Secret Service agents were also allowed to carry side-arms in the State.

All Garda leave was cancelled, and members were directed to get a haircut, wear their best uniforms to look 'first-class', and to display 'efficiency, smartness and courtesy'. Members unlucky enough not to have received the 'current issue of uniform' would be 'detailed for duty at places away from the presidential route'. Costigan stressed that 'the eyes of the world' would be on Ireland. Buses were hired from CIÉ and extra trains laid on to transport Gardaí to various locations. A memo from Crime Section warned members about named Russian correspondents who had arrived in Ireland and whose 'movements and associates' should be 'discreetly watched'. Gardaí assigned to duty at the various locations were directed to ensure that 'placards, slogans, or other offensive matter be removed'.

ARRIVAL IN DUBLIN

Air Force One touched down at Dublin Airport at 7.55 p.m. on 26 June. Almost half of the entire Garda service was deployed on duty between the airport and Áras an Uachtaráin. Each day of the visit saw an average of 2,969 Gardaí being deployed to various locations. Two traffic units – each comprising one Sergeant and eight Gardaí on new motorbikes – escorted the motorcade for the duration of the visit. An estimated quarter of a million people – half the population of Dublin at the time – turned out to see the President in the capital. Gardaí stood side by side every five yards and stood closer near the centre.

This signed photograph recalls the crowds who lined the streets of Dublin to see the US President in the capital.

At all times, five US Secret Service agents accompanied the President, with an additional five being assigned if he was going to a function. Agent Gerard Blaine later recalled how 'everyone on the detail loved Ireland', and said that they had received 'the greatest support from the law enforcement officials'. They were, however, concerned about the President injuring his back, especially on a few occasions when the motorcade was swamped by adoring crowds. Gardaí had been told to keep their backs to the motorcade and survey the crowd, the overhead windows, and rooftops, but occasionally crowds rushed towards the President's car, 'led by police officers looking for an autograph'.

On 27 June, *The Irish Times* quoted an unnamed Garda on duty in the city centre as saying that he 'wouldn't be sorry when the Kennedy visit was over'. On duty in Westmoreland Street, young Garda boxer Tony Ruane was admiring a pair of suede boots in a shop window when he was abruptly admonished by an Inspector for 'window shopping'. Tony recalled being 'transfixed' by the sight of President Kennedy as he passed a few minutes later. Four years later, whilst working with the Special Detective Unit (SDU), Tony would find himself protecting Kennedy's widow, Jackie, and her children, during their Irish vacation. Kevin Street's legendary Detective Sergeant Jim 'Lugs' Branigan turned out that June morning in 1963, dressed in a

crisp new suit after his Superintendent had, tongue in cheek, told him that only men of outstanding physique, wearing lounge suits, would be allowed on protection duty.

As the motorcade passed through Dublin, tens of thousands of people pressed forward, while the motorcycle escorts, uniformed Gardaí and US Secret Service agents pushed them back. Swallowed up in the surge was a protest group from the 'Belfast Republican Prisoners Committee' led by a brass band. The CIA had anticipated anti-partition protests, but this group was barely noticed in the sea of people. Another crowd awaited the motorcade in the Phoenix Park. In the scramble to get near the President, Garda motorcyclist Mark Hearne had the windshield of his bike broken off, while others had to lift the President physically out of his car. The 'guest of the nation' rested well in the US Ambassador's residence in the Phoenix Park after a hectic day.

VISIT TO WEXFORD

The following morning, Kennedy was looking forward to visiting his Dunganstown ancestral home, to meet with the cousins whom he had last seen in 1947. New Ross was first on the schedule, though, and the US Secret Service had received an anonymous threat to the President; plainclothes Gardaí swamped the area around the podium on the Quay. After the speeches, the President freely mixed and shook hands with the crowd, to the consternation of Gardaí and his Secret Service escort. At one stage, Jim Rowley, head of the US Secret Service, was briefly barred by Gardaí from getting into his car, but after some 'furious words' the matter was resolved.

A short drive brought Kennedy to Dunganstown, where he toasted with a cup of tea all those who had left and all those who had stayed. His cousin, Mrs Mary Ryan, had assured Gardaí that only twenty people would be invited to the house, including the parish priest and curate. But once Cousin Jack arrived, the yard got rather overcrowded. A Garda Inspector decided to clear people from the yard. According to the following day's *Dallas Morning News*, his 'energetic entreaties were reinforced with a cane, which at one point punched at the chest of one of the most respected White House reporters, Merriman Smith'. A reporter from the *New York Times* wrote that 'the Irish cops were pretty rough'.

Garda recruit Pat Kirwan, a nephew of Mrs Ryan, stood in uniform in the yard to meet his cousin, President Kennedy. As the President shook hands with the nervous young Garda, he asked, 'Are you here to mind me for the day?' Earlier, Pat had been looking with curiosity at a red telephone beside the cow house when he was confronted by a Secret Service agent who warned him not to touch it as it was a 'Hot Line to the White House'. The US President was never more than two minutes away from a direct line to Washington.

A quick helicopter ride brought the VIP to Wexford, where he laid a wreath at the memorial to Commodore James Barry. An estimated 30,000 people turned out to greet him as he received the Freedom of the City. More headaches followed for his security team when he ordered the motorcade to stop no fewer than three times before leaving Wexford. The first stop was at the Loreto Convent, to meet the Mother Superior who was a third cousin, the second was at the County Hospital to meet the nuns and staff, and finally they stopped at the Convent of Mercy Orphanage.

RECEPTIONS IN DUBLIN

Back in Dublin, the US President attended a garden party at Áras an Uachtaráin. In attendance were 1,500 of the 'great and the good' of Dublin society. The event turned out to be an embarrassment for the hosts, though, as the guests jammed in, attempting to shake Kennedy's hand. A planned walkabout had to be cancelled, but he did manage to plant a tree while Secret Service agents held the crowd back. Patrick Hillery, who would later occupy the residence as President of Ireland, said of the event that 'top society did not behave well'.

That evening, there was a formal dinner at Iveagh House, and a crowd of over 2,000 waited on the street to get a glimpse of Kennedy. Garda crash barriers failed to keep them back, and to the horror of his security, the President decided again to walk over to meet them, resulting in something of a heave. Another crowd awaited him on his return to the Ambassador's residence.

THE FREEDOM OF CORK

The following morning, there was panic in Cork when the President's limo failed to start. It had been parked in the yard outside Union Quay Garda Station. Fortunately, Inspector Joe Ainsworth sourced a 1937 Rolls Royce from a funeral home in the city. Meanwhile, a bus transporting Gardaí from Kerry broke down in Mallow, resulting in a three-hour wait for a replacement.

As around 100,000 people lined the streets, some of the 900 Gardaí on duty linked arms to keep them back. On the street outside City Hall, where President Kennedy received the Freedom of the City, Gardaí were obliged to get 'more forceful' when the leader of the free world found himself jammed up against a wall. Through all this, the President continued to smile, saying, 'It's all right, these are my people'. When one man caught Kennedy's hand as the car pulled off, a Secret Service agent loosened the grip but lost his balance, falling into the car on top of his charge.

BACK IN DUBLIN

Back in Dublin, after a formal lunch at the Ambassador's residence, the President visited Arbour Hill Cemetery to pay homage at the grave of the 1916 leaders. In a moving ceremony, a class from the Irish Army Cadet School performed a series of drills, including the poignant Queen Anne drill. Kennedy later recalled this event as the highlight of his visit. Five months later, at the request of Jacqueline Kennedy, Irish Army Cadets would perform the same drill at the US President's graveside.

In Leinster House, at a joint session of the Dáil and Seanad, Kennedy reflected on the historical ties between Ireland and the United States, and on Ireland's role as a global peacemaker. At Dublin Castle, he received the Freedom of the City and was conferred with honorary degrees from University College Dublin and Trinity College. That evening, following a dinner at the Áras, the crowds were still waiting in the rain. As the US President's car approached the gates of the Ambassador's residence, a man ran towards it, forcing a Garda motor-cyclist to swerve to avoid hitting him.

John F. Kennedy addressing a joint session of the Dáil and Seanad at Leinster House.

SAYING GOODBYE

The following morning, President de Valera was at the Ambassador's residence to say good-bye. Before leaving Ireland, Kennedy visited Galway, where 600 Gardaí lined out for duty. After receiving the Freedom of the City, he gave a speech in Eyre Square, following which he again mingled with the crowds, and the Secret Service were 'quite rough' in knocking away hands that held on a little too long. A Garda Sergeant at one stage called on his radio for back-up, 'quick or they'll be wanting to shoulder him into town!' People in the crowd heard him and a chant spread outward: 'Shoulder him! Shoulder him!'

In Limerick, the Greenpark Racecourse proved the perfect location for the most effective crowd management of the entire visit. Finally, at Shannon Airport, the US President gave a short poignant farewell. To a tearful audience, he said: 'This is where we all say goodbye'. Quoting lines from a poem given to him by Sinéad Bean de Valera, John F. Kennedy promised that he would 'come back and see old Shannon's face again'. To the booms of a 21-gun salute, he inspected an Army guard of honour, before boarding the plane which would take him away forever.

On his way to the plane, he took time to speak to Assistant Commissioner Michael Wymes, saying: 'The police did a mighty fine job, thanks very much. I would like you to thank them all for me.'

CONCLUSION

In a report to the Department of Justice, Commissioner Costigan stated that, 'Mr Jim Rowley, head of the US Secret Service, said to me that in all his experience of presidential journeys, his staff never received from any other police force as much co-operation in planning the security arrangements or as much help in carrying them out as they did here.' He added that it was Mr Rowley's considered opinion 'that An Garda Síochána was the most efficient police force at crowd control, acting on the force of personality and self-confidence'.

The State Papers from 1963, released in December 2006, revealed the facts relating to the Kennedy/Costigan letter. In the letter, JFK wrote: 'Not only you, but also the members of your entire department, were most co-operative and worked many hours assisting the preparations for the visit'. He asked for his gratitude to be passed on to Assistant Commissioner Wymes, Chief Superintendent James Moore and Superintendent Philip MacMahon. He concluded:

'Ireland will long remain a fond memory and you, as well as all the men in your command, have my deepest thanks for making this possible'.

Commissioner Costigan drafted a reply and sent it to Minister Haughey for approval. He also sought permission to publish the letter in the *Garda Review*, so that the message could be passed on to all members. In a note to Minister Haughey, Department of

Family members of the then Commissioner Daniel Costigan, presenting the original framed letter of thanks from President Kennedy for display in the Garda Museum. (L to R) Donal Costigan, Brenda Costigan McDonald, Commissioner Noel Conroy, Mary McDonnell, Mark Costigan.

Justice Secretary Peter Berry revealed his anger that 'a Head of State should write to a public servant' and recommended that the letter should not be published. He also added that, 'The Minister for External Affairs, too, might feel that protocol is being brushed aside too rudely'. Permission to publish the letter in the *Garda Review* 'or any other publication' was refused. Daniel Costigan had been Assistant Secretary in the Department of Justice, and a colleague of Peter Berry's, before being appointed Garda Commissioner in 1952. He died in 1979, and some years later, his family generously presented the JFK letter to Commissioner Noel Conroy for display in the Garda Museum, where it is today a treasured exhibit.

THE WHITE HOUSE
WASHINGTON

July 19, 1963

Dear Commissioner Costigan:

On behalf of myself, the members of the White House staff who accompanied me, and the United States Secret Service, I wish to extend my sincere appreciation and gratitude for the many splendid public receptions and motorcades during my recent trip to Ireland.

I have been informed by Mr. Emory Roberts of the White House Secret Service Detail that not only you, but also the members of your entire department, were most cooperative and worked many hours assisting in the preparations for my visit.

Would you please extend my appreciation and gratitude especially to Assistant Commissioner Michael Wymes, Chief Superintendent James Moore, and Superintendent Phillip McMahon for the fine cooperation and assistance given Mr. Roberts.

Ireland will long remain a fond memory and you, as well as all the men of your command, have my deepest thanks for making this possible.

Sincerely,

John Kennedy

Commissioner Daniel Costigan
Garda Siochana
Phoenix Park
Dublin, Ireland

Letter from US President John F. Kennedy to Commissioner Daniel Costigan, thanking An Garda Síochána for their handling of his visit to Ireland.

CHAPTER 15

'TWO DEPOTS': A BRIEF HISTORY OF GARDA HEADQUARTERS AND THE GARDA COLLEGE

Sergeant John Reynolds
Michael Reynolds

An Garda Síochána of the twenty-first century is a national, primarily unarmed policing service which covers the 26 counties of the Republic of Ireland. It has a presence in every community and deals with a wide range of policing tasks, from the security of the State to walking a beat and responding to calls. Since 1922, the number of Garda stations and premises has varied to meet the operational requirements of a particular time. Some stations have closed, new ones have opened, and many older stations have been renovated to provide modern facilities to both Garda personnel and the public they serve. Historically, some iconic buildings are inextricably linked with An Garda Síochána, including the Phoenix Park Depot and the Garda College in Templemore.

PHOENIX PARK DEPOT

As discussed in an earlier chapter, the Constabulary (Ireland) Act, 1836 brought significant changes to the existing structure of policing in Ireland. While the city of Dublin retained a separate unarmed force, the Dublin Metropolitan Police (DMP), the County Constabularies were merged into one new national organisation, the Constabulary of Ireland, which policed all 32 counties of Ireland and was commanded by an Inspector General based at Dublin

Castle. Modern facilities were required for the new organisation, not only to cater for the training of recruits, but also to accommodate a reserve of up to 200 men who could respond at short notice to any part of Ireland where land-related violence or other incidents were taking place.

The Phoenix Park in Dublin was chosen as the most suitable location for the new training depot, and the recently established Office of Public Works was given responsibility for planning and construction. 'The Depot' was completed in 1842 at a cost of over £10,000, with the most notable features being the three stone buildings facing onto the large gravel parade square. As the Constabulary evolved over the years, so did the Depot, with the addition of features such as railings and sentry huts at the entrance in 1861, a riding school to train members of the mounted constabulary, an infirmary, officers' club and the 'wet canteen' (bar) which catered for the hundreds of men who lived, worked and trained inside the railings.

Following the War of Independence, a formal disbandment parade for the Royal Irish Constabulary (RIC) took place at the Depot on 4 April 1922, after which the force ceased to exist. Training of recruits for their successors in the new Civic Guard (Garda Síochána), which was founded on 9 February 1922, took place at the Royal Dublin Society (RDS) in Ballsbridge, Kildare Artillery Barracks and Collinstown Aerodrome (now Dublin Airport). The Civil War was taking place as the Civic Guard was trained and deployed throughout the 26 counties, so the Depot was not fully occupied until early in 1923. The Depot initially served as both Garda Headquarters and a recruit training centre, but HQ was then moved to the Royal Hospital in Kilmainham where it remained until the early 1950s, when the Commissioner and his staff returned to the Depot. Garda Headquarters has remained there ever since.

In 1960, Charles Haughey TD told the Dáil that training facilities at the Depot and another site at the Soldiers' Hall in Parkgate Street were 'no longer considered suitable for the accommodation of Garda recruits'. The decision to move recruit training out of Dublin was taken, with the small town of Templemore in north Tipperary being chosen. A garrison town since 1814, Templemore had the large McCan (formerly Richmond) Barracks, with plenty of accommodation, and was centrally located with a railway station, making it accessible from all parts of Ireland. Minister Haughey told the Dáil that Garda recruitment would increase to 700 per year as the men who had founded An Garda Síochána in 1922 were starting to retire in large numbers. To keep the service at the authorised strength of 6,400, a substantial number of new recruits would be needed. While news of increased recruitment was generally welcomed, there was some adverse comment, with one newspaper lamenting the 'passing of the big policeman' and querying whether new recruits would be the 'same strapping fellows we saw in uniform in the past' (*Connaught Sentinel*, 9 August 1960).

THE GARDA TRAINING CENTRE

The Templemore skyline is still dominated by the imposing structure of McCan (Richmond) Barracks. Since 1964, thousands of Garda trainees have travelled there from all counties of Ireland and even further afield to begin their careers in An Garda Síochána. McCan Barracks has now become the Garda College, a modern and vibrant third-level institution, but generations of young Irishmen who enlisted in the British Army during the nineteenth century would recognise much of the barracks, which has a remarkable military history.

HISTORY OF RICHMOND BARRACKS

Following unsuccessful rebellions in 1798 and 1803, the British Government built dozens of new barracks throughout Ireland, including several in Tipperary, a county with a long history of rebellion and lawlessness. Robert Peel, MP for Cashel in 1809 and the politician later responsible for introducing a constabulary to Ireland and forming the London Metropolitan Police, credited the high level of disorder in the county to 'a natural predilection for outrage and a lawless life which I believe nothing can control'. Construction began in 1809 and had been completed by 1814, at a cost of £42,500, which was £500 under budget. The 'Peninsular War' between France and Britain was taking place in Portugal and Spain while the barracks was being built, so to commemorate British military victories, streets in Templemore were renamed after locations in Portugal, such as 'Talavera', 'Vimeiro Mall' and 'Bussaco Street'. The presence of a barracks in Templemore allowed local men to enlist, as Richmond was primarily a recruit-training depot.

Soldiers in Templemore Barracks in the 1850s. (Capel Croft collection)

In 1847, 16-year-old Ensign Harry Loft joined the 64th Regiment in Templemore, and in a letter to his mother, written on 28 May 1847, described Richmond as:

Splendid barracks, with two large squares, and all the buildings three storeys high.… The town is a wretched place; there is only one street with three or four respectable shops.

The outbreak of the First World War, in August 1914, brought significant change, as Richmond was chosen as the site for a large prisoner-of-war (POW) camp. The magazine of the RIC reported that the POWs were received 'with much cordiality by the townspeople'. Over 2,300 prisoners were eventually detained in Templemore, and the barrack squares were divided into compounds, each with observation towers complete with machine guns and search lights and surrounded by barbed wire. In March 1915, the prisoners were suddenly moved to POW camps in England. A report from the RIC stated that Pierce McCan, a senior member of the Irish Volunteers, had 'attempted to visit the POWs in Templemore'. It was also reported that the Volunteers planned to attack Richmond and free the prisoners, so that they could assist with the upcoming rebellion, the 1916 Easter Rising. After the POWs left Templemore, it became a training barracks for Irish recruits to the Munster Fusiliers and the Leinster Regiment. Thousands of young Irishmen destined for the trenches of the Western Front did their basic training in Templemore.

In August 1919, at the height of the War of Independence, the Northamptonshire Regiment arrived in Templemore, unaware that it would be the last regiment of the British Army ever to serve there. When the Irish Republican Army (IRA) killed District Inspector Wilson of the RIC in August 1920 in Templemore, 'wild scenes were witnessed' as the military and police carried out reprisals. The town hall was burned down and compensation claims totalling £184,000 were lodged with north Tipperary County Council in respect of the burnings and other damage. In October 1920, another reprisal attack took place in Templemore following the deaths of three soldiers in an ambush.

Cavalry in Templemore, 1913.

McCan Barracks

Following the truce of July 1921, in February 1922 the Northamptonshires handed Richmond Barracks over to the IRA, thus ending 107 years of continuous occupation by the British Army. An uneasy peace had come to Templemore, but much of the town lay in ruins. Richmond was renamed McCan Barracks to commemorate Pierce McCan, who had died in a British prison in 1919. When the Civil War began in June

1922, the situation in Templemore was very tense, with anti-treaty IRA members, known as 'irregulars', occupying the barracks. Preparations were made by the Free State army to storm the barracks, but a truce arranged by Dr Harty, Archbishop of Cashel, allowed the barracks to be vacated by the irregulars, and the Free State army took possession peacefully.

When the Second World War began in 1939, a state of emergency was declared in Ireland, which remained neutral. McCan Barracks was occupied by the 10th Uisneach Battalion, and until the emergency ended in 1945, a large garrison was stationed in Templemore. McCan was then vacated except for Defence Force Reserve camps during the 1950s, and it later became the Headquarters of the 3rd Field Artillery Regiment. The current premises in the Garda College used by the Defence Forces is still known as 'McCan Barracks'.

The 'Templemore Special', 1964

By October 1963, the building of new facilities in Templemore had been completed at a cost of £560,000. Works included the construction of outdoor handball alleys, basketball courts, a lounge, a new gym, and renovation of the old gym into a recreation hall. The cost of the indoor heated swimming pool at £50,000 was justified on the basis that 'every member of the force should be a first-class swimmer with knowledge of life-saving'. The February 1964 issue of *Iris an Ghárda* reported that the new Garda Training Centre (GTC) was 'truly a milestone in Garda advancement'.

The formal transfer of 190 recruits and their instructors took place on 14 February 1964. On that cold, wet St Valentine's Day, recruits gathered on the Depot square for the last time and marched towards Kingsbridge (now Heuston) railway station, led by the Garda Band. On arrival at Kingsbridge, the group boarded a train temporarily renamed the 'Templemore Special'. One newspaper reported that the centre aisles of the Catholic church in Templemore would in future 'be reserved for GTC personnel at 9.30 a.m. mass each Sunday, and the public are asked to use the side aisles only'.

The formal opening of the GTC took place exactly one week later. In his speech, Garda Commissioner Daniel Costigan thanked the Minister for the 'magnificent new accommodation' and stated his belief that the new GTC would 'turn out first class guards, drivers and highly trained officers, Inspectors, Sergeants and detectives'. In March 1964, during the first passing-out ceremony in the GTC, Commissioner Costigan told the new Gardaí that to be good police officers they 'must have a vocation as they would for the ecclesiastical life and must conform to standards higher than people in other walks of life'. Recruits and serving members alike referred to the new training centre as 'The Depot', carrying on the tradition which went back to 1842.

Top left: Garda College fitness training, 1981.
Top right: Parading at Templemore, c. 1981.
Above left: A lecture in Templemore in 2001.
Above right: Garda College Attestation ceremony, 2003.

THE GARDA COLLEGE

In 1989, a two-year training programme for students and probationers was introduced, and a major building programme saw the facilities modernised. The Garda Training Centre became the Garda College. In 1992, the National Council for Educational Awards designated the Garda College as an institute of higher education. Since then, ongoing construction and modernisation have allowed the Garda College to evolve constantly and to improve the standards of training provided, ensuring that it remains a world-class third-level police training facility.

Recruit Garda Gary Sheehan

The greatest tragedy in the history of the GTC took place in December 1983 when Recruit Garda Gary Sheehan was killed at Derrada Wood near Ballinamore, Co. Leitrim. Originally from Carrickmacross in Co. Monaghan, Gary joined An Garda Síochána on 7 September 1983, following in the steps of his father and grandfather. When businessman Don Tidey was kidnapped in Dublin in November 1983, a nationwide search was undertaken by An Garda Síochána and the Defence Forces. Garda recruits in training were taken from Templemore to assist with the search, which eventually focused on the Ballinamore area.

On 16 December, a joint Garda and Defence Forces operation located the kidnappers at Dromcroman Wood. Don Tidey was released, but both Recruit Garda Gary Sheehan and Private Patrick Kelly of the Defence Forces were shot dead during the rescue operation. Gary Sheehan is the only Garda recruit to have been murdered in the line of duty. A commemorative plaque is located at the gate of the Garda College, and at each graduation ceremony, the Gary Sheehan Memorial Medal is awarded to the best overall trainee Garda. In September 2021, Gary Sheehan was posthumously awarded a Gold Scott Medal for bravery.

Policing a Pandemic

One of the most historic days in the history of the Garda College took place on 20 March 2020. In response to the global pandemic caused by COVID-19, 319 trainee Gardaí, some of whom had only begun their training several weeks earlier, were attested early and became full members of An Garda Síochána. The ceremony was attended by An Taoiseach Leo Varadkar, Garda Commissioner Harris, and all staff of the Garda College. No family members or friends were present to witness this 'passing out'. There was no drill display, the Garda Band was absent, and the atmosphere sombre. All of those present realised the historic nature of this ceremony, and the seriousness of the situation that Ireland faced. It was one of the most momentous occasions to occur in the remarkable 200-year history of Richmond Barracks. When it was over, Garda trainees and college staff alike departed for their new temporary stations all over Ireland.

CHAPTER 16

THE SCOTT MEDAL

Geraldine Du Berry

'Real valor consists not in being insensible to danger; but in being prompt to confront and disarm it.' (Walter Scott)

The Scott Medal is awarded to members of An Garda Síochána, who have, as Scott himself put it, 'distinguished themselves for valor in the performance of their duty'.

Born in Canada in 1862, Walter Scott, the eponymous donor of the medal, was brought up in Boston. At the age of 15, he joined Butler Brothers Wholesalers where he was employed as a manager for 55 years. In addition to being a successful businessman, Scott had a philanthropic nature; he sponsored several academic scholarships, endowed numerous hospital beds, and was a generous patron of many charities.

Scott's lifelong interest in police work was recognised when the New York City Police appointed him as Honorary Commissioner. It was in that capacity that he met Eoin O'Duffy, then Commissioner of the fledgling Irish police service. That meeting resulted in Scott's offer of an endowment in perpetuity of a gold medal for bravery to members of the service deemed deserving of the award. Walter Scott had already originated the award of Scott Medals in the New York, Boston and Detroit police departments. Within a matter of months, the dies for the Irish Scott Medal had been cast by the firm of Dieges and Clust in New York, and the first gold medal struck from them – a medal that was awarded to Garda James Mulroy in 1924. The first presentation of the Scott Medal, at Garda Headquarters in the Phoenix Park, was attended by Walter Scott. *Guth an Garda* reported:

> General O'Duffy, Chief Commissioner, said that before introducing Colonel Walter
> Scott he wished to thank the many distinguished people who had honoured them
> with their presence. It was fitting that when a great man like Colonel Scott from
> a free country like America honoured them with his presence that he should be

received by people who had done their bit to bring about freedom to their own people.

The Scott Medal is designed to acknowledge both its American and Irish influences. In the form of a Celtic cross, there are five panels on the face of the medal containing: the words 'The Scott Medal' and 'For Valor', the eagle and the shield of the USA, the harp and sunburst, and the Garda Crest. (As a point of interest, 'valor' is still spelled in the American way). The reverse of the medal carries the inscription, 'Garda Síochána na h-Éireann'. The four outside panels are the arms of the four provinces of Ireland – Ulster, Munster, Leinster and Connaught.

By 1926, provisions had been made and criteria established for the awarding of Silver and Bronze Scott Medals. The first

In 1924, the first Scott Medal was awarded to Garda James Mulroy.

Silver Scott Medal went to Garda John Whelan, and the first Bronze to Detective Garda James Hanafin in 1926. Chief Superintendent John Collins was the first member of the service ever to be awarded two Scott Medals, a Gold in 1940 and a Bronze in 1942. In 1998, Garda Yvonne Burke became the first female recipient of a Scott Medal.

Gold, Silver and Bronze Scott Medals.

In his book, *An Garda Síochána and the Scott Medal,* Gerard O'Brien writes of the medals, which are still held in the highest esteem:

> They represent the reality that courage is not confined to any particular generation or gender or age or rank but are a permanent and integral feature of the Garda Síochána and of all who wear its uniform.

Walter Scott died in 1935 at the age of 74, laden with honours at home and abroad. He was a knight of the French Legion of Honour, a member of the Belgian Order of Leopold and held the Silver Grand Cross of Austria.

A list of all the recipients of the Scott Medal can be found at: https://garda.ie/en/about-us/our-history/the-scott-medal/

The writer acknowledges Inspector Deborah Marsh (Silver Scott Medal recipient 2017), Sergeant John Reynolds PhD and Sergeant Frank Lavin for their kind assistance in researching this chapter.

Garda Yvonne Burke was the first female recipient of the Scott Medal.

CHAPTER 17

THE UNITED NATIONS

Garda Stephen Moore
Retired Sergeant Martin Drew

HISTORICAL PERSPECTIVE
Garda Stephen Moore

In 1956, a year after Ireland joined the United Nations (UN) the Government received a request to supply personnel to serve as security officers on UN missions. As the Garda Síochána Act, 1924 precluded serving Gardaí from serving outside the State, the twenty members who accepted positions with the United Nations Truce Organisation resigned from An Garda Síochána, on condition that they would be permitted to re-join on completion of their UN service. Sergeant Frank Eivers was one of the first Gardaí to resign and take up a UN post in 1956. On 18 September 1961, he lost his life while working as personal security guard to the then Secretary General of the United Nations, Dag Hammarskjöld. Both were killed when their plane crashed on the way to peace talks.

In response to a UN request to send members of An Garda Síochána to Namibia, to take part in a mission to oversee the withdrawal of South African troops, and to supervise the holding of free elections, the Irish Government passed the Garda Síochána Act, 1989. This allowed serving members of An Garda Síochána to participate with the United Nations Civilian Police Components on overseas missions. That year, thirty-five members of An Garda Síochána took part in the United Nations Transition Assistance Group (UNTAG) Namibia.

AN GARDA SÍOCHÁNA'S ROLE IN PEACEKEEPING DUTIES

One of the primary objectives of police missions is the restoration and maintenance of peace in conflict-affected/post-conflict states. The peacekeeping missions in which Garda Síochána personnel are deployed have a community policing focus. Their role is to resolve conflict at ground level, restore law and order, ensure civil rights, and implement mission mandates.

Since 1989, An Garda Síochána has participated in 28 international peacekeeping missions/operations, deploying 1,118 personnel across the continents of Africa, Asia and Europe. An Garda Síochána deployed 429 members to UNFICYP Cyprus Mission and fifty-two members to EULEX Kosovo mission. On 2 October 2021, following a competitive interview process, Superintendent Jarlath Duffy was selected and appointed to the position of Deputy Senior Police Advisor (DPSA) to UNFIYCP at Mission Headquarters.

The contribution of An Garda Síochána to peacekeeping missions and operations has been internationally recognised and reflected in the appointment of senior Garda officers as police commissioners of United Nations-led missions. An Garda Síochána also assisted commissions of inquiry into the facts and circumstances of the assassinations of Indian Prime Minister Mohtarma Benazir Bhutto and Lebanese Prime Minister Rafic Hariri.

PEACEKEEPING MISSIONS WITH THE EU AND OSCE

An Garda Síochána has participated in civilian police missions with the European Union and the Organisation for Security and Co-Operation in Europe (OSCE) in the following mission areas:

- ICFY, Former Yugoslavia: 1994–1995
- EUEU, Palestine: 1995–1996
- OSCE, Eastern Slavonia: 1998–2001
- OSCE, Macedonia: 2001–2001
- EU COPPS ESDP, Palestine: 2005
- EULEX, Kosovo: 2008–ongoing
- EUPOL, Afghanistan: 2010–2011
- ECOMSA, South Africa: 1992–1994

EULEX KOSOVO MISSION

EULEX supports Kosovo on its path to a greater European integration in the Rule of Law and continues to concentrate on the fight against organised crime and corruption, working closely with local counterparts to achieve sustainability and EU best practices in Kosovo. The main role of the organisation is as monitors, mentors, and advisors to local counterparts in the police, justice, and customs fields.

MY MISSION
Retired Sergeant Martin Drew

On a Friday morning in April 1993, fifteen members of An Garda Síochána boarded an aircraft at Dublin, bound for Zagreb in Croatia. We were on our way to be the second Garda contingent to the United Nations Protection Force (UNPROFOR) in the former Yugoslavia. UNPRO-FOR had been set up a little over a year earlier to intervene in the Yugoslavian wars of secession.

Since 1956, Irish Defence Forces personnel had served with distinction in places such as Kashmir, Syria, Congo, Cyprus and New Guinea. In the few short years since the Garda Síochána Act, 1989, Gardaí had served in Namibia, Angola, Mozambique and Cambodia. When I was called to attend for a medical examination to serve with the UN, I did not know where I would serve.

Although slightly disappointed not to be going to Africa, I was not too dissatisfied. Having been born on the anniversary of the shooting of Archduke Franz Ferdinand, I was fascinated with the Balkans. I knew how the plucky Serbs had fought off the Austrians, and later, how the Partisans under Tito had fought off the Germans during the Second World War, with Tito resisting both Stalin and the West and forming the Movement of Unaligned Nations. I was, however, unaware of the darker history of Chetnik, Ustase and the Partisan atrocities that had kept Yugoslavia together.

On passing the medical examination, I attended a week's training course in Templemore. We were briefed by Superintendent John McElligott, who was serving at that time in Zagreb, and his predecessor, Superintendent McGowan. An Irish Army officer briefed us on the complicated political situation. Yugoslavia had been a country of six republics with two autonomous regions, five major languages, three religions and two alphabets. If you believed that you understood the situation, we were warned, you had not been given all the facts.

Another Army officer briefed us on the military situation. Yugoslavia, on its disintegration, had one of the largest armies in the world, with over 100,000 men under arms, and over a million men in reserve. The country was awash with landmines, and we learned about the different landmines we were likely to encounter.

FIRST IMPRESSIONS

Landing in a balmy Pleso Airport, we encountered a plethora of uniformed personnel – army and police dressed in their national uniforms, all wearing the blue beret and badge of the United Nations. Some of our Garda colleagues who had trained to be deployed in Western Sahara had been deployed to the former Yugoslavia instead, because of the emerging humanitarian crisis. That night, we were billeted at the Babylon Hotel on the outskirts of Zagreb. There we met Russian police monitors who were also awaiting deployment.

The following day, we learned that we were all being deployed to the UN Protected Areas within Croatia. These were Serb-controlled areas with small Croat minorities; they had seceded by force from Croatia when Croatia and Slovenia had declared independence from the Federal Republic of Yugoslavia. Militant Serb nationalists had wrested control of the federation, suppressing the rights of minorities within the autonomous regions of Kosovo and Vojvodina, in Serbia.

On our first night, we were billeted at the Babylon Hotel on the outskirts of Zagreb.

Accompanied by several colleagues, I joined our Russian counterparts on a UN bus, and we travelled south to the self-proclaimed Republic of Serbian Krajina (RSK), the UN Protected Area in which the Serbs were in the majority. We were waved through a Croatian Army checkpoint on the outside of Karlovac about 50km south of the capital. What we saw in Karlovac astounded us: the buildings straddling the river Korana that had not been destroyed by fire or explosives were heavily pockmarked with bullets; no window was left intact. Across the river, we were in Serb-controlled territory. On the outskirts of the deserted town, we were stopped at another checkpoint, this time manned by the police of the RSK. After they had checked our UN identity cards, we could proceed.

Having driven through miles of gentle countryside populated with small farms, we eventually arrived at Knin, a medium-sized town which had been proclaimed capital of the RSK. Overlooked from the hill by a medieval castle, Knin was situated at a major railway junction in the heart of the country. As the Serbs in this area had declared independence, the Croatians now had no railway connection between Zagreb and their second city, Split, or the western city of Zadar. The Croatians also wanted the return of Knin for symbolic reasons; in the early Middle Ages, it was the seat of King Zvonimir and was known as the city of Croatian kings. The UN Headquarters for Sector South was also in Knin. On arrival, I learnt that I was being deployed to the Duty Office at HQ.

LIFE IN KNIN

We got accommodation on the outskirts of the town on the upper floor of the residence of Davorka, a dentist who lived there with her husband, Mladen, and their children. It was a large house, like so many in the town, designed to accommodate an extended family, but because of the economic strain that the conflict had placed upon the people, the children had moved out of the upper apartments to accommodate UN personnel who could supplement the family's meagre income with the dollar, a valuable non-degradable currency.

In the supermarkets in Knin, the shelves were almost empty. Serbia was under a trade embargo and goods were scarce. Electricity was in short supply, too; it was provided by a hydroelectrical generator, and during the summer, which was extremely hot and dry, we had no electricity at all. We quickly learnt one phrase used by the inhabitants: *nema voda, nema struja, nema nista* – no water, no power, no nothing.

My first job at HQ was to take statements from local people, mainly Serbs, who had lost their money in Croatian banks. As I wanted to see more of the country and meet its people, I requested a transfer, and soon found myself working as a liaison officer with the local police, my main duty being to ensure that crimes against ethnic minorities in the region were thoroughly investigated. I liaised with a Serb policeman named Dragan. He had been in the police in Zagreb but had been dismissed as Croatia attempted to Croatianise the largely Serbian police force.

I was the sole member of the Irish contingent amongst about twenty monitors in the station, from many different countries. One of the Russian police monitors, with whom I was friendly, was a former member of the KGB. I remember the Russians looking on in horror at television footage of their parliament building being attacked by the military during the Russian constitutional crisis of September 1993.

Below left: Martin Drew with some of the multinational team of about twenty monitors at Knin Station in the summer of 1993.
Below right: Martin Drew (right) with a retired schoolteacher and his wife who lived outside Knin and with whom he had formed a friendship.

At Plitvice, Croatia, in 1993 (L to R): Tom Mansfield, Martin Drew, Mary Aldridge, Peter Foley, Bob Noonan.

Although very poor, the inhabitants – both Serbs and Croats – were hospitable and always made us feel welcome. Local smoked meats and cheese were always on offer, with Turkish coffee, or their wine or plum brandy. I developed a friendship with a retired schoolteacher and his wife who lived in his ancestral home some distance outside Knin. Amongst the family photographs he showed me was one of his grandfather in the uniform of the Austro-Hungarian army; another was of his brother, an officer of the Yugoslav army, serving with the UN in Sinai in the 1960s. A Partisan during the Second World War, his father had been killed in the house by Chetniks (Serb royalist fighters), and his sister had been killed outside the house by a shell fired by German troops from Knin.

Gradually, I acclimatised to living in a country where a low-intensity war was in progress. On daytime patrols, we sat with locals, drinking coffee, and playing *baloti* (boules), listening to shells falling on the neighbouring village. The attitude of the locals seemed to be: 'Today we live, tomorrow we shelter.'

While Knin was out of artillery range of the Croatian military, the adjoining towns were not so lucky. According to ceasefire arrangements, the Serbs were not supposed to have access to heavy artillery or large automatic weapons, but this was not always the case. A no-fly zone was also in operation; however, while driving on the road towards Korenica one day, we were bewildered by a great roaring sound as we were overtaken from above by a Serb MIG fighter, flying at rooftop level, which skimmed along the road past us, like a huge swallow, before disappearing beyond the horizon.

We had been warned to be wary of encounters with the military on the road; they would try to intimidate UN personnel, and there had been attempts by military personnel to hijack UN vehicles. One car being driven by UN military observers was riddled with bullets when it failed to stop during a hijack attempt; both occupants of the car escaped unharmed, but I saw where one bullet had gone through the middle of the driver's seat, miraculously missing the driver. These encounters reached their inevitable conclusion when a Czech military observer was killed in August 1995.

WORSENING HOSTILITIES

During that summer, two colleagues, Tom Mansfield and John Drumm, were transferred to Sector Sarajevo in Bosnia, one of the most hazardous postings in the whole mission. The airport was under shelling on their arrival, the plane had to perform a violent corkscrew descent, and they had to run to get cover in the airport buildings. As they sped towards the city, Tom could hear small-arms fire pinging against the Armoured Personnel Carrier (APC), which reversed up to the door of the PTT building (UN protection force headquarters) to deposit them safely. He was later assigned a room and was advised to crawl across the floor to the bed. The window of the room had been blown out, and in the morning, he discovered that the walls were pockmarked with bullet holes. Our Garda Colleague, Paul Reid, was to meet his death in Sarajevo in 1995 when his vehicle was attacked in 'Sniper Alley' in the city. His companion, Philip Carr, was seriously injured in the same incident.

In early September, there was an escalation in hostilities and shelling became more frequent and widespread. On 9 September, I was to accompany a UNHCR convoy to transfer several elderly Croatian civilians from the village of Matasi across the confrontation lines to the Croatian town of Gospic, where they were to be resettled. Having delayed our departure to avoid an artillery barrage at the town of Gracac, we learned at a military checkpoint on the outskirts of the next town, Korenica, that a full military assault was under way by Croatian forces. It was my first experience of hearing shellfire close up; the explosions sounded to me like beer kegs being dropped from a height.

As Serb civilians began to gather around our vehicles, we drove to a nearby Czech UN camp in case the Croatian civilians we were escorting became targets of violence. At the Czech camp, near the famous Plitvice lakes, the civilians were given shelter, but they became pawns in the escalating hostilities, with the Croatians and Serbs refusing to call a ceasefire to let the convoy through. Over a week later, the Czechs finally smuggled the civilian group through the confrontation line on a military convoy in armoured cars.

I later learned that the Croatians had attacked and taken several hamlets around the village of Medak, before the UN negotiated a withdrawal. I joined other civilian police monitors and accompanied a Canadian army sweep team into the area. Our task was to interview survivors to establish whether war crimes had been committed. It had been agreed that we would enter the area on the withdrawal of the Croatian forces at 12 noon. However, there was no sign of the Croatians withdrawing, and after some time, we heard a series of explosions and shots. Eventually the Croatians withdrew, allowing us to proceed. We encountered a scene of devastation. All the houses had been destroyed; dead livestock had been thrown into wells; there were earth-movers in the fields. Among some Croatian army personnel, one of our interpreters pointed out an army officer who had been a teacher in her school before the hostilities. There appeared to be no survivors of the attack.

It being late, it was decided that we would wait until the next morning to begin the gruesome task of body recovery. During the night, we came under an artillery barrage. Having been woken by my Swedish colleague, Stikkan, I got up and donned my flak jacket and helmet to avoid the danger of shrapnel, then went to shelter in the bathroom, which had the smallest window in the house where we were staying. I sat there with Stikkan and the elderly landlady, listening to shells whistling over the house. The barrage subsided after about an hour but resumed later during the night. It was by no means a restful night's sleep.

The following day, we removed the charred remains of two elderly women to a temporary morgue – the village school in Medak. The women had been burned to death in a chicken coop. Other bodies were found as the days progressed, including that of an elderly woman with a rope tied around her torso, her fingers appearing to have been severed. She had been dead for some time, her body was bloated, and maggots fell from the wounds in her body when she was being moved. During the search, the body of a man who had been missing for some time was found; there was a suicide note in his clothing.

The post-mortem examinations of the victims were conducted on a basketball court in the yard of the school, as there was no electricity and insufficient light to conduct the examinations indoors. We wore surgical face masks doused in aftershave to cover the sickening stench of decomposing flesh; the local magistrate and doctor who carried out the examinations drank plum brandy liberally during their investigations. I was to attend about a dozen such post-mortems there, and I was later called upon in Dublin by an investigator from the war crimes tribunal in the Hague to make a statement regarding this episode.

TENSIONS IN KNIN

On my return to Knin later that month, the situation had greatly changed; the atmosphere was extremely tense because of the Croatian attack and no military assistance from Belgrade.

Goran, one of our interpreters, was picked up by the military and conscripted into the army. On patrol to Matasi, we found the road blocked by a Serb military checkpoint. Although refused entry to the village, we found an alternative route.

The Matasi villagers told us that after the Croatian attack, Serb military had rounded up some middle-aged Croatian men who had been put lying on the ground where they had been kicked in the ribs. One of them had then been taken away and we were unable to get any information from Serb authorities as to his whereabouts. I finally received information that he might be in the hospital in Knin. I found him there, and I was able to speak with him when his military guard stepped out of the room temporarily. He was overjoyed to see us, having feared that he would be secretly killed. He was released from custody after several weeks.

The winter was very severe, with heavy snowfalls throughout the sector. Although Knin itself was not affected by heavy snow, it did get ice storms, a phenomenon I had never encountered before. I used to walk to work, and the family I lived with – the Vuckovics – would look on in amusement as I attempted to make my way up the steep hill outside their house, slipping and sliding on the ice, and eventually scrambling up the hill on all fours. The extremes of temperatures in the country were astounding. While Knin could be frozen solid, Split, on the coast, could have glorious sunshine and temperatures of 20°C.

AN INTERLUDE IN BELGRADE

On my next CTO (compensatory time off), I decided to travel to Belgrade. Getting there would prove difficult, though, and would entail a long trip by bus overland through Bosnia or, rather, Republika Srbska (RSK).

The atmosphere darkened palpably on entering Bosnia. It seemed a sullen place, bristling with hostility. There were uniforms everywhere and frequent checkpoints; it was the first time during the conflict that I had encountered uniformed female soldiers. By chance, I crossed the border near Obljaj, a mountainous village from where, in 1914, Gavrilo Princip had set out to slay Archduke Franz Ferdinand, tipping the world into the Great War. I was the only foreigner on the bus, and the locals craned their necks to catch a glimpse of my passport as it was passed up for frequent inspection.

Before breaking the journey at Banja Luka, we passed through the town of Prijedor, on either side of which were miles of houses that had been systematically destroyed; not a house stood intact. An elderly man, seeing my astonishment, gave a blood-curdling laugh and, drawing his thumb across his throat, chortled, '*Muslimani*' (Muslims).

It was well after dark when we arrived at a remote border crossing on the Serbian frontier. This time, my Irish Service passport caused some surprise and confusion amongst the border guards. After some delay, I was allowed to proceed and return to the bus. I learnt from my travelling companion that the bus driver had wanted to leave without me, but the Serbian policeman had refused to allow the bus to proceed, leaving a fellow policeman behind.

I found Belgrade to be a charming city. Although labouring under the same trade embargo as Knin, it did not appear to suffer the same level of privation. I stayed in the stately Hotel Moskva in the centre of the city, where I met a porter with an affinity for Celtic music. He presented me with a tape of a local band called Orthodox Celts, and I gave him a tape of Four Men and a Dog in return.

SREBRENICA

On returning to Knin, I volunteered to serve temporarily in Srebrenica in Bosnia; conditions there were particularly challenging, and monitors were asked to serve there for only short periods. I was joined on the trip from my sector by Antonio, a Portuguese police monitor. We left Knin early one morning, driving north to Zagreb where we stopped at HQ to collect supplies and fuel. We then set out for the Serbian border, driving along the ironically named Highway of Brotherhood and Unity. It was raining heavily, and the road was deserted. We passed turn-offs to Osijek and Vukovar, cities that had become bywords in the west for barbarity and cruelty; the war was to teach us that we had yet much to learn about the meanings of these words.

Having crossed the Serbian border, we stayed overnight at a hotel in Sremska Mitrovica, in Vojvodina. The following morning, we drove along the river Drina and crossed into Bosnia near Bratunac. As we drove along desolate mountain roads, passing numerous bombed-out houses, a Serb military checkpoint finally emerged out of the mist, revealing that we were approaching Srebrenica. After crossing the checkpoint, we passed the derelict Potocari battery factory that would become notorious the following year, the desperate population gathering for shelter there as the Serb military rolled through Srebrenica.

Srebrenica was a Bosnian Muslim enclave, nestling against the Serbian border and surrounded by the Bosnian Serb military. The UN offices and accommodation were in the town post office where, the previous year, General Morillion had declared the town a UN Protected Area. The population had swollen to over 40,000 from a pre-war population of 15,000 and the people lived a hand-to-mouth existence. There was no electrical supply to the town nor any reliable supply of water. All food and supplies were provided by aid convoys, which had to pass through the Serb cordon. Many people lived in villages of lorry containers, which had been converted for human habitation. Others lived on shop floors and in the disused petrol service station, their daily lives on full view to passers-by. The town had been situated

in a wooded valley, but the trees had been cut down for fuel. The ingenuity of the people astounded me. Along a small stream, many had set up small hydroelectric generators where they charged car batteries, which were then used to provide lighting in houses. The local cinema was a used VCR player run from a car battery.

At the post office, we had a large electric generator and there was elementary heating in the sleeping quarters. On our daily patrols into the country, we collected drinking water in large containers from a mountain spring. We also visited the minute Serbian population living in the enclave, to establish whether they were getting adequate rations from the Red Cross committee there. The school was operating in particularly challenging conditions, and there was an overwhelming smell of urine from the latrines because there was no adequate water supply to flush them. There were heavy falls of snow while I was in Srebrenica, and the children, although ill-clad to withstand the severe cold, had a sled and entertained themselves by sledding down a steep slope in the centre of the town.

We also visited the station of the Bosnian police, where a portrait of Marshal Tito was displayed prominently on the wall. I wondered why he was so revered still in Bosnia and discovered that he had declared the Bosnian Muslims a distinct nation in the 1960s. This reverence was widely held by the local population. On entering the homes of Muslims, it was customary to remove one's shoes to demonstrate respect to the household. I once attended the scene of the murder of a man in a Muslim household, and every one of the local police and the investigating magistrate removed their footwear before entering the house.

THE END OF MY TOUR OF DUTY

After a short attachment in Srebrenica, I returned to Knin; I had one month remaining before my tour of duty came to an end. My intention was to return in the future to visit both Knin and Srebrenica and the people I knew; however, fate was not to be kind to the people of either town. The following year, hostilities escalated considerably. In August 1995, the

Croatians attacked along the whole Sector South towards Knin. The Serb military machine crumbled as the Croatians advanced, and almost the entire population of 250,000 Serb civilians fled into Bosnia in face of the onslaught, many of them never to return. Many old people who did not flee were killed in their homes by advancing troops.

However bad the plight of the people of Knin, it was little in comparison to what was endured by the Muslim population in Srebrenica. In July, the Dutch UN contingent having been pushed aside by advancing Serb troops, the hapless population made their way to the Dutch compound at Potocari for protection. But they were left to the tender mercies of the advancing forces. All the men of military age and boys as young as 12 years of age were separated from the general population, taken away and secretly murdered – over 7,000 in all. It was the biggest massacre in Europe since the end of the Second World War.

HOME AGAIN

My involvement with the United Nations ended almost as suddenly as it had begun. In April, I said goodbye to the Vuckovics and my friends in Knin and took the bus north to Zagreb with all my comrades who were being rotated out. Gardaí serving on UN missions were still a relative novelty, and there were TV cameras awaiting us on our arrival in Dublin Airport.

On flying home, we were entitled to a month's leave, during which time I adjusted to being home again. It had been the most momentous year of my life. I had been involved in war crime investigations and prisoner-of-war exchanges; I had met with Government ministers

Members of An Garda Síochána at the 1994 Overseas Service Medal Parade.

Martin Drew (centre) with Garda colleagues Bob Noonan and Mary Aldridge at the 1994 Overseas Service Medal Parade.

An Garda Síochána medal awarded for Overseas Service.

and secured the right of police monitors to visit prisoners of war. I wondered how I was going to settle down to more mundane policing matters. However, I need not have worried: I paraded for duty in Mountjoy Garda Station at 6 a.m. on a bright June morning. I had barely time to greet my unit colleagues when I was climbing in the window of a public house in Dorset Street in pursuit of suspected burglars. And so I gradually consigned my year with the United Nations to the past.

I have returned many times since to the former Yugoslavia. I have found the Bosnians, Croatians and Serbs to be warm and generous people. Yet, close to 30 years later, I still struggle to comprehend the enormity of the horror committed in their names. What happened there should serve as a reminder to us here in Ireland that the tribal drum can lead us down dark paths and onwards to deeds that can never be undone.

CHAPTER 18

A History of Legal Powers

Detective Garda Darren Martin

The establishment of An Garda Síochána in law can be seen in the Acts and legal provisions of the new State from 1922 onwards. A new police force required men, uniforms, equipment and, more importantly, the foundation 'laws' to give it its powers to keep the peace. The new Civic Guard should not be seen as a replacement for the Royal Irish Constabulary (RIC); rather, it should be seen that this was the new state's policing authority in every rural and urban part of the country. It was also important for the new Government to ensure that in giving authority to the Civic Guards, legal powers were not used inappropriately.

The Indemnity (British Military) Act, 1923 provided a legal bar to commencing civil or criminal proceedings in Saorstat Éireann against any person for any act, matter, or thing, done after 23 April 1916 and before the enactment of the act. This was important following an end to the conflict and the establishment of the new state. Legal provisions were passed to establish the new courts system and the rules for governing its operation. The District Justices (Temporary Provision) Act, 1923 gave the new executive the power to appoint district judges and peace commissioners, with the latter given powers to sign and enforce legal documents in prosecution, such as summonses. Section 7 gave legal recognition to the Civic Guard.

The first reference to the new name, An Garda Síochána, came in the Garda Síochána (Temporary Provisions) Act, 1923. Section 7(1) provided the power to distribute An Garda Síochána throughout the State, except within the limits of the Dublin Metropolitan District, where the Dublin Metropolitan Police (DMP) still policed. This Act also provided for the investigation of complaints against police officers for neglect or a violation of duty. It established the representative bodies for members and prohibited membership of unions. Section 21(1) recognised An Garda Síochána and established that any reference to the RIC in previous legislation was to be taken as including An Garda Síochána. This Act was replaced by the

Garda Siochana Act, 1924. The DMP continued as a separate police force and the first legislating indication of closer and eventual amalgamation of the two forces was evident in the Dublin Police Act, 1924, which permitted DMP members to assist members of An Garda Síochána outside Dublin and granted them the same legal powers.

The Public Safety (Powers of Arrest and Detention) Temporary Act, 1924 granted the power of arrest and detention for several scheduled offences, including possession of firearms or explosives, robbery, inciting violence to overthrow the Government, and the obstruction of the administration of justice. These powers were needed in such a politically charged environment. By 1925, the decision was made to amalgamate the DMP and An Garda Síochána. The Police Forces (Amalgamation) Act, 1925, Section 5(2) provided that the police force for the State would now be An Garda Síochána, alone.

THE ADMINISTRATION OF JUSTICE – THE INVESTIGATION AND PROSECUTION OF OFFENCES

The investigation and prosecution of criminal offences, and ultimately bringing offenders before the courts, is the main role of any police service. The Prosecution of Offences (administration) Act, 1924, Section 9(1) provided that the more serious offences – indictable offences – were to be prosecuted in the name of the Attorney General. Section 9(2) provided that less serious or minor offences, known as summary offences, would be prosecuted by a Minister of the Department or a person authorised on their behalf in any court of summary jurisdiction, i.e. the District Courts. This remained the case until the establishment of the Office of the Director of Public Prosecutions (DPP) in 1974 by the passing of the Prosecution of Offences Act, 1974.

In rural areas, the District Superintendent was responsible for the prosecution of cases before the District Court. The prosecution for minor offences was still within the legal capacity of individual members of An Garda Síochána who commenced a prosecution as the 'common informer' to the court. The decision to commence a prosecution must now be at the suit of the DPP in all matters. In 1975, the Office of the DPP issued a directive to An Garda Síochána permitting prosecution to be taken on certain minor offences at the suit of the DPP. This directive has changed to include or remove certain offences. It is now required that all prosecutions be taken at the suit or on the directions of the Office of the DPP and the 'common informer' is no longer utilised by members of An Garda Síochána.

CHANGES IN SOCIETY AND THE LAW

In the early years of An Garda Síochána, the investigation of offences was in the main with public order offences and occasional thefts. In the latter years of the 1920s, new regulations and duties fell to members of An Garda Síochána to enforce, such as that of the Intoxicating Liquor Act, 1927. This set out the trading hours of licensed premises, and it was the duty of An Garda Síochána to ensure compliance with it.

The 1930s saw an increase in the use of mechanical vehicles. The Road Traffic Act, 1933 introduced the requirement to hold a driving licence for certain classes of vehicle and gave the police the power to demand production of that licence. The Act also set restrictions on the speed of vehicles. Section 55 required more than a single witness to give evidence of their opinion of the speed of the vehicle at the time of the alleged offence – a little different from today. Traffic Control became the responsibility of An Garda Síochána. In the time before traffic lights, this meant point duty directing traffic in towns and cities.

The end of the 1930s saw the introduction of the Offences Against the State Act, 1939. This Act granted the power of arrest and detention for the purposes of interrogation. It is the first legal provision that permitted the legal detention of a suspect for the investigation of an alleged offence; the suspect can be detained for a period of up to 24 hours. With the shadow of war in Europe and the Emergency in Ireland, the legislation provided the power for the prosecution of scheduled offences under the Act and associated Acts. These include offences relating to the

Seizure of illicit distillation equipment in the 1930s.

possession of firearms or explosives, as well as membership of unlawful organisations. Still in use today for the investigation of certain offences, this Act was one of the first to give a power of detention for the purpose of investigating suspected criminal offences in the State.

After the Second World War, the Censorship of Publications Act, 1946 was introduced. Section 17 permitted a Chief Superintendent to apply to the District Court for a warrant to search a premises where he believed there to be censored publications or periodical publications for distribution, and to seize them. Although the health crisis was different at that time, the Health Act of 1947 provided powers of detention of persons suspected of having a commutable disease. This primary legislation would once again be used during the health crisis resulting from the COVID-19 pandemic.

By the end of the 1940s and into the 1950s, large-scale urbanisation was taking place, with many leaving rural areas seeking paid employment in urban settings. With population increases in cities like Dublin and Cork, policing was much concerned with maintaining the public peace. The 1950s saw the rise of youth gangs in the urban areas of cities. It was in this decade that members of An Garda Síochána took to the streets to ensure that public fighting and disorder were curtailed. By the 1960s, the media had begun to report the incidents of street violence in urban areas, leading to a robust response from An Garda Síochána with the establishment of specific public order patrols.

Members of An Garda Síochána seize equipment at a poitín distillery in Westport in 1979. (L to R): Detective Garda John Joyce, Sergeant Michael Ferry, Garda Dermot O'Flaherty, Garda Paul Joyce.

The Road Traffic Act, 1961 saw new powers and statutory requirements being introduced which had a lasting impact; it included laws to prohibit driving whilst intoxicated. This remains one of the most amended and extensive pieces of legislation still in everyday use. It is also one of the most challenged and litigated Acts.

The Criminal Procedure Act, 1967 introduced and amended criminal court systems and procedures for the conduct of criminal trials and hearings. Section 31 refers to the member of An Garda Síochána in charge of the station, and bail was introduced. This decade saw an increasing number of statutes being passed which in turn increased the number of criminal offences. Amendments to the Intoxicating Liquor Act and the introduction of the Street and House-to-House Collections Act saw members of An Garda Síochána taking on new duties regarding their enforcement.

In the 1970s, new legislation such as the Gaming and Lotteries Act, 1970 and the Garda Síochána Act, 1972 came into law. The Offences against the State Act, 1972 saw the inclusion of opinion evidence of a Chief Superintendent that a person was a member of an illegal organisation. As mentioned above, the Prosecution of Offences Act, 1974 saw a major new change to the prosecution of criminal offences in the State. The Act created the Office of the Director of Public Prosecutions (DPP), who would be required to make independent decisions on the prosecution of criminal offences. Investigation files were now sent to the DPP, seeking a direction on how the case was to proceed. The independent position of this office is essential in determining if an accused is to face a criminal charge before the courts, and in serious cases the venue in which the trial is to be heard. The DPP has in subsequent years issued directives to investigators that outline several minor criminal offences which may be taken without forwarding a file for directions.

The Garda Siochana Act, 1977 amended the statutory rules concerning the various Garda representative organisations. Also in this year, and to reflect the emergence of a new and dangerous threat to society, the Misuse of Drugs Act, 1977 was passed; it remains the primary legislation used by An Garda Síochána and other law-enforcement agencies such as Irish Customs to investigate the sale and supply of illegal drugs.

By the 1980s, the level of recorded crime in the State was increasing. The number of armed incidents rose dramatically as robberies of financial institutions and cash-in-transit became customary. The Criminal Justice Act, 1984 saw the introduction of many new requirements for the arrest and detention of persons at Garda stations for the investigation of criminal offences. It introduced the power to detain a person for a specific period for the purpose of questioning, and to take forensic samples and take cautioned statements in the investigation of these crimes. The Act necessitated the creation of the custody record and made it a requirement that a detained person be given a notice of their rights while detained in a Garda station. In 1986, the Garda Síochána (Complaints) Act established the Garda Complaints Board to investigate complaints against members. The Garda Siochana Act, 1989 permitted members of An Garda Síochána to serve outside the State, as part of a UN peacekeeping mission.

In the 1990s, the activities of criminal gangs and unlawful organisations saw several high-profile incidents, resulting in public outrage. Although the science of criminal investigation was always part of policing, the Criminal Justice (Forensic Evidence) Act, 1990 introduced additional legal provisions for the collection and retention of forensic evidence which assisted in the investigation of crime. The Firearms and Offensive Weapons Act, 1990 introduced new and expanded criminal offences relating to the possession and use of firearms and other offensive weapons. The political agenda was still very much focused on crime when the Criminal Justice (Public Order) Act, 1994 passed, introducing offences relating to public order. This Act has become the bedrock of everyday policing in Ireland.

The year 1996 became a watershed moment and a tipping point in the fight against crime. The murder of journalist Veronica Guerin and the shooting dead in Adare of Detective Garda Jerry McCabe and the serious injury of his colleague, Detective Garda Ben O'Sullivan, led directly to the introduction of legislation to combat criminal enterprise. The Criminal Assets Bureau Act, 1996, and the Proceeds of Crime Act, 1996 introduced new procedures in law, which permitted the State to confiscate the ill-gotten gains of criminal enterprise from those who profited from crime. By 1997, the Criminal Law Act provided additional powers of arrest and search. It also abolished the legal definitions of misdemeanour and felony; criminal offences would now be defined as minor and indictable. The legal definition of an arrestable offence was now any offence that carried, on conviction, a penalty punishable by imprisonment for a term of five years or by a more severe penalty; it included an attempt of any offence. The Non-Fatal Offences Against the Person Act, 1997 introduced new classifications of assault, which increased in severity depending on the injury caused. The Offences Against the State Act, 1998 introduced offences for directing an unlawful organisation. Drawn up after the Omagh bombing, it introduced inferences which the court may draw concerning membership of an unlawful organisation.

A NEW CENTURY

The Criminal Justice (Theft and Fraud Offences) Act, 2001 saw the introduction of offences concerning theft and fraud, replacing the obsolete Larceny Act, 1916. The Garda Síochána Act, 2005 set out the statutory functions and responsibilities of the service and established the Garda Síochána Ombudsman Commission (GSOC) to investigate complaints concerning members of the service. The Criminal Justice Acts of 2006 and 2007 enhanced the preceding Acts relating to certain offences. The financial crash of the closing years of the decade witnessed an increase in reported financial crimes, and the birth of a new form of crime – cybercrime. The extent of criminal activity was becoming borderless, with criminals using online avenues for their personal gain. Advances in technology saw the exploitation and sharing of information on vulnerable persons. Legislative tools to combat this – such as the Criminal Justice (Money Laundering and Terrorist Financing) Act, 2010 – were introduced, which made provision for offences that occurred outside the State.

The laws were further enhanced with the Criminal Justice (Forensic Evidence and DNA Database System), Act 2014. This provided for the establishment of a database to assist in the investigation of criminal incidents. The Criminal Justice (Victims of Crime) Act, 2017 introduced specific rights to victims of crime. The Harassment, Harmful Communications, and Related Offences Act, 2020 made it a criminal offence to publish intimate material concerning someone online without the knowledge of that person. The Criminal Justice (Mutual Assistance) Amendment Act, 2017 provided for evidence to be transmitted to this jurisdiction from another for the purposes of a criminal investigation. Older legislation continues to be amended, as seen with the Criminal Justice (Amendment) Act, 2021. The legal requirements to identify, retain and ultimately present technical and digital evidence to the courts in cybercrime investigations necessitate having highly skilled investigators, with expertise beyond the traditional skillsets.

CONCLUSION

The decade leading up to the centenary of An Garda Síochána saw amendments to legislation reflecting the service's new global outlook on fighting crime. Policing has moved from the local policeman concerning himself with only local issues to Gardaí playing our part in the fight against large criminal networks. However, community-based policing will always be at the forefront of everything we do. The job and the law may have changed, but the essence of policing remains the same: to prevent crime, to seek out evidence and to present it to the courts, and to perform our duties to the best of our abilities, without fear, favour or malice, treating every person with respect through every action we undertake, ensuring that those actions are legal, proportionate and necessary.

CHAPTER 19

A LIFE IN THE GUARDS

Retired Assistant Commissioner Pat Leahy

I t was early on 12 May 1982 when I boarded the Templemore train, a borrowed suitcase my only companion. Deep in thought since leaving Cork, I tried to rationalise why I was making the journey. I had not applied to be a member of An Garda Síochána; my mother had completed all the paperwork for me. I had never considered a job in the service, but I was here now, standing on the platform at Ballybrophy. I remember reading the platform sign – 'BALLYBROPHY' – and taking it as a sign from God that this was just not meant to be. Having missed the Templemore stop, I contemplated jumping on the next train back to Cork, but I did not have the heart to let the folks back home down. There and then, I made a pact with myself: I would complete the six months' training and then give up. This way I would not be seen as a failure; I would just be saying that I did not want *that* job.

A CHANGE OF HEART

Having been in the FCA (Fórsa Cosanta Áitiúil – local defence force) for years, I liked the militaristic lifestyle in Templemore of the 1980s – three to a room, bed-blocks, polishing floors, shining shoes, marching, saluting and discipline. In the FCA, I had enjoyed the camaraderie of that kind of lifestyle. My time in Templemore was even better, and at the end of the six months of training, my attitude to a job with An Garda Síochána had changed. I had changed, and my outlook on life would never be the same again. Just before my passing-out parade, I changed my pact: I would give An Garda Síochána a real shot to see what happened; Dublin would be exciting, and I had friends there, so there would be a bit of adventure as well.

When the station list came out, and I learned I was being sent to Ennis, it felt like being back at square one again. Arriving in Ennis Garda Station with a handful of other recruits, I was terrified of making it to Ennis and no further. That afternoon, I listened to the Chief Superintendent tell me what was expected of me and how to stay out of trouble. And then it happened: 'You're going to Killaloe Garda Station.'

I had never heard of Killaloe. I did not even know which direction it was in. But I knew that I had to fix it there and then. I went back up the stairs and knocked on the Chief's door. He looked surprised to see me.

'I'm getting married, and I need to get a transfer to Dublin,' I blurted out.

After a brief but frank discussion, he agreed to keep me in Ennis until a transfer option to Dublin could be explored. Twelve months later, I arrived (free and single) in the Dublin Metropolitan Region (DMR) South Central, parading at Donnybrook for the late shift. I had enjoyed my time in Ennis – a beautiful town with some fabulous people – but as I saw it, at 21 years of age, my life and my career were only just about to start.

A Significant Step

My service in Donnybrook would prove to be a most significant time in my life: a great Sergeant as a mentor to provide the first guide rails in my career; a great unit to work with; and individuals who would become lifelong friends. I learned my trade there and was provided with opportunities that would change my life.

From Donnybrook I was seconded, along with approximately ninety others from across the city, into the Central Detective Unit to work on the Tango Squad, tackling organised crime associated with Martin 'the General' Cahill and his gang. I remember sitting beside a colleague and great friend from Donnybrook, Paul Casey, as we listened to our first serious crime briefing in Harcourt Square. We were told that if we were not prepared to stand up to these criminals, then we should go back to our stations. This was why I had persevered with An Garda Síochána as a career, why I had transferred to Dublin. I knew right then and there that I had made the right choice.

The following eighteen months were challenging, exciting, demanding and rewarding. I created professional links and friendships with colleagues that would endure throughout my career. Eventually I was promoted to the rank of Sergeant. Then, after a wonderful year stationed in Bunclody, I returned to Pearse Street where I remained for some years as a Sergeant and as an Inspector.

Academic Qualifications

Pearse Street introduced me to the concept of major event planning and management – an element of policing that would become a key focus for me right up to this day. Large operations, large briefings, and the capacity of the police to work as a team enthralled me. Planning and managing large events at district, divisional or regional level and preparing for emergencies influenced me to consider education, and An Garda Síochána delivered. I had not had the

opportunity to attend college before joining An Garda Síochána but when the opportunities presented themselves, I jumped at the chance. I attended Harvard and MIT, studying leadership and strategy, completed a primary degree in Public Management, an International Executive MBA and a PhD, supported by Garda-funded programmes. I had the opportunity to contribute to the planning and implementation of some of the most momentous events in our history, including the visits of Queen Elizabeth II, US President Barack Obama, Pope Francis, and the 2016 Commemorations, all of which stretched us to our limits. We briefed nearly 3,000 members at the 3Arena on the first day of the Queen's visit, and later that day we were dealing with a riot not far from the Garden of Remembrance.

Above: Members of An Garda Síochána on duty for the visit of Queen Elizabeth II to Ireland in 2011.

OPERATIONS SUPPORT UNIT

From Pearse Street, I was promoted to the position of Superintendent in Castlebar and later took over the national Operations Support Unit with responsibility for the Air Support, Water, Mounted and Dog units. The Operations Support Unit brought me great personal satisfaction; I was happy there and had a great affinity for the individual units, their expertise, and their willingness to get the job done, no matter what.

We had some great days there, but we also had some sad ones. Calling off the search for the sunken trawler, *Honey Dew II*, sticks in my mind to this day. Telling the families that we had completed the search and had not found their loved ones was extremely difficult, and my mind sometimes wanders back to that final day on the deck of the dive platform off the southeast coast. The sea was flat calm, and we said a silent prayer before shutting the operation down. We were so disappointed that we could not bring the crew home, but I had watched day after day as our divers got tangled in the drifting nets while searching, and I was glad that we had come through without further tragedy. The members of An Garda Síochána attached to the water unit were amazingly professional throughout this difficult time; they were an inspiration, and I remain proud of what they did and what they continue to do every day.

THE NORTH CENTRAL DIVISION

After a period as Chief Superintendent at the Professional Standards Unit, I was lucky to be offered the Chief's job in the North Central Division at Store Street. My only reservation was that almost all my previous service had been in the South Central and I had formed the view that Pearse Street was the epicentre of policing in the city. I was soon to learn that they were two vastly different places, and it did not take long before I became totally immersed in the north inner city.

It was here that I experienced the real effects of the drugs trade on communities. Open drug dealing, intimidation and drug-related violence were taking a daily toll on the lives of the people living and working in the area. The most amazing people – both residents and elected representatives – were fighting an uphill battle, attempting to create a normal, healthy living environment. It was here that I really came to understand the necessity for a change in policing from a traditional reactive approach to a proactive community orientation.

Austerity was beginning to take hold when I first arrived in North Central, and in a strange sort of way it helped to focus the minds of stakeholders and the Gardaí. We all knew that significant change was required, but we also knew that there was no cavalry coming to help us. We were losing numbers, wages were cut and there was no extra money, with very little new training and no recruitment. The question was whether to let police–community relations slip back to how things had been in the 1980s, or to work hard to ensure that things moved forward on our watch. We chose the latter, and through the hard work of the Gardaí on the ground, local stakeholders, and local elected representatives we were collectively awarded European Best Practice in community-oriented policing in 2015.

However, within a year, the city was plunged into a violent feud following the attack and murder at the Regency Hotel. The north inner city became the epicentre for violent attacks and, instead of visible community policing, the residents and businesses in the area were subjected to armed checkpoints and intense investigations; 24-hour static checkpoints were established in certain areas, with a view to preserving life and protecting the community. The violence and intimidation were relentless, until key arrests were made, and the main agitators were either incarcerated or left the country. Nearly twenty people would be murdered before the city and the North Central returned to some form of normality. The residue and the memory will take much longer to disappear as those who have suffered most try to come to terms with their loss. The fabric of the community was damaged during this time, and it represents one of the most challenging periods of my career. I had developed a great fondness for the people and the place during my time there, and I took some of the North Central with me when I left.

THE PINNACLE

In 2017, I was appointed to the position of Assistant Commissioner with responsibility for the Dublin Metropolitan Region (DMR). This appointment marked the pinnacle of my career. I had left Cork with a borrowed suitcase at the age of 20, and the idea of becoming a Sergeant would have been enough; Assistant Commissioner was never on my radar.

The people in the DMR office were exceptionally committed. The Chief Superintendents across the city were colleagues and friends whom I trusted, having worked with them for years. Drugs had become a scourge across the city, and turf wars were springing up between rival gangs; extreme violence accompanied the change. Funding was a constant struggle, with access to overtime becoming a daily issue. Districts and Divisions were operating on multiple fronts just to maintain a respectable balance within communities, and it took its toll. Very few would admit it, but I could see it during our frequent meetings and conversations. It was not the work that was causing the stress, however; it was their desire to deliver the best possible service to their respective communities, and the constant battle for the resources to do that.

Retired Assistant Commissioner Pat Leahy.

Their days were spent juggling a selection of balls, and their first job each day was to identify the balls and keep them in the air.

It was also in 2017 that I became Chairperson for 'European Capitals Policing', and hosted an international conference in Dublin. In attendance were chiefs of police for the capital cities of 35 nations. The conference focused on two key policing areas – the 'Strategic Response to Mass Casualty Events' and 'Community Oriented Policing'. The themes continued to be developed at conferences across Europe for the following three years. This was not my first foray into the realm of international policing, however; this aspect of policing had developed much sooner in my career.

INTERNATIONAL POLICING

An Garda Síochána gave me more opportunities than I could ever have imagined. How nice Ennis seemed when I found myself abandoned in the bush in Southern Angola by a South African Defence Forces helicopter crew. I was there to investigate a reported incursion and firefight between the Koevoet (the counter-insurgency branch of the South West African Police) and PLAN (People's Liberation Army of Namibia). I spent hours wandering around trying to locate evidence and a potential way out before being rescued by a Malaysian

Army patrol who had got lost and had unintentionally driven into Angola from neighbouring Namibia, where the United Nations were operating.

I was working there with An Garda Síochána, having joined thirty-four of my colleagues from Ireland in a year-long mission to prepare for and preside over free and fair elections in Namibia. It was while preparing in Dublin to travel to Namibia that I first met Peter Fitzgerald, who was a Superintendent at the time. He later retired as Deputy Commissioner of An Garda Síochána, having served on several missions with the United Nations. I had not known Peter previously, but he was to become my friend and mentor for the rest of my career. I vividly remember our first encounter.

Peter, accompanied by half the Irish contingent, was detailed to take responsibility for the Oshakati region in Ovamboland, just south of the Angolan Border. This was a volatile area, where PLAN and the Koevoet were most active. On arrival into Oshakati, we were greeted with machine-gun fire and mortars. Peter had been requested to take the UN-appointed Police Commissioner and his Deputy to the Angolan border the following morning, and he was looking for a volunteer to drive him. After a prolonged silence, I put up my hand and said, 'I'll drive you, Super, but only if we can turn back when I feel that it is unsafe to proceed any further.' Peter agreed and the next day we set off towards the border. We eventually turned back after several hours when we met a South African military patrol, who had just been in a firefight and were showing the signs of it. This was to be the start of a long and exciting professional relationship and a deep friendship which will see both of us out the far end. I subsequently travelled with Peter to Cambodia, Bosnia, and the Middle East.

Namibia brings back memories of adventure-filled, six-day patrols in the bush, sleeping in the sand, surrounded by fire circles to keep out the snakes. It was an extraordinary adventure which defined many of us, and great friendships developed.

Cambodia was different, however, with more ominous challenges and dangers. The natural environment was incredibly beautiful but tough, the country was heavily mined, and the Khmer Rouge remained active. We had executive powers there and enforcement always brings a response. On the outskirts of Phnom Penh, I witnessed the great bravery of Peter Fitzgerald. It was during a forced evacuation of a shanty town by the military, who had launched an assault in the early hours of the morning. We became separated very quickly in the chaos and my last glimpse of Peter was standing between soldiers and civilians with his hands in the air, demanding that the shooting stop. It would be about an hour later that I next saw him. He was remonstrating with a soldier who was dragging a person from his home. As the soldier began to beat the person, Peter stepped between them and grabbed the soldier by the front of the shirt. The soldier pulled a handgun from his holster and pointed it at Peter's head. A silence descended in the immediate vicinity as everyone took in the sight of a Cambodian soldier holding a gun to the head of a uniformed UN officer. The picture stopped everyone in their tracks until eventually the soldier stepped back and slipped away into the crowd. While there had been other challenging times with the United Nations, this features right up there at the top.

On St Patrick's Day 1996, I was on duty in a cemetery in Vogosca, just outside Sarajevo, where the locals were disinterring the bodies of their deceased loved ones so that they could be moved to the other side of a line that had been drawn on the new map of the former Yugoslavia. It was a tense and emotional time, the pain was palpable, and the atmosphere was one of intense sadness. I remember thinking about home, realising how lucky we were, and then redoubling my efforts to make a difference in the lives of these people. I left Bosnia exhausted after a year. It had been the most intense, the most demanding, but also the most rewarding year, and to this day I remain in contact with many people from Bosnia. I lost my father when I was there and missed my chance to say goodbye, but I know that he was proud of what I was doing.

In 2005, I found myself in Beirut, working with Peter Fitzgerald and Martin Donnellan. Peter had been requested by the United Nations Secretary-General, Kofi Annan, to assemble a small team to conduct a fact-finding mission into the Circumstances, Cause and Consequences of the assassination of former Prime Minister Rafiq Hariri. Mr Hariri had been killed along with twenty-one others in an explosion in Beirut on 14 February 2005. Less than ten days later, we were in Beirut at the scene of the bombing. After a challenging and eventful four weeks, we travelled to New York and briefed the Secretary-General and his senior team on the content of our report (the Fitzgerald Report), which subsequently prompted a full international investigation.

I later returned to Africa – both Uganda and Malawi – on behalf of the Department of Foreign Affairs (Irish Aid programme), to conduct capacity-building assessments on policing in these countries. Looking back on my travels, Africa left the biggest mark on my life – the landscape, the freedom, the unspoiled beauty, the tastes and especially the smells. The smell of the earth in Africa stays with me to this day. No matter where in Africa I have gone, that smell of fresh African earth lights up my senses; it has always been a wonderful experience.

An Garda Síochána was the first choice in policing for the United Nations on many occasions. Our tradition of being unarmed, together with our culture of communicating and engaging fairly and without agenda, endeared us to many nations. We should defend this natural orientation in policing robustly; it has served us well.

CONCLUSION

My time in An Garda Síochána represents an exceptionally lucky journey through life for which I am eternally grateful. I have learned that policing is a noble profession and is one worth pursuing; it offers a wide array of opportunities for life-changing experiences. While it is not without its challenges and its ups and downs, I would recommend it without reservation or hesitation.

When I reflect on my career, I think the trick for me was finding a blend of 'living' and 'being' – finding a balance between living for today while preparing with one eye on the future. I had always planned to retire from policing at 55 years of age; I reckoned that I would still have the strength and determination to get a new life experience under my belt before I was forced to slow down. I stayed on for two years longer than I had expected, but the time was right when I did go.

MODERN POLICING

Garda Robbie Peelo shakes hands with a PSNI officer on the Louth/Armagh border prior to the setting up of a joint checkpoint, as Garda Emma Kelly looks on. Co-operation between the two police services has never been as strong; they work closely together in many areas from crime detection to state security.

Mar chuid dá dtiomantas leanúnach don Ghaeilge, thug An Garda Síochána Tionscnamh an Fháinne isteach in 2022. Tá mar chuspóir aige seo an pearsanra go léir a spreagadh pé Gaeilge atá acu a úsáid agus bealach éifeachtach a chur ar fáil do bhaill den phobal pearsanra a labhraíonn an Ghaeilge a aithint gan stró.

CHAPTER 20

——'THE PERFECT MURDER'——

Retired Detective John Cribbin

* Reader discretion advised as this chapter contains graphic content that some may find upsetting.

Over many years, different men and women of An Garda Síochána have pitted their investigative minds with distinction against all types of criminal endeavours. I hope that I have left my own mark 'with distinction' on this illustrious policing history.

I was born in Mayo in the early 1960s, in a county that was relatively crime-free when I was growing up. That all changed with the brutal murder of Mary Duffy in September 1976. She was one of two victims murdered by Englishmen John Shaw and Geoffrey Evans. Fascinated as I was by the successful Garda investigation, an interest in bringing violent criminals to justice was awakened in me. The double murder of Garda Henry Byrne and Detective Garda John Morley, whom I personally knew, reinforced my desire to join the service.

I joined An Garda Síochána on 30 May 1984. On 3 November, I arrived from the training centre in Templemore to the 'A' District. Assigned District number 99A, Kilmainham Garda Station was my first posting. There I soon found that my policing exuberance was channelled towards detective work, solving crime, and chasing down its nefarious perpetrators. Detective Garda Brian Gilmartin (now retired), aided by the late Detective Sergeant Kevin Ward (formerly of the Murder Squad) and the team in the Kilmainham Detective Unit, nurtured in me the skills required to be a good detective. I was taught that a mistress called truth had always to be served first by those of us lucky enough to serve. I also discovered that sometimes the truth is a difficult thing to unearth, no matter the effort.

After a couple of years in uniform, I was elevated to work in plainclothes, within the Crime Prevention Unit, based in Kevin Street. This eventually led to my dream appointment to Kevin Street Garda Station as a new detective in July 1991. Tremendous places to work for any detective, Kevin Street and Kilmainham stations provided many varied and professional challenges. I replaced a retiring legend, Detective Garda Cathal Murphy, instrumental in convicting the infamous Malcolm MacArthur for the murder of Bridie Gargan in July 1982.

I worked alongside many great men and women of all ranks, in both uniform and plainclothes. Our leader was Detective Inspector Michael Connelly, and he referred to his unit as 'Family'. After safely carrying out an early-morning strike, the 'Family' would regularly sit down together to a breakfast cooked by that gentleman detective, the late Ray McEneaney. Dolly Mixtures of memories flood my mind, of stalwart colleagues, victims, witnesses, and perpetrators – times spent together working, in court, at weddings, sporting endeavours, work-related social events and, sadly, sometimes burying our dead.

I have worked on a great number of murder investigations during my career. People sometimes ask me, 'What is the perfect murder?' Martin Richards QPM, Chief Constable of Sussex, put it most elegantly when he explained, 'The perfect murder is the one we never hear about.'

Mary Cummins is Reported Missing

On 26 July 1992, Gardaí at Kevin Street received a report that 36-year-old Mary Cummins, a local single parent with one young daughter, was missing. She had last been seen on 23 July, leaving local pub Carr's at 6 p.m. Preliminary enquiries by uniformed Gardaí proved unsuccessful. With the aid of the Garda Dog Unit, all waste ground and derelict buildings in the vicinity were searched, without success. It was as if Mary Cummins had dropped off the face of the earth.

When the case was passed on to me, I quickly established that Mary had returned to her apartment on Nicholas Street with her grocery shopping after leaving Carr's. Nothing in her apartment indicated that any criminal behaviour had taken place. She was not seen coming back or leaving her apartment again. Unfortunately, CCTV cameras were not common back then, and this hindered our investigation initially.

Beside myself with exasperation, I returned to Carr's, where I had the good fortune to find a new witness, a former British soldier, who provided vital new information regarding events on the evening of 23 July. He recalled seeing Mary Cummins having a drink in the company of the caretaker of a local girls' school in Warrenmount, Dublin 8. Mary's daughter and this man's daughter had played together in the pub until Mary's friends collected her daughter. The caretaker had told the witness that the mother of his children had abandoned him and their two daughters by running off to England in 1991 and said that there had been no contact since. The witness had suggested that he would go with the caretaker to the British Embassy to ask for help in locating his wife. To his amazement, the other man had turned down this offer.

I identified the school caretaker as Michael Bambrick of Ronanstown, Dublin 22. The girls' mother, Patricia McGauley, was indeed missing. In the early hours of 12 September

1991, a neighbour had heard the couple arguing violently, which was not unusual. That evening, at about 8.30 p.m., the neighbour had seen Patricia McGauley from behind, leaving the house, wearing a dress and high heels. This sighting would later become significant.

In early August 1992, my partner, Michael Mellon, and I interviewed Bambrick in Kevin Street. On the surface, Bambrick seemed to be an ordinary working man, struggling to raise two small kids on his own. He admitted meeting and drinking with Mary on 23 July in Carr's pub. Blatantly, he claimed not to have seen her again. During the interview, he removed his shoes, filling the room with a very unsavoury pungent smell, akin to rotten eggs. When I put the following question to him: 'Isn't it strange the way two women in your life have disappeared, Michael?', Bambrick retorted, 'Yes, it's a terrible coincidence. It is just a misfortune and pure bad luck. But I had nothing to do with it.'

There was something ominous in the way he delivered this reply. Detective Mellon and I were not fooled. Good detectives never believe in 'terrible coincidences'.

TIME PASSES

Nevertheless, leads petered out completely and we had nothing to move forward Mary Cummins's missing person's case. Over the next two years, my investigation was desultory, carried out alongside my everyday duties. However, after reinterviewing family and friends of both women, I discovered more leads and witnesses. I assembled detailed knowledge of the two women's lives and of Bambrick's background, and I gained an insight into his psychological mindset. Witnesses were all steadfast in their belief that neither woman would abandon her children without a word. However, no new evidence linked Bambrick and Mary Cummins after their meeting in Carr's. No new suspects manifested themselves either. Everything about the case ended up in a big black document box; over time, it overflowed.

Even after changing her name and moving address, Bambrick's former wife was still in fear that he would come back into her life after 20 years. Her evidence was vital as it tragically corroborated information that Bambrick was to relate to Gardaí later in 1994. She revealed that he was a cross-dresser and said that he also had worryingly abnormal sexual behaviour in his background, including a fetish for bondage and choking female partners during intimate relations. Having experienced at first-hand his dangerous fetish, and fearing for her life, she had left Bambrick, on the advice of a psychiatrist.

New unanswered questions regarding the disappearance of Patricia McGauley now surfaced. Who had left the house wearing the dress and high heels on the evening of 12 September 1991? I now believed that it was Bambrick. If he had murdered Patricia, then, very possibly, he had killed Mary Cummins as well. But we had no bodies. With no hard evidence to support my suspicions, I consulted a state forensic psychologist. He explained that Bambrick's removal of his shoes during our interview with him in Kevin Street in August 1992 had been an attempt to control the interview. The psychologist's reflections on all the evidence presented led him to believe that both women were dead, and very probably buried in or near Bambrick's home.

Despite our belief that we had prima facie justifiable grounds to do so, there was no legal solution found to permit a search of the homestead for a body or evidence of murder. Back in 1994, a serious gap in Irish criminal law was tying our hands. Desperately trying to circumvent it legally, senior Gardaí had even contacted the Gloucestershire Police incident room, investigating serial murderers Fred and Rose West.

A New Witness

It was then that a courageous young girl – Bambrick's daughter – walked into Ronanstown Garda Station in Clondalkin, with an adult neighbour, giving us our next breakthrough. Garda Mary Bushell gained her trust. The girl made several serious allegations of abuse against Bambrick: he had assaulted her, not fed her, violently killed her pets in a depraved way, and neglected her welfare. Gardaí who called to her home to collect her clothes found the interior of the house uninhabitable.

Interesting facts about the comings and goings at the child's home were disclosed. The visit a few years earlier of an unknown woman – nicknamed by the girl as 'the Coca-Cola woman' – riveted Gardaí. The child recalled playing with the woman's daughter in Carr's pub. When leaving Carr's, the woman had taken her shopping home to her apartment. In the apartment, the woman gave the child some Coca-Cola memorabilia. She then accompanied them to Ronanstown on the bus. Bambrick and the woman went out drinking in Clondalkin. The child recalled seeing the woman return to the house late that night. The next morning, she saw her father burning what appeared to be the woman's runners in an open fire in their sitting room. Was it possible that Mary Cummins was 'the Coca-Cola woman'?

Garda Mary Bushell showed the child a montage of photographs of women including one of Mary Cummins. Mary was identified as 'the Coca-Cola woman'. It was a major breakthrough, which contradicted her father's story.

Detective Sergeant Walter Kilcullen provided the next vital link. He introduced me to a local man, an acquaintance of Mary Cummins. The man's son worked for Coca-Cola and had given him several Coca-Cola promotional items, which he had then passed on to Mary prior to her disappearance.

In January 1995, Michael Bambrick was arrested by Garda Mary Bushell on foot of the serious physical allegations made against him by his daughter. While in custody, he was asked again about the two missing women. Steadfastly he stuck to his earlier narratives.

The family home became vacant after a family subletting the house moved out. Dublin Corporation took back ownership of the property and gave permission to An Garda Síochána to search it. Detective Inspector Michael Byrne, now in charge of Kevin Street Detective Unit, liaised with colleagues in Clondalkin, and formed a joint search team. On 12 and 13 April 1995, amid a media frenzy that filled many inches of the tabloids, the team started searching the home, and digging up its back garden. Bones from several dead dogs were found buried in the garden. However, nothing else of evidential value was found then.

Former Garda Commissioner Pat Byrne, then a Deputy Commissioner of Operations, met Detective Inspector Michael Byrne and Superintendent Michael Carolan (Clondalkin) in charge of Ronanstown Station. He appointed Detective Chief Superintendent Kevin Carty, head of the Central Detective Unit (CDU) in Harcourt Square, to lead the investigations. Carty formed an investigation team made up of detective personnel from Kevin Street, Ronanstown and the CDU. The Kevin Street team comprised Detective Inspector Michael Byrne, Detective Sergeant John Doyle (senior), Detective Gardaí Mick Mellon, Tom Flanagan (junior) and myself. The Investigation Incident Room was based in Lucan Garda Station.

THE INVESTIGATION CONTINUES

Detective Chief Superintendent Carty was one of the most skilled investigating minds with whom I have ever had the good fortune to work. Led by him, we sifted through the sands of Michael Bambrick's life, seeking out new evidence. Countless conferences were attended as over 300 leads were followed up, generating close to 500 witness statements, numerous reports, and searches. Other possible suspects were identified, investigated, and eventually eliminated. The interior of the two-storey house was minutely forensically examined by staff from the Forensic Science Laboratory in Garda HQ. Disturbingly they found a lot of human blood and staining, not visible to the naked eye. Dried blood was discovered on about 50 floorboards partially within the box room. Having established Michael Bambrick's character and his psychology, there was no doubting the identity of the only suspect left in the frame.

At this point, Bambrick was living with another woman in Dublin 7. Her safety became a grave concern, putting added pressure on the investigation team. When interviewed, she claimed that Bambrick had told her he had killed a woman in Clondalkin.

We interviewed all known prostitutes working the Benburb area close to Bambrick's new residence. One of these women recognised Bambrick from our description. She claimed that he had purchased her leather miniskirt from her for £20, after giving her a pair of ladies'

Above left: Photographing floorboards at a crime scene. Above right: A Garda photographer examines evidence.

leather pants (the property of the woman with whom he was living) to replace her skirt. He had been wearing these under his jeans. He modelled the skirt on himself for her by walking up and down. Gardaí also received credible information that Bambrick had possession of an illegal shotgun and spear gun.

Detective Chief Superintendent Carty assembled several detectives from around the country, some of whom had been in the old Murder Squad, now incorporated into the CDU. All were accomplished interviewers of serious crime suspects. On the morning of 24 June 1995, Michael Bambrick was arrested by Detective Sergeant John Melody (CDU) on suspicion of the illegal possession of a firearm; he was detained at Kevin Street Station. It is interesting to note that throughout his detention, Bambrick did not have one person who visited or rang the station enquiring about his welfare, with the exception of his solicitor. The weapons were never located by Gardaí.

THE BREAKTHROUGH

During an interview on the evening of his arrest, Detective Sergeant Pat Lynagh and Detective Garda Gerry Dillon told Bambrick that they knew all about him. He was reminded how, as a boy, he had topped every flower in his mother's garden in a fit of jealous rage when his mother's attention was directed to his brother during a visit home from England. They told him that they also knew of his purchase of the leather skirt. Guilt is a gift which always keeps giving, and Bambrick's earlier reticence now disappeared. He needed to tell all, and he proceeded to make a lengthy confession.

Bambrick gave the detectives details of how he had killed both women and how later in his home he had carried out the vile task of dismembering their bodies. The cause of their deaths, according to Bambrick, was his dangerous bondage fetish, which he had indulged for personal erotic gratification, choking his female partners during intimate relations. His account could be neither forensically corroborated nor denied, due to the time elapsed. Bambrick said that he had used his bicycle and a wheelbarrow to carry the dismembered body parts of his victims to two different burial sites. That wheelbarrow had for many days sat in our Incident Room, its morbid future as an exhibit as yet unknown.

Later that night, Bambrick voluntarily accompanied Gardaí to Balgaddy in Ronanstown, identifying two burial sites quite near his home. I recall standing captivated as the inky black fingers of that mild summer night gently caressed the Dublin city skyline, cocooning me in my own thoughts, fully aware as I was of the grisly tasks ahead. A strained speechless reverence observed by Gardaí was broken briefly by the hum of intermittent traffic in the distance, the raised voices of distant shouting youths and a barking dog, as we waited for Bambrick to speak.

That night, the 42-year-old Bambrick wore a light, long-sleeved, black, four-buttoned sweater. The top buttons were open, revealing part of his dark-haired tanned chest. He also wore not-so-clean beltless blue jeans and dirty lace-less white runners. This smallish man, with the makings of a future pot belly evident, and his strong workman's hands by his side, was now somehow childlike, giving up because the game was over; and he was revealing all his clever moves to us.

The illumination afforded by the light from a few Garda torches under the guidance of Bambrick's fingers marked the spot. First, the resting place of Mary Cummins. Then, at a different location, that of Patricia McGauley. Mary Cummins's dismembered body, having been cut up by Bambrick with a paper knife and a junior hacksaw (confirmed by forensics), was recovered near a ditch over the next few days. Bambrick had callously disposed of the body of Patricia McGauley, the mother of their children, in an open drain. Dublin Corporation had regularly cleaned out this drain during the preceding years, clearing it of discarded rubbish, inadvertently removing Patricia's decomposed body parts. Only seven small skull fragments were recovered.

My all-consuming competitive mental struggle with Bambrick over the previous years was finally at an end. I had won. I felt elation – victory even – as the full headlight beams of an unmarked Garda car or two manoeuvred into place, focusing on Patricia's resting place. Now a profound professional debt of honour could be paid by giving answers and some form of closure to two heartbroken and grieving families. This sad and personally emotional task fell to Garda Mary Bushell (Patricia's family) and me (Mary's family) to perform much later that night. The elation subsided and was replaced altogether by an intense empty feeling in my heart. Mary and Patricia, two women whom I had never met, but yet had known so intimately over the years, would now definitely never be coming home.

CONCLUDING THOUGHTS

It was not my first time to stand in the presence of a cold-blooded, evil, self-centred killer. Sadly, nor was it my last. In a soft Dublin inner-city accent, Michael Bambrick's flat, unemotional voice had articulated with workman-like detail where he had placed each body part. I noted his total lack of emotional empathy and remorse. He showed no regard whatsoever for the destructive effect of the loss of those two women's lives on their loved ones left behind. In many ways, Bambrick appeared so normal to me that night, as he narrated his depraved past deeds to us, that I remarked to myself how he was not much different to look at from any other man in Dublin.

> True evil has a face you know and a voice you trust. (Anonymous)

The flick of a switch that separates one from the other. A chance crossing of paths. We can never know what influenced Mary Cummins into her fatal decision to go off with the school caretaker on that summer's evening. But through the work of members of An Garda Síochána, her senseless murder ensured that Michael Bambrick received justice not only for her murder but also for 'the perfect murder' of Patricia McGauley.

On 26 July 1996, one day short of four years after meeting Mary Cummins, Bambrick was sentenced by the late Judge Paul Carney to 18 years in prison for the manslaughter of Mary Cummins, and 15 years for the manslaughter of mother of two, Patricia McGauley. Judge Carney said that his preference would have been to sentence 'this dangerous accused' to life imprisonment for the 'horrific homicides', but 'constitutional problems' prevented him from doing so. Bambrick served his sentence in Arbour Hill prison until his release in April 2009. Had these murders not been successfully solved when they were, the evidential value of both burial sites might have been lost forever. Twelve months later, they were both construction sites.

The old policeman in me still likes to believe that there is no such thing as 'the perfect murder'. It is a contradiction in terms. In my experience of criminality and its participants, there is no such thing as a perfect plan or crime either. A shadow is always left as you pass. Because, simply put, 'something always goes wrong'.

CHAPTER 21

THE INVESTIGATOR

Assistant Commissioner John O'Driscoll
with Garda Stephen Moore

INVESTIGATION OF CRIME

When I joined An Garda Síochána in April 1981, not much had changed with regard to the investigation of crime from 1940 when my father joined the organisation. Many of the criminal charges prosecuted in 1981 were contrary to the provisions of legislation enacted prior to the foundation of the State in 1922. Both my father and I were involved in the prosecution of offences that were contrary to legislation that included the Offences Against the Person Act, 1861, the Malicious Damage Act, 1861, and the Larceny Act, 1916.

Throughout my father's career in An Garda Síochána and in my earlier years of service, the investigation of serious crime involved considerable reliance on technical examination of crime scenes – the Garda Technical Bureau is the longest-established specialist unit in An Garda Síochána – and on obtaining admissions from those identified as suspects.

However, as I approach the end of my career in An Garda Síochána, the investigation of crime, and serious crime in particular, has been subject to considerable change. The focus once placed on identifying suspects and obtaining statements of admission has shifted to ensuring that An Garda Síochána fulfils its duty with regard to the investigation of crime, as referred to by the Supreme Court, in *Braddish v. DPP* – 'to seek out and preserve all evidence having a bearing or potential bearing on the issue of guilt or innocence'.

REGULATIONS

The treatment of persons in custody is governed by regulations made under the Criminal Justice Act, 1984, as amended. These regulations are designed to provide safeguards for persons in custody from improper behaviour by members of An Garda Síochána. They are also intended as safeguards for members of An Garda Síochána against whom unjustified allegations may be made.

Solicitors were first permitted to attend garda station interviews in 2014. Prior to this,

The investigation of serious crime relies considerably on technical examination of crime scenes.

solicitors were allowed to attend garda stations only to provide legal advice to detained persons. Provision has also been made for the electronic recording of interviews.

A HUMANS-RIGHTS-BASED APPROACH

The adoption of a human rights-based approach has also given rise to change over time in how An Garda Síochána undertakes the investigation of crime. An Garda Síochána has endeavoured to ensure the embedding of human rights standards within policing in general and, in particular, with regard to its participation in the investigation of crime.

In Ireland, the European Convention on Human Rights Act, 2003 requires An Garda Síochána to perform its functions in a manner compatible with the State's obligations under the European Convention on Human Rights (ECHR). A human-rights-based approach puts the rights of individuals and protected groups, enshrined at law by the ECHR, at the centre of every decision and action of An Garda Síochána.

The duties governing a criminal investigation arising from the ECHR impact on such matters as thoroughness, effectiveness and independence. In particular, the deprivation of liberty of a person reasonably suspected of committing an offence will give rise to issues of compatibility of the detention with Article 5 of the Convention. When searching and surveillance are involved, potential interference with respect for private life, home and correspondence arises – impacts of Article 8. Meanwhile, interrogation of suspects may give rise to issues under Article 3.

FOCUS ON VICTIMS

In the past, there was minimal focus on victims in the course of investigation of crime. The introduction of victim-impact statements under the Criminal Justice Act, 1993 was a significant landmark in the recognition of victims' rights. It guaranteed victims a voice at the sentencing hearing.

More recently, the Criminal Justice (Victims of Crime) Act, 2017 confers a wide range of rights on victims of crime. The 2017 Act gives effect to the European Union Victims' Rights Directive. The most important characteristic of this legislation is that it confers *rights* on victims, irrespective of the nature of the crime.

UNDERTAKING INVESTIGATIONS

An Garda Síochána has ensured that it is has a capacity to undertake investigations in a manner that complies with all relevant obligations placed upon it, including those relating to human rights and victims. A typical investigation relating to serious crime will now involve the appointment of a senior investigating officer (SIO) and an incident room coordinator (IRC) along with a family liaison officer (FLO). The necessary decision making is done in compliance with a Garda decision-making model (GDMM).

In 2009, An Garda Síochána introduced a Garda Síochána Interviewing Model (GSIM) and later, in 2014, an Interview Policy and *Manual of Guidance for Investigative Interviewing*. The primary goal of investigative interviewing is stated as being to obtain accurate, complete and reliable information from interviewees for the purpose of establishing facts about matters under investigation.

TRAINING

An SIO, who will typically be of Inspector rank, undertakes a lead role in any investigation to which they are assigned. The SIO will undertake a course of study leading to a Postgraduate Diploma in Serious Crime Investigation, considered the flagship of the Crime Training Faculty, located within the Garda Síochána Training College. The SIO programme is designed to develop the expert knowledge and leadership and management skills of middle managers within An Garda Síochána and other public bodies, to equip them with the expertise necessary to investigate serious crime in Ireland. The Crime Training Faculty provides a suite of training programmes to support the investigative function in An Garda Síochána in the areas of interviewing, canvass coordinating, crime scene investigation and the investigative management.

SURVEILLANCE

The Criminal Justice (Surveillance) Act, 2009 provides the legal basis for covert surveillance measures. It sets out in clear terms by whom, to whom and the parameters within which authorisations may be sought for conducting covert surveillance. The powers under the 2009 Act are available only to An Garda Síochána, the Defence Forces, the Revenue Commissioners and the Garda Síochána Ombudsman Commission.

THE INTERNATIONAL DIMENSION

As An Garda Síochána enters its second century, it is frequently required to undertake investigations that have a transnational dimension. Consequently, co-operation at an international level in the undertaking of investigations is commonplace; this will involve participation by An Garda Síochána and the law-enforcement authorities in other jurisdictions. This co-operation is facilitated by the use of such investigative tools and instruments as the mutual legal assistance (MLA) process – the formal means of requesting assistance in another country, whereby an international letter of requests (ILOR) is utilised to ask the requested state to obtain specific, identifiable evidence.

The requirement to provide for an international dimension to investigations is reflected in enactment of such legislation as the Criminal Law Jurisdiction Act, 1976; the European Arrest Warrant Act, 2003 (as amended); the Criminal Justice Joint Investigation Team Act, 2004; the Criminal Justice (Mutual Assistance) Act, 2008; and the more recent Criminal Justice (International Co-operation) Act, 2019. The 2009 Act made further provision in relation to mutual assistance and facilitating the participation of members of An Garda Síochána in joint investigation teams.

In 2019, An Garda Síochána and the Police Service of Northern Ireland (PSNI) established a Joint Investigation Team, under Article 20 of the Second Additional Protocol to the European Convention on Mutual Legal Assistance in Criminal Matters. This was the first Joint Investigation Team (JIT) in which An Garda Síochána took part and was established to investigate a crime gang suspected of abducting and torturing a company executive who worked and resided close to the border with Northern Ireland.

Soon afterwards, arising from an illegal migrant-smuggling operation which left thirty-nine people dead, An Garda Síochána, through the Garda National Immigration Bureau (GNIB), participated in a second JIT. The international evidence used in the trial held in the United Kingdom was the result of a JIT that had been quickly set up between Belgium, France, Ireland and the UK, with the participation of Eurojust and Europol. The Netherlands also provided evidence to the trial.

In the trial, eight men were found guilty of involvement in an illegal migrant-smuggling operation which had resulted in the death of the victims from oxygen starvation. Their bodies had been discovered on 22 October 2019 in a lorry container in the town of Grays in Essex, They had been sealed in the airtight container for nearly 12 hours.

INTERVIEWS CONDUCTED BY GARDA STEPHEN MOORE

With more than 2,000 serious investigations completed between them, Retired Assistant Commissioners Tony Hickey and John O'Mahony, together with retired Detective Superintendents Tony Sourke and Michael Byrne, were ideally placed to answer my questions about investigations, from how they are conducted to what, in their opinion, makes for a successful outcome.

Retired Assistant Commissioner Tony Hickey (left) and retired Detective Superintendent Michael Byrne.

WHY IS AN INVESTIGATION TEAM SET UP?

An investigation team is set up to coordinate all the various strands of the investigation in accordance with best practice. Most commonly, investigation teams exist to investigate serious crimes such as murders, armed robberies and kidnappings – those crimes that require immediate responses. However, they are also used for a broad range of other crimes such as aggravated burglaries, serious assaults, historical cases, sexual abuse cases, fraud cases, unusual crimes with obscure legislation and, at times, in response to findings in tribunals.

WHO FORMS AN INVESTIGATION TEAM?

Senior officers within the Region or Division in which the crime took place act in an advisory role; they also provide resources and attend conferences. The SIO has all operational control of the investigation and is responsible for the collection and preservation of evidence and the transfer of evidence. The SIO is the person responsible for the investigation.

The Incident Room Coordinator (IRC, formerly known as 'The Bookman') plays a pivotal role in any investigation. Every piece of evidence comes through the IRC who records everything, filters everything, and gives jobs to be conducted by other teams. The most important relationship the SIO will have in any investigation is with the IRC.

Other critical people involved in investigations include scenes-of-crime officers. Local scenes-of-crime personnel will be used, but for serious crimes the Technical Bureau will be brought in for their expertise. A scenes-of-crime manager will be appointed, who will liaise closely with the SIO.

Search teams will be utilised if required, headed by a search team manager. A search can be conducted in anything from a house to 20 square miles of forestry. Teams will be set up to run enquiries. House-to-house questionnaires may be conducted; these are very important and tend to give the overall comings and goings of everyone in a particular area at a particular time. CCTV and telephone teams will also be set up, if required, to collect evidence.

Further along an investigation, arrest teams and interview teams will be formed to arrest and question suspects. Family liaison officers and other supports which the Gardaí provide are also vital in many investigations. For some investigations, specific outside specialists may be required, and their expertise can sometimes provide the crucial evidence needed.

The initial stages of an investigation are absolutely critical to its success. If it transpires that a particular crime is not so serious after all, it is easier to stand down the investigation than to catch up if the first 48 hours are lost.

HOW IMPORTANT IS TEAMWORK?

No investigation has ever been solved by one person alone. Good investigators are team players. They are ever willing to share their knowledge and experience with younger less experienced personnel, to achieve higher standards. It is very important that outside teams coming into an unfamiliar area build rapport quickly with the local Gardaí and management in that area, involving them and using their local knowledge to assist in the investigation. Teamwork also travels outside the investigation team, and all experts brought in to help with the investigation are quickly made to feel part of the team. It is vital to create an atmosphere where everyone's opinion matters, and feedback is welcomed from every member of the team. It is also important to acknowledge that a local person may not want to speak with a local Garda whom they may know personally; they might prefer to speak with an external Garda. This can sometimes work the other way too.

Investigations are never solved by one person alone.

WHAT IS CONSIDERED A SUCCESSFUL INVESTIGATION?

An investigation is considered successful when every member of the investigation team plays a part in dealing with the facts of the case and establishing where the truth lies. Every investigation is looking for the truth of what happened. It is not the job of an investigation team to decide on the guilt or innocence of a person; that is decided by a judge in the District Courts or by a judge and jury in higher courts.

Any investigation has a better chance of success if you 'throw the kitchen sink at it' from the very beginning. Preparation is key, and it is important not to presume anything, to have total regard for the law of the land, and to adhere to all human rights laws. Investigators must not discriminate, and they must always make sure that every action they take is proportional and legal; investigators must be personally accountable for all their actions. If these standards are adhered to, there is better chance of achieving a successful outcome.

However, even the best investigators make mistakes. They learn from those mistakes, but sometimes, despite all their efforts, there simply will not be enough evidence to have a successful outcome.

Generally, a successful investigation will bring closure to injured parties, and it will bring a certain amount of satisfaction if and when the truth is proven beyond a reasonable doubt. However, on occasion, and in particular in murder investigations, there can be no closure for either the victim or their families – the victim cannot be brought back.

WHAT UNIQUE SKILLS ARE NEEDED TO BE A GOOD INVESTIGATOR?

Crime investigation is a craft – an investigator must serve an apprenticeship, watching, listening and learning in order to establish the necessary expertise. Anyone who wants to be a good investigator must have a great interest in the investigation process and be willing to learn from the mistakes that they will undoubtedly make. They need to make themselves available and be there every day, working as part of a team, always remembering that the devil is in the detail.

Good investigators have the ability to establish a good rapport with their colleagues on the team, but also with suspects, injured parties, experts, and any person with whom they have dealings as part of the investigation. They must be empathetic, have integrity and be ethically sound in everything they do. They should have the ability to analyse every situation and the confidence to get their opinion across. Good investigators always keep an open mind and are willing to ask the hard questions. They won't accept the first answer or become tunnel visioned and will always maintain their focus in reaching their target, which is establishing the truth. A good investigator needs to stay the course – any particular investigation may take a week, months or years, and stamina and perseverance are essential.

As a police service, how can An Garda Síochána become better at investigations?

It is important to ensure both that the legislation is adequate and that investigators are provided with appropriate resources. Training and education are key. New members of An Garda Síochána need more and earlier exposure to the workings of the courts and the judicial system. Past members with an interest in investigations used to spend days in courtrooms, learning. Every day in court is a learning day, and anybody who wants to be an investigator should be in court as often as they can. New members with a specific aptitude for an investigative role should be identified as soon as possible and trained to the highest level.

Investigators can get better at sharing information; this shared information will only benefit future investigations – knowledge is power. We can learn from the experiences of our international partners and maybe send more Gardaí to be trained in other jurisdictions, especially in countries dealing with crimes that could have a significance in this country, such as terrorism.

Although An Garda Síochána has improved greatly when dealing with victims of crime, the service can still do better and should always be at the forefront of developing and maintaining high levels of supports for these victims. An Garda Síochána must continue to learn from past mistakes and make sure, through training and education, that the next generation of investigators has the necessary tools to achieve more and more successful outcomes.

The opinions expressed in these interviews are those of the named persons who took part and answered my questions. They do not come directly from An Garda Síochána. Each interviewee was quick to add that they themselves have made mistakes in investigations, but that they always learned from their mistakes. Each one wanted to thank the investigators who preceded them and who helped them during their careers.

CHAPTER 22

─ROADS POLICING ─

Garda Damien Duffy

By 1953, the phenomenon of motorised traffic in Dublin city had become so commonplace as to necessitate the establishment of a novel Garda unit, with responsibility for regulating and controlling the myriad transport methods of the day, which included cars, animal-drawn vehicles, bicycles and trams. An initial eight-man team of specialist motorcyclists, some of whom had previously served with the Irish Army's motorcycle corps, began to patrol the city streets, using maroon 500cc Triumph motorcycles. According to an *Evening Herald* article of 3 April 1953, their aim was 'helping to ease traffic congestion and to educate offenders, with courtesy'. The unit may have grown to over 100 Garda and civilian staff members; the tools, the training, and the transport may have changed; but the basic role has not – keeping people safe on the country's roads.

Stationed in the impressive accommodations of Dublin Castle, the Garda Traffic Corps – known since 2018 as the Garda Roads Policing Unit – has, for almost seventy years, provided

Early vehicles used by An Garda Síochána.

a constant uniform presence at the former seat of British power in Ireland. From this city-centre location, the unit patrols and responds to incidents across the entirety of the county of Dublin, and further afield when required.

While initially established to deal with the rising levels of traffic in Dublin, Roads Policing Units are now well-established nationwide. Although the geography and urban/rural ratios may vary, these units share the common goals of ensuring public safety, through a high-visibility presence, education, and enforcement where necessary. The women and men of the Roads Policing Units nationwide work tirelessly, often in hazardous conditions, to keep road-users safe. Instantly identifiable by their Battenberg-pattern vehicles, Roads Policing Gardaí take a particular pride in the turn-out of their equipment and personal presentation.

Sadly, despite efforts to reduce road deaths through education and enforcement of road-traffic legislation, road-traffic collisions continue to rob families of loved ones. The investigation of these incidents falls to the Forensic Collision Investigation Unit of the Roads Policing Units. The Gardaí specialising in this role are highly trained in the examination and investigation of fatal and serious-injury road-traffic collisions. Fulfilling a role that requires a particular constitution and level of fortitude, they employ cutting-edge tools, including airborne drones, to photograph and survey incident scenes, with a view to providing investigators and victims' families with the facts surrounding an unfortunate death on the roads.

GARDA NATIONAL ROADS POLICING BUREAU

The Garda National Roads Policing Bureau was established in July 1997 as part of An Garda Síochána's contribution to reducing the number of road fatalities and improving safety on our roads. We have seen a significant reduction in the number of fatal road-traffic collisions over recent years. In 2010 and 2019, Ireland was the winner of the European Transport Safety Council Road Safety Performance Index (PIN) annual award, which is presented to a European country that has demonstrated continued progress on road safety, combined with a strategic approach to tackling the problem across Government. Although every road fatality is one too many, Ireland now has one of the lowest levels of road deaths per capita in Europe.

The following table illustrates the decline in fatal road-traffic collisions since 1972.

Year	Fatal Collisions
1972	640
1982	533
1992	415
2002	376
2012	162
2021	137

This is achieved in large part through high-visibility mobile patrols, concerted media campaigns with partner agencies, and target enforcement of the key lifesaver offences.

The Government Road Safety Strategy, 2021–2030 aims to reduce the number of deaths and serious injuries on Irish roads by 50 per cent over the next nine years. The main goal is to reduce deaths on Ireland's roads annually to 72 or lower, while reducing serious injuries from 1,259 to 630 or lower by 2030. The Strategy contains high-impact actions for An Garda Síochána to take, including assisting partner agencies in achieving the targets.

High-Visibility Patrols

High-visibility patrols by the Roads Policing Units are designed to create deterrence and change unlawful traffic behaviours. In addition, Roads Policing Units carry out checkpoints such as speed checkpoints, intoxicated-driving checkpoints and general road-traffic checkpoints.

Speeding

Gardaí use a range of speed-detection technology to reduce speed across Irish roads, including handheld and tripod-mounted laser speed guns and van-mounted Go-Safe vans, which are operated by civilians.

A reduction in speed will lead to a reduction in the incidence of fatal and serious injuries and will improve road safety for all road-users.

An Garda Síochána works closely with a range of partner agencies, including Government departments, the Road Safety Authority, Transport Infrastructure Ireland, and the community, in order to develop a national culture of safe road use.

Gardaí use a range of technology to reduce speeding on Irish roads.

INTOXICATED DRIVING

Modern technology has assisted An Garda Síochána in enforcing intoxicated-driving legislation. The legislation has advanced reducing legal limits and increasing penalties. Mandatory intoxicated testing is conducted by Gardaí under legislation empowering them to test any driver stopped at a mandatory intoxicant testing checkpoint without the need to form an opinion in relation to the driver of the vehicle. In 2011, mandatory alcohol testing for drivers involved in road-traffic collisions was introduced.

Breath testing has progressed from the 'blow in the bag' test to the use of the Dräger Alcotest 7510, which is a handheld breath-alcohol measuring device. Penalties for drink-driving offences range from disqualification periods from three months to six years, depending on the classification of driver (learner, novice, professional), level of alcohol detected, and whether it is a first or subsequent offence.

Drug testing was introduced in 2017 and Gardaí can carry out roadside drug testing using a Dräger Drug Test 5000, which can analyse a saliva sample to detect the presence of four different types of drugs, namely opiates, cocaine, benzodiazepines and cannabis. Failing the test can result in the driver being arrested and brought to a Garda station to provide a blood sample, which will be sent to the Medical Bureau of Road Safety for analysis.

AUTOMATIC NUMBER PLATE RECOGNITION (ANPR)

A key focus of the Roads Policing Units is denying criminals the use of the road network. Recent years have seen investment in Automated Number Plate Recognition (ANPR) cameras. ANPR uses optical character recognition technology to read vehicle registration plates; it is used in patrol vehicles by many police services worldwide. The technology can read number plates at a rate of six per second on vehicles travelling up to 180km/h. First introduced in 2008 as vehicle-mounted cameras, the ANPR cameras allow Gardaí to check a vehicle registration plate instantly against a database of vehicles that may be stolen, in the possession of criminals, or are uninsured or otherwise of interest to a criminal investigation.

All vehicles fitted with ANPR camera systems will be able to identify vehicles as being stolen, untaxed, uninsured, having no NCT/CVRT, or suspect. The systems therefore make a significant contribution to the target of denying criminals the use of our roads and increasing safety for all road users.

MOBILITY

An Garda Síochána recognises the importance of providing modern technology to allow members to spend time on active patrol, as opposed to on administrative duties. To this end, the Active Mobility Project was introduced. A key component of the project was to provide frontline Roads Policing Gardaí with mobility devices – personal-issue mobile phones – giving them access to key Garda systems on the roadside. With a range of applications, these devices allow Gardaí to check vehicle and driver details at the side of the road, accessing up-to-date criminal intelligence that will also include instant information on disqualified drivers. The technology also allows for the creation of fixed-charge notices (FCNs). In 2021, the first FCNs were issued to motorists at roadsides using the mobility devices and by year end over 160,000 had been issued this way.

While this technology is only an aid to Roads Policing Gardaí in the execution of their duties, it goes a long way towards identifying criminals and denying them the use of our roads.

COVID-19

On its arrival to these shores, the COVID-19 pandemic had a major impact on the lives of almost everyone on our island. One of the key Government strategies in the battle against the virus was encouraging people to limit their travel to essential journeys only, and to be responsible in their social interactions. Responsibility for the enforcement of the resultant health regulations fell to An Garda Síochána and the Roads Policing Units in particular, whose members manned checkpoints in all seasons, providing a constant presence on the roads, encouraging, and sometimes enforcing, public health measures when appropriate.

A Garda checkpoint in Dublin in March 2021 during the COVID-19 pandemic.

MY CAREER PATH

A constant feature of the Roads Policing Unit since its inception has been the use of motorcycles. This mode of transport allows members to navigate congested urban traffic quickly while responding to emergencies. It was the draw of these impressive machines and the equally impressive skill of the riders that drew my interest to this strand of policing. In 2007, joining the smaller divisional Roads Policing Unit at Pearse Street, I soon found myself doing standard motorcycle training – a four-week course at Garda HQ in the Phoenix Park. By the end of the course, I had learned how to operate a 700cc Honda Deauville motorcycle safely and competently; this was a testament to the course instructors, as I had never so much as sat on a motorcycle before. The standard motorcycle course had a high failure rate, partly because some students decided that motorcycles were not suited to them, and partly because of the exacting standards the instructors required from participants to pass. Only when you had proven your ability to operate the machine to the highest standards of safety and control could you expect to be deemed competent. My initial training would be a constant emotional rollercoaster of apprehension, fear, excitement and, ultimately, a sense of accomplishment.

In January 2010, I transferred to the Roads Policing Division at Dublin Castle where I completed the advanced motorcycle course – two more weeks honing the basic skills provided by the standard course – and then the escort course. The tool of choice for the advanced Garda motorcyclist was the Yamaha FJR 1300cc sports tourer – an impressive machine, which has since been replaced by the BMW R1250RT police special. The skills these courses developed would be required for a key feature of the division – the provision of vehicle escorts under a wide variety of circumstances.

The use of motorcycles has been a constant feature of the Roads Policing Unit.

Roads Policing Unit waiting at Dublin Airport for the arrival of Pope Francis in August 2018.

My first escort job was as a member of a three-rider team providing the ambulance escort of a critically ill child being transferred from Galway to Temple Street Children's Hospital in Dublin. Our role was to get the ambulance through rush-hour traffic safely, smoothly, and as quickly as possible – an adrenaline-fuelled experience, to say the least. I had to draw on every aspect of my training, while keeping myself, my colleagues and the public out of harm's way as we completed our objective in horrendous weather conditions, all the time having to navigate all sorts of hazards. At times along the journey, I wondered what had possessed me to follow this career path. At the hospital, there was no time to engage in conversation with the medical team in the ambulance, but the look of gratitude on the ambulance driver's face was enough to convince me that I *was* on the right career path. Other escorts, fortunately, come with a little more notice.

The Roads Policing Unit has provided the escorts for US presidents, for Queen Elizabeth II, and for other visiting dignitaries. Just as importantly, we have provided escorts for children attending urgent medical procedures, the Army Explosive Ordnance Disposal team, and expectant parents who find themselves stuck in traffic at precisely the wrong time.

CONCLUSION

While the white gauntlets and baton of the Garda regulating traffic on O'Connell Bridge in the 1950s are gone, one thing has not changed. The members of the Roads Policing Unit are often the first at the scene of incidents that have a huge impact on people's lives – sometimes life-saving and sometimes tragic; it would be wrong to suggest that it is 'just work'. While entry to the unit is voluntary and often very competitive, it takes a certain kind of individual to turn up every day, presented to the highest standard, and deal so frequently with life-and-death incidents. I am proud to be one of them.

CHAPTER 23

TACKLING THE SCOURGE OF DRUGS

Retired Assistant Commissioner Michael O'Sullivan

I was 20 years old when I joined An Garda Síochána in 1977. My training complete, I was sent to Omeath Garda Station in Co. Louth. Omeath was originally a station with a Sergeant and a Garda, but with the Troubles it had become a hub of activity. Work consisted of endless checkpoints, interspersed with Irish Republican Army (IRA) attacks across the border using the Omeath catchment area as a base.

Over a year after I joined, I was transferred to Garda HQ and later was selected to join the newly established Special Task Force – the forerunner of the Emergency Response Unit (ERU). Our role was to act as an armed back-up, frequently working along the border and throughout the country, in an effort to curb IRA activities.

While working in Dublin, I became increasingly aware of the prevalence of heroin in the inner city and the effect that it was having on crime rates. Put bluntly, it brought devastation to the inner-city communities.

THE DUBLIN DRUG SCENE IN THE 1980S

Prior to the 1980s, the drug scene in Dublin consisted mainly of 'hippie-types' selling cannabis resin, and a small number of hard-drug users breaking into pharmacies to steal prescription drugs. Formed in 1968 by Detective Sergeant Denis Mullins, who at the time was attached to the Special Detective Unit in Dublin Castle, the Garda Drug Squad consisted initially of four Gardaí. By 1971, the Drug Squad had increased to two detective Sergeants and ten men, and they were transferred out of Dublin Castle and into the then Central Detective Unit (CDU).

Towards the end of the 1970s, the drug scene changed dramatically. After the invasion of Afghanistan by the Soviet Union, the Dunne organised-crime group, led by Larry Dunne, began flooding Dublin with cheap Afghan heroin. Before this time, Ireland had few heroin addicts. The city became more violent, with a huge increase in aggravated robberies and widespread heroin dealing in the flat complexes of the inner city, making it almost impossible for An Garda Síochána to detect or prevent. A survey carried out at the time found that the heroin problem was worse in Dublin, per head of population, than in a corresponding New York ghetto, with 12 per cent of young people (between the ages of 15 and 19) heroin abusers. An Garda Síochána was struggling to deal with the problem and the rising crime rates.

It was against this background that I arrived, together with Nóirín O'Sullivan, Aidan Reid, James McGowan, Oliver Claffey and Janet Russell. We were all stationed in the inner city and could see at first hand the devastation caused by heroin. Without any official sanction, we formed a small unit and carried out surveillance on some known locations inside various inner-city flat complexes. It soon became apparent that the only way to operate was for one of us to pose as an addict and to buy drugs from the dealers, with the other members of the team maintaining a covert presence. We sought advice on the legality of the proposal and were told that it had never been tried before and probably would not be a practice that would be recognised by the courts. More senior detectives saw it as a crazy and unworkable idea.

Undaunted, in May 1982, we put the operation into practice and began buying drugs and arresting the dealers at an opportune time. The cases were subsequently subjected to legal challenge but upheld in the courts. The number of arrests dramatically increased in the following months. As the success of the operations became evident, the unit was officially recognised, and we were all transferred to the Drug Squad at the Central Detective Unit (CDU) where we began operating with increased resources. Some elements of the media dubbed the unit 'The Mockies', playing on the fact that we were disguising ourselves as 'mock addicts'.

The increase in operations yielded many high-profile targets, the first casualties being the senior members of the Dunne organised-crime group, which imploded after their arrests. At this stage, the Drug Squad was managed by two excellent Detective Inspectors, John McGroarty and Denis Mullins. As the drug problem escalated, additional detectives were allocated to the unit.

New groups began to fill the vacuum left by the Dunnes. The Kinahan organised-crime group began in 1986 but was quickly dismantled on the arrest of its founder, Christopher Kinahan, who was uncovered in a luxury 'safe flat', with a large amount of heroin. The unit, working within the CDU, went on to arrest many of Dublin's most prominent criminals.

At the same time, a policy of establishing District Drug Units was introduced. Soon local units were carrying out their own operations, with great success. However, Irish society was beginning to realise that the drug problem was rapidly spreading throughout the cities and countryside and bringing an unprecedented crime wave in its wake.

The Lucan investigation team at the unveiling of a memorial plaque in Dublin Castle in honour of Veronica Guerin. Back row (L to R): John O'Driscoll, Brian Woods, Tom Fallon, Robert O'Reilly, Pat Bane, Bernard Masterson, Mick Murray, Noel Browne, Michael Gaynor. Front row (L to R): Mick McElgunn, Paul Curran, Len Aherne, Tony Sourke, Assistant Commissioner Tony Hickey, Commissioner Pat Byrne, Catherine Clancy, Bernie Guerin, Todd O'Loughlin, Paudric Kennedy.

THE GARDA NATIONAL DRUG UNIT

I left the unit in 1989, upon promotion to the rank of Sergeant, and returned in 1995, when it became the Garda National Drug Unit (GNDU), with its first Chief Superintendent, Kevin Carty; heretofore the highest rank within the Drug Squad had been that of Inspector. Carty took the new national unit to great heights. For the first time in the history of An Garda Síochána, drugs were given an equal priority to other serious crimes. The unit became a focus for all national and international investigations, and through his contacts Chief Superintendent Carty formed closer bonds with other international law-enforcement investigators. An Garda Síochána's international reputation in the investigation of drugs was becoming established.

The first target of the new unit was John Gilligan, who had become a household name through the work of Veronica Guerin. Operation Pineapple, as it was called, began with a proactive investigation into the Gilligan organised-crime group. However, following the murder of Veronica Guerin, the murder investigation took priority, and the operation was subsumed into the investigation.

The Criminal Assets Bureau

One of the many outcomes of Veronica Guerin's murder was the establishment of the Criminal Assets Bureau (CAB) under the then Chief Superintendent Fachtna Murphy. The foundation of CAB had a major effect on the criminal underworld, with most of the higher echelons of the illegal drug trade moving to the Netherlands and Spain. This brought them closer to the source of drugs, and it also increased their collaboration with their foreign counterparts, leading to the formation of international organised-crime groups, many of which operate to this day.

At that time, cannabis was the most prevalent drug being imported into the country, followed by ecstasy and heroin (cocaine was imported only in small quantities). The increased importation of drugs into Ireland by the cartels began to create criminal empires and increased wealth among many new criminal groups. One lasting memory is the search of John Gilligan's Equestrian Centre, 'Jessbrook', in Enfield, Co. Meath. A vast building resembling an aircraft hangar, it was a symbol of how ineffective the law had been, when an unemployed individual had been able to amass such wealth through crime, in full public view. The GNDU continued to target high-profile criminals nationally and internationally, with increased collaboration from European police services.

I left the Unit on promotion to the rank of Inspector and spent several years working on investigations in Kevin Street and the National Bureau of Criminal Investigation (NBCI). Many of the murder investigations resulted from feuds between the new rival drug gangs.

Growth of the Drug Problem

I returned to the GNDU in 2010 as Detective Superintendent and was surprised to see the growth in the drug problem at a national level. With heroin now available throughout the country, the number of heroin users had more than doubled. The number of organised-crime groups had greatly increased, and the number of deaths from inter-gang feuds was at an all-time high.

The Celtic Tiger provided a lucrative market for the growing cocaine trade. Cocaine had now become the most common drug of choice in Ireland, spanning all social groups. It

A seizure of drugs in Finglas, Dublin, in April 2022.

yielded greater profits than other drugs and rapidly became the lifeblood of criminal gangs, the wealth accumulated from its sale enriching criminals at all levels and giving power and status to those even at the lowest level of the criminal hierarchy.

The level of co-operation between international law-enforcement agencies and An Garda Síochána greatly increased. Irish criminals abroad had expanded their drug market and their global criminal influence. The importation of controlled drugs into Ireland had increased to record levels; seizures of large quantities of drugs, cash and firearms had risen dramatically and were a reflection of the increased success of An Garda Síochána and its international partners.

FORMATION OF THE DRUGS AND ORGANISED CRIME BUREAU

I left the GNDU on promotion in 2012 but returned as the Detective Chief Superintendent in 2016, by which time the unit had grown substantially. Drug distribution had continued to increase in both scale and violence, with an increasing number of gang-related deaths. In the same year, the then Commissioner, Nóirín O'Sullivan, organised the merging of GNDU and the Organised Crime Unit (which was then part of the NBCI). The formation of the Drugs and Organised Crime Bureau (DOCB) reflected the levels that organised crime in Ireland had reached. Most criminal groups were involved in the supply of cocaine, and the use of firearms was an integral part of their operations. The influence of the drug cartels at national and international level had reached new heights, and they were displaying a contempt for the law and an arrogance not seen before.

In February 2016, a group of heavily armed men, carrying Kalashnikov assault rifles and dressed as members of the ERU, disrupted a boxing weigh-in at the Regency Airport Hotel in Dublin. A man was shot and fatally wounded, sparking the Kinahan/Hutch feud which led to a series of murders over a two-year period. The murders were organised by drug cartel members residing outside the jurisdiction and were carried out by an assortment of 'hit teams'.

A dismal milestone in the history of criminality in the country, these events were a catalyst to An Garda Síochána's receiving additional resources, which assisted them in apprehending the majority of those responsible. DOCB was particularly successful in subsequent seizures of nearly €20 million in drugs and significant amounts of firearms, and in preventing over forty murder attempts.

The success of An Garda Síochána in combatting the most lethal criminal feud in the history of the State is a reflection of the resilience, professionalism and bravery of the Gardaí involved. The murders and subsequent successful investigations highlighted the power and ruthlessness of the Irish drug cartels operating at an international level.

CONCLUSION

In 2016, I was promoted to Assistant Commissioner. Following my retirement the following year, I took up the position of Executive Director of the Maritime Analysis Operations Centre (Narcotics) (MAOC.N), an international law-enforcement agency comprising law-enforcement personnel from several European countries and the US Drug Enforcement Agency (DEA). The Agency is tasked with coordinating the interception of maritime drug shipments coming to Europe. In 2020, it was responsible for the interception of 23 vessels and the seizure of €2.3 billion worth of drugs.

In this role, I worked in close collaboration with the team at DOCB. After over four decades working in law enforcement, and having collaborated with many law-enforcement agencies throughout the world, it is a source of great pride to me to see the esteem in which An Garda Síochána is held. All those who have worked with An Garda Síochána in international investigations regard the organisation as a highly professional and effective agency, and many former members now hold important positions in Europol, Interpol and the United Nations.

Some of the individuals I arrested in the back streets of Dublin over thirty years ago are now in charge of international drug cartels responsible for the large-scale importation of drugs to their homeland and to many other countries. It is because of the proactivity of An Garda Síochána that their operational base is now located outside Ireland. But despite their power, wealth and the sophistication of their criminal networks, they are constantly reminded of one principle: they have to be lucky all the time; law enforcement has to be lucky only once.

Retired Assistant Commissioner Michael O'Sullivan.

CHAPTER 24

CAB – A SUCCESS STORY

Garda Stephen Moore in conversation with former Minister for Justice, Nora Owen
Retired Garda Commissioner Fachtna Murphy

The Criminal Assets Bureau (CAB) is an independent statutory body, established on 15 October 1996 by the enactment of the Criminal Assets Bureau Act. The Bureau is a key part of the armoury the State uses in tackling criminal activity; in particular, it tackles serious and organised criminal activity, through depriving persons of their ill-gotten gains and disrupting the resources available in supporting this activity.

The Bureau is a multi-disciplinary body, staffed by members of An Garda Síochána, officials from the Revenue Commissioners (both Taxes and Customs), officials from the Department of Social Protection, together with staff from the Department of Justice, which includes the Bureau Legal Officer, Forensic Accountants, Financial Crime Analysts, IT Experts and Administrative staff.

The Criminal Assets Bureau is rightly heralded as a Garda success story. Since its inception in 1996 to the end of 2020, the Bureau had transferred in excess of €32,357,685 to the Exchequer under the Proceeds of Crime legislation.

The Bureau's roots lie in the realisation that criminals had the upper hand and that laws were inept at dealing with the proceeds of crime. It was established at a time when the public saw the battle between justice and lawbreakers ebbing in the wrong direction. I spoke with two of the main orchestrators in the formation of the Bureau who told me the story of CAB, 25 years on from its inception.

When Nora Owen became Minister for Justice in December 1994, she was a member of what became known as the 'Rainbow Coalition' Government, comprising Fine Gael, the Labour Party and Democratic Left. Inheriting her portfolio from Máire Geoghegan-Quinn of Fianna Fáil, she was, she says, 'immediately put on the back foot'. Negative headlines of the day directed at the Department of Justice featured the right to silence, bail laws, prison spaces, the seizure of assets, the drug problem throughout the country, the split in the Garda

Representative Association, contract killings and rural killings. Major events such as the Brinks Allied robbery and the Lansdowne Road riots rocked the country just months into her ministership, and opposition from coalition partners initially delayed reforms to bail laws and the building of more prison spaces. She sets the scene:

> Every second newspaper headline at the time was calling for my resignation; you have
> to remember the times – the economy was starting to move out of a terrible recession
> and when the economy is off the table, the opposition to government will always focus
> on either Health or Justice to gain support.

According to Nora, the first early steps in tackling the money-laundering issue came with the passing of the Criminal Justice Act, 1994. This had been brought to the Dáil by her predecessor, but Nora Owen was instrumental in implementing sections 32 and 57 in 1995 when she took over as Minister. She explains:

> This started the ball rolling; it made financial bodies take certain steps in identifying
> those suspected of money laundering and it set out obligations on financial institu-
> tions to make a report to the Gardaí if they suspected individuals.

In January 1996, a memorandum of understanding (MOU) between the Revenue Commissioners and An Garda Síochána was agreed:

> Myself and Ruairi Quinn [Minister for Finance] were able to get Revenue and An
> Garda Síochána to sign the MOU; this was essentially the first bit of CAB. Before,
> Revenue would not share information with the Gardaí, and the Gardaí could not
> demand information from Revenue.

She goes on to tell how a presentation by senior Gardaí, led by Deputy Commissioner Pat Byrne and Chief Superintendent Tony Hickey, on the drugs problems the country faced really solidified opinion within Government that action was needed:

> It was May 1996 when they briefed me and six other members of Government. The
> briefing really opened the eyes of the Government to the drugs problem; more money for
> Justice was needed to tackle this problem and we knew we had to put a package together.

In June 1996, two events occurred which led to an outcry from the public for action. First, on 7 June, Detective Jerry McCabe was shot dead in Adare, Co. Limerick and his partner, Ben O'Sullivan, was seriously injured when the Provisional IRA attempted an armed robbery of a post-office van. Less than three weeks later, on 26 June, journalist Veronica Guerin was murdered while she sat in her car in traffic on the Naas dual carriageway. Owen recalls:

The funeral of Detective Garda Jerry McCabe. His murder and that of journalist Veronica Guerin were a catalyst to setting up the Criminal Assets Bureau (CAB).

Jerry and Veronica's deaths came as such a shock. Veronica was the first journalist murdered in Ireland – a young mother who everybody knew. Both these murders led to the purse strings being loosened for Justice, and the whole kitchen sink was thrown into the programme to tackle crime.

Fachtna Murphy was then a Chief Superintendent in the DMR Eastern Region, having been a Superintendent over the fraud squad; he would later become the first head of CAB. He describes this time as:

> …a sad month – there was a perception that people were getting away with acts like these and giving two fingers to the State. Something had to be done. These two events – and in particular the murder of Veronica – were a catalyst to set up a bureau to target the proceeds of crime.

Three pieces of legislation were quickly brought before the Dáil. These were the Proceeds of Crime Act, 1996; the Disclosure of Certain Information for Taxation Purposes Act, 1996; and the Criminal Assets Bureau Act, 1996. Fachtna Murphy describes how this occurred:

> The first two acts were enacted but the Government decided to set up the Bureau in an ad-hoc administrative manner. This allowed the Bureau to see what was required and to see if any changes were required before being enacted.

He continues:

> When it was decided to set up the Bureau, I was appointed Chief Bureau Officer and Barry Galvin, who was state solicitor for Cork and who had a history of speaking

openly about the issues with drug trafficking and the need to seize the proceeds of crime, was appointed as the Bureau legal officer.

Fachtna goes on to tell me how the Bureau was originally set up:

The Bureau would be a stand-alone body, headed by a senior member of An Garda Síochána with an experienced legal officer, and we took a multi-agency approach. I wanted a team-based approach and we established teams within the Bureau comprising of members of An Garda Síochána, members of the Revenue Commissioners, from both Tax and Customs, and officials from Social Welfare. We brought in civilian support by way of accountancy and technology experts, alongside clerical supports and members from the Chief State Solicitor's Office.

When I ask Fachtna about learning on the job and whether anything came up before the legislation for the Criminal Assets Bureau was enacted, he replies:

Normally when something is set up, you have a year or so to bed in, but we didn't have this time – there was huge urgency to see us up and going and we needed to hit the ground running. Very soon, we saw the need for anonymity provisions, and the need for a Garda to have the same powers as a revenue official and vice-versa. These were added to the Act before it was enacted in full on 15 October 1996.

Fachtna Murphy was CAB's first Chief Bureau Officer.

When I ask if any legal challenges were made following enactment, he continues:

When we started using the Proceeds of Crime legislation, there were regular constitutional challenges. One challenge against the use of the Chief Superintendent's opinion was heard in court for 29 days.

In response to the suggestion that CAB was a success story from the outset, Fachtna replies:

From the start it was clear that a number of people were engaged in criminal activities; Gardaí had intelligence that these people had obvious assets which far exceeded any legitimate earning capabilities they would have. There were people claiming social welfare who lived in big houses, who were buying state-of-the-art cars with cash and travelling abroad on expensive holidays. The Gilligan case was a classic example of this when he was found with £300,000 in his suitcase on his way to Amsterdam. So, yes is the answer

to your question, and it has held up to this day, and the reason it has held up is because of the multi-agency approach and the way the different agencies work as teams – they blended well, but they were also busy times, and we had a 24/7 approach.

A Success Story

When asked to look back on his time in CAB and to give me his thoughts, Fachtna Murphy says:

> I look back on it with a considerable amount of satisfaction. Cynics at the time who challenged the Government of the day, saw the Bureau as just another gimmick, but it wasn't; it was a success from the off. I remember the first day well and a photoshoot which took place at Government Buildings, I was alongside the Commissioner Pat Byrne, Minister for Justice Nora Owen, Minister for Finance Ruairí Quinn and Barry Galvin – the people who made it happen – it is hard to believe that was over twenty-five years ago.

Nora Owen remembers going to the CAB offices and seeing first-hand the work the Bureau was undertaking:

> I went into the office and saw a huge whiteboard split into three sections – Gardaí, Revenue and Social. For the first time, all three were able to link the chains together: if person A was a criminal, if they were taking money from the state through Social, and if they were paying any tax to Revenue. It was very rudimentary, but what was significant was this was the first time all three could share information.

I ask what the most satisfying aspect was for her when it became clear that CAB was a success:

> For me, it was getting the money that was driving the big crime; it was getting the power into our laws where we could go after this money. It made the criminals' job harder, and it drove many criminals away from Ireland.

Fachtna Murphy went on to become Garda Commissioner and served in this office from 2007 to 2010. Nora Owen remained Deputy Leader of Fine Gael in opposition until 2001.

Conclusion

Since its inception, the Criminal Assets Bureau has become a world leader in asset investigation. Many police services from around the globe have studied CAB and many countries have tried to establish similar bureaus of their own. Twenty-five years later, CAB continues to be one of the most successful arms of law enforcement in this country. It is at the forefront of the battle against criminality, with the demand for its expertise seeing staff numbers more than tripling since its formation, from just thirty-one in October 1996, to ninety-nine today.

Over its 25-year history, the Bureau has had to adapt and change in response to the changing patterns of criminal behaviour. Notwithstanding this, the Bureau has demonstrated its effectiveness and its ability to meet the challenges posed by these developments and remains central to the overall law-enforcement response to serious and organised crime in this jurisdiction.

The Bureau continues to upgrade and enhance the training needs of Bureau Officers and staff. In September 2020, in conjunction with the University of Limerick, it commenced the Proceeds of Crime and Asset Investigation (POCAI) course, which provides participants with an academically recognised qualification for their skillset in the area of proceeds of crime, asset identification, seizure, confiscation and recovery.

Chief Superintendent Michael Gubbins, Chief Bureau Officer, CAB, at the Bureau's twenty-fifth anniversary press conference in Garda Headquarters in 2021.

CHAPTER 25

RURAL POLICING

Garda Brendan O'Connor

Having commenced training in April 1996, I enjoyed a Phase II placement in the Bridewell Station, DMR (Dublin Metropolitan Region). After my attestation in July 1997, I was sent to Donnybrook Station in the 'E' District, where I served until January 2002. My early career in Dublin – both as a student in some of the most socially deprived communities in the north inner city and a subsequent probation in the leafy surroundings of Dublin 4, surrounded by corporate prosperity and personal wealth – exposed me to experiences that I found fascinating and gave me an appreciation for the uniqueness of policing.

Something that really stood out for me was the contrast between the different calls I attended. One might be someone struggling with addiction or homelessness, while the next would involve attending one of the most valuable properties in the State. Exposure brings perspective and balance to those who choose policing as a career; it gives a unique insight into other people's lives. Apart from the personal experiences attained through interacting with such a variety of individuals from different cultures and backgrounds, city policing also involved exposure to all kinds of social, cultural, and sporting events of national and international significance. The adrenaline rush and the buzz of policing a vibrant 24-hour city cannot be matched. Responding to a major incident or assistance call, with multiple units rushing to a location, sirens wailing and lights flashing, brought a level of excitement and sense of purpose different from anything else.

TRANSFER TO DONEGAL

Much as I enjoyed those early years in the city, a holiday in Donegal with my wife convinced me to take the plunge, and I made an application to transfer to the country. Carndonagh in north Inishowen would be my first country station; it was somewhere I knew nothing about and had never visited.

My first shift was a night tour. On arrival at the station, I let myself in. I was the only person there: no bustling parade room, no banter and slagging in the locker room, no Sergeant to tell me exactly where to be and at what time to be there – just me on my own in a little building. The one thing that stood out was the silence: no radio chatter, no constantly ringing phone, no noise from reluctant guests in the custody area. It was a completely alien environment that bore no resemblance to what I had come to know as a work setting.

After a while, the phone did ring. My colleague in Malin Station needed transport to carry out an inquiry. I made my way and located Ireland's most northerly Garda station, where I received a warm welcome from my new partner, Padhraig. Seated in a very old building – the ancient single-bar electric fire taking the chill off the air was possibly the most modern appliance in it – Padhraig was attending to the 'Super's Post', a function and ritual embedded in the daily routine of rural stations big and small. Every item of correspondence is carefully documented and recorded by hand in a register, assigned a file number and its destination noted.

Other books and registers sat on shelves. There were books for everything: warrants register; insurance and driving licence production book; a postage book that recorded and accounted for every stamp expended; JLO (Juvenile Liaison Officer) book; vacant houses register; licensed premises inspection register – the list seemed endless. And for everything that didn't have a register, there seemed to be a file: District Instructions; Divisional Instructions; HQ Circulars; Fógra Tora; CT 68s; Collator Bulletins; Executed Warrants; Summonses for Service. These were all books and files with which I would become familiar as I spent more time in rural stations.

Once the paperwork had been attended to, Padhraig took me on my first rural patrol. The most striking thing initially was the sheer geographical size of the area to be policed. Rural districts and sub-districts can be vast, with hundreds of kilometres of roads to be patrolled and policed – a stark contrast to the sometimes claustrophobic and repetitive nature of patrolling a small geographical portion of a large city. Given the distances to be travelled, dealing with the most straightforward of calls can be extremely time-consuming.

NO SHORTAGE OF VARIETY

While the sheer volume of calls in an urban area is not replicated in rural areas, this does not mean that the incidents attended by rural Gardaí are any less serious than those attended by members stationed in urban areas. It is necessary only to look at the incidents dealt with over the years in the Buncrana district to see that police personnel can be confronted by anything on any given day, whether that be the discovery of 100 Kalashnikov rifles, 100 lb of commercial explosives and 50,000 rounds of ammunition at Five Fingers Strand near Malin in 1988, the single biggest loss of life in a traffic collision in Ireland when eight lives were lost on the

Scenes of rural policing in bygone days.

Clonmany-to-Buncrana Road in July 2010, or the tragic drowning of five members of the one family in an accident at Buncrana pier in March 2016.

One thing that struck me after a short time spent working in country areas was the wealth of experience and knowledge of members 'on the regular' (i.e., working on a regular – not specialised – unit). At that time, there were very few specialised units operating outside large urban centres. While the downside of this might have been an absence of career opportunities, multi-tasking led to an accumulation of knowledge and experience. The regular can at times be expected to be the response unit, the traffic unit, the crime unit, the drugs unit, the public order unit, and the community engagement unit. Of course, not everyone can excel at everything, and individual Gardaí naturally veer towards spheres of policing that interest or motivate them. But there is a freedom to working in the country that allows individual members' personalities to shine as opposed to being perceived as just a member of an anonymous uniformed group.

INVESTIGATING A TRAFFIC ACCIDENT

Around the time I transferred to the Milford District, a particularly horrific traffic accident took the lives of two young women, which had a huge impact on the local community. In a time that predated divisional scenes of crime units, forensic collision investigators, senior investigating officers, and appointed family liaison officers, I observed a member from the regular put together a meticulous investigation file that led to convictions on serious charges and lengthy custodial sentences. Observing this investigation from the first members on the scene to the conviction was my first real insight into just how capable, professional, and compassionate my colleagues could be, and the genuine connection between Gardaí and the communities in which they worked and lived.

'Accountability' is a word that we often hear bandied about in discussions about modern policing. To me, real accountability exists when you regularly interact with the people who rely on you in their time of need. This can occur simply bumping into them when buying a pint of milk in the town, sitting beside them at mass on a Sunday, or meeting them at the school gate. When you must look a person in the eye and stand over what you have done or have not done, it brings a quality assurance that no oversight can match.

THE DYNAMICS OF RURAL POLICING

My time spent in Carrigart Station allowed me to develop and experience the dynamics of rural policing. It was there – working in a small station with just two Gardaí and a Sergeant – that I was exposed to aspects of policing of which I had never even been aware. On arrival, I was briefed about the importance of keeping the door open for a couple of hours every shift; and 'dole day' was identified as the most important day in the month.

At that time, anyone in receipt of unemployment assistance had to present at their local Garda station on a particular day each month, with a form issued from social welfare, which was countersigned by the local Gardaí. Initially, I didn't understand how this practice could be anything other than a distraction and inconvenience. After a few months, though, the penny dropped: having a significant portion of the young male population obliged to present at the station to maintain their income was a very effective way of addressing the phenomena of unanswered doors or ignored phone calls when following up on other matters or trying to serve a summons. It was a remarkable coincidence that names appearing in other files or registers in the station would be amongst those slipped under the door each month rather than being presented in person. Of course, most forms processed were from people who would have no other dealings with Gardaí. In those instances, the ritual provided a great opportunity to meet with people in person and develop the single most effective tool in the armoury of any Garda – local knowledge.

By simply being around a place, you get to know the people personally – you interact with the clergy, the GP and the teachers, and you get to know the postman, the taxi drivers and everyone else who is a cog in the wheel of how that community functions on a daily basis. This works both ways – rural people suss you out, too, and make up their minds on whether they will trust or engage with you. Something that happened to me quite often when new to an area was that someone would come into the station, see an unfamiliar face, and say, 'Sorry, I thought it was so-and-so that was working.' Initially, I would almost take offence and wonder whether they wanted a Garda or not. But over time, people got to know me and would start asking for me.

Sitting in a patrol car on the main street of any town or village in Ireland at closing time acts as a magnet for those seeking conversation and can lead to interesting appraisals of colleagues, and how efficient or strict they are perceived to be. A particular terminology exclusive to Donegal is the description of the Roads Policing Unit, which is referred to with a certain reserve as the 'County Patrol'. The threat of 'the County' as some form of anonymised bogeyman was always a useful tool when persuading an otherwise law-abiding citizen of the virtues of regularising a minor road traffic matter.

FEWER ARRESTS

Another differentiating characteristic of policing a small community is a much lower dependence on making an arrest to deal with an issue, particularly when policing the night-time economy. I remember initially feeling that the Gardaí were shying away from the issue when they weren't reaching for someone obviously committing an offence. I soon learned that issuing a summons is more effective than having to make an arrest and travel long distances – leaving the area without a presence – to process a prisoner. When local knowledge means that you know who you are dealing with, there are more options. In my experience, the patrol car at someone's door the following day – giving the news that a person's behaviour was unacceptable and a summons is on the way – has often been much more effective than arresting or trying to reason with an intoxicated person.

THE CHALLENGES

While in general I have found my time in rural policing enjoyable, it can also be challenging. Working on your own has limitations and dangers. The sheer isolation and distance from back-up bring a vulnerability and a need for constant vigilance. Policing is, by its nature, unpredictable, and volatile situations can develop in an instant. However, if we had become overly risk averse, the unique style of Irish policing that generations of Gardaí have delivered, with the overwhelming support of local communities, would never have evolved or survived.

Improvements in technology and communications have enhanced the safety of members working alone in rural areas, but no technology can overcome the distances involved. This is something you are very aware of when working on an offshore island such as Arranmore or Tory Island, both of which are in Milford District. Whether attending to an incident on the islands or staying out to perform a tour of duty, this is an experience unlike anything else. Calls for service are not overly common, but they do occur, and sometimes involve incidents and tragedies of a serious nature. If rural policing was a new experience for me, performing duty on an island is on a whole different level. Travelling on the ferry to Arranmore Island on the Saturday evening of a busy bank holiday weekend, with the same revellers who create the policing requirement, is a somewhat unique experience, as is carrying a tetra radio that is chirping with transmissions from the mainland. You are still part of policing in the Division, yet what you are tasked with could not be more different from what colleagues in busy towns are dealing with.

CONCLUSION

On a personal level, rural policing can be a little claustrophobic at times – there is no anonymity. When I changed out of my uniform in Donnybrook and walked out of the station yard, nobody knew who I was, or anything about me. In the village I live in today, I am 'the Guard', my house is 'the Guard's house', my car is 'the Guard's car'. Even my wife and children have a small bit of their own identity eclipsed and identified by my job.

The sheer isolation and distance bring a need for constant vigilance.

Rural policing is definitely unique. It can be intrusive when people call to your home on official business because the station is unmanned, or someone approaches you in the shop about work when you just want to buy a Sunday paper. However, it is the essence of what community policing is all about. I hope that we remain as ingrained in our communities in the next hundred years as we have in the first.

CHAPTER 26

THE SUPER,
THE INSPECTOR,
THE SERGEANT AND
THE GUARD

Superintendent Chris Grogan, Inspector Ailish Myles,
Detective Sergeant Dara Kenny, Garda Billy Horan

THE SUPER

Superintendent Chris Grogan, Carrick-on-Shannon Garda Station

'For every one of you here, there's another fourteen outside wishing they were in your place' – those were the words of one proud instructor on 7 February 1994, the day I entered the Garda College, Templemore, part of an intake of 105 newbies from all over the country.

A late vocation to An Garda Síochána, I had already completed a degree in marketing and dabbled in a computer programming course, in between working in the Marketing Department at Guinness, laying cables for Sierra Construction, and spending a couple of summers in the United States, working as a doorman and playing GAA with Connemara Gaels. However, some of my friends and teammates from Roscommon GAA were commencing their careers in An Garda Síochána and the feedback from them was good. My sister, Karen, had already taken the initiative in our house, following in the footsteps of our dad, Christy, who had served for 33 years, and 'made the job easy' for us, as he has reminded me on numerous occasions.

In the late 1970s, I walked alongside my dad in the annual Garda Pilgrimage to Knock Shrine. Encased in a sea of blue, surrounded by 'polis' (Garda slang for 'Gardaí'), I felt indirectly inducted into the organisation. I also recall the dark days when my father's colleagues, Detective Garda John Morley and Garda Henry Byrne, were shot dead in the line of duty. In my own career, I was to experience a similar devastating loss when my two colleagues, friends and former teammates, Detective Garda Adrian Donohoe and Detective Garda Colm Horkan, paid the ultimate sacrifice with their lives.

I am now starting my twenty-ninth year in this wonderful and varied career. However, spending the first two days of that career on prison security duty at the rear of Portlaoise Prison, seeing nobody except the Inspector who came to inspect me, I did question my vocation. The variety kicked in after that, though, and it's been a blast ever since. Having served as a Garda in Portlaoise, Mountrath, Boyle and Roscommon, I was promoted to Sergeant in 2003, and transferred to the Garda College, lecturing in the Legal and Policing section. Big numbers were being recruited at that time and the place had all the energy of a third-level institution, with some fantastic people passing through the doors. In 2006, I returned to frontline policing, serving in Athlone.

In 2009, I transferred to the Armed Support Unit in Mullingar, with a regional role of policing the Eastern Region under the expert leadership of Detective Superintendent Mick Hoare. I am extremely proud of the pioneering work conducted by my unit in this challenging time. It was a huge departure in policing practice to have uniformed members carrying firearms in their daily duties. In the early days of this new policing response, I encountered some resistance, both internally and externally, but my unit persevered, working solidly and professionally at our duties. This unit is a now a jewel in the crown of the organisation.

Superintendent Chris Grogan.

Seven years later, in 2016, I was promoted to Inspector and transferred to the 'B' District, Pearse Street. It was a fantastic place to work, with a tremendous blend of dedicated Gardaí and Garda staff keeping the show on the road, led by the ever-inspirational Superintendent Joe Gannon.

With the onset of COVID-19 restrictions, I was seconded full-time into the Garda National Public Order Unit, tasked with public order policing in the Dublin Metropolitan Region (DMR). It was an eerie feeling on patrol with a scattering of people going about their business – very different from the bustle normally associated with the Grafton Street/Dame Street area. Gardaí were fantastic in the application of community policing across the State during these tough times, with appropriate implementation of the four Es: Engage, Explain, Encourage and Enforce.

In 2020, I was promoted to Superintendent in Baltinglass, spending just over five months there prior to transferring to Carrick-on-Shannon where I am responsible for the efficient administration and policing response in Leitrim District. It is a fantastic district, and I am grateful to the talented and dedicated personnel serving in my area of responsibility. The Leitrim District has a unique blend of urban and rural policing challenges, between the entertainment popularity of Carrick-on-Shannon, the busy N4 as the gateway to the northwest, the various lakes and waterways associated with the river Shannon, the rural beauty of places like Kinlough and Drumkeeran, and the proximity to Northern Ireland. In common with other local Superintendents, I have the routine areas to address, including Joint Policing Committees, cross-border co-operation, crime investigation, Court, complaints, liquor licensing and media requests. My Chief Superintendent is Aidan Glacken whom I have always found to be very professional and a true leader; we work well together.

To date, my career has included frontline, academic, specialist and management roles across the country. I have worked alongside the finest of people who are a credit to the organisation and ensure the healthy position that it holds in Irish society. This must be respected and continuously addressed in terms of the wonderfully diverse nature and composition of Ireland's population today. The next hundred years will be every bit as challenging as the century that went before. Neither time nor society stands still, requiring an agile, proactive and professional policing response for the citizens of Ireland.

Notions of reinventing An Garda Síochána's unique policing skillset are misguided and unnecessary. Throughout my service to date, I have endeavoured to use that skillset to serve the people, and I will continue to do so. My wish for the next hundred years is for the future incumbents to continue the wonderful and unique provision of a policing service to the people of Ireland.

THE INSPECTOR

Inspector Ailish Myles, Nenagh Garda Station

I am an Inspector in An Garda Síochána with 26 years of service. I am also a married mother of two boys and one girl. I hail from Knockanroe, just 6km from the gates of the Garda College in Templemore, Co. Tipperary. After achieving my Leaving Certificate in 1989, I followed my passion for hairdressing and worked professionally in a hair salon off Grafton Street in Dublin.

My greatest inspiration and influence in life comes from my late parents, Mick and Brid Delaney, who believed in the value of community, hard work, fairness and decency. I decided that An Garda Síochána offered a great opportunity to give life to the values of my upbringing and, in April 1995, at 23 years of age, I made a short – but lifelong – journey when I walked through the gates of the Garda College and signed up as a Student Garda. Two years later, I graduated, having been awarded the prestigious Gary Sheehan Memorial Medal for the best overall student. It was a memorable day for me and for my family.

I was appointed to Inspector rank in 2018, having previously contributed as a Garda in Rathmines and a teacher/trainer at the Garda College at both Garda and Sergeant rank, delivering Student Garda training, and progressing to deliver major contributions in numerous specialised areas, from tactical training to leadership and management. My experience in the Garda College helped to nurture and develop my skillset and I am delighted to have the opportunity to lead by example and demonstrate these skills in the operational field at the rank of Inspector.

My initial transfer as Inspector was to Anglesea Street in Cork city, where I was assigned to the Governance Hub – a pilot project which informed some of the outcomes of the Future of Policing in Ireland Commission. I held divisional responsibility for policing plans, risk assessments, inspections, data quality and promoting excellence in governance and accountability in policing across the division. A critical part of my responsibility was engaging with internal and external stakeholders and empowering my management team to initiate operations.

In April 2019, I took up my current role as an Inspector in Nenagh District, with special responsibility for Roscrea Sub-District. A microcosm of modern Irish society, Roscrea is a bustling, busy town, and in many ways is a 'melting pot' of cultures. Having an understanding and appreciation of the socioeconomic factors in which the community operates is key in my role, particularly when planning and delivering a policing service that must evolve and transform with the needs of the community.

Inspector Ailish Myles.

My role has a broad remit, with accountability ranging from administration to hands-on operational management and quality assurance. Judgement calls are required when responding immediately to investigate incidents such as sudden, unexplained, or violent deaths, assaults or serious public order disturbances; planning searches for missing persons; and searching for suspected offenders, drugs and stolen property. Enforcement of road-traffic legislation and quality-of-life offences are high on my list of priorities. For me, the one constant is adapting to changing demands – prioritising issues and targeting resources to the most critical areas. Listening to the community is vital when deciding on priorities, and working in partnership with the community and problem-solving as part of multi-agency teams are of the utmost importance. My educational studies in the areas of governance and human rights grant me further insight into how to deliver on my role and responsibilities.

I like to lead by example, and I am a strong believer that teamwork and participation form the best approach to getting things done. I see leadership as empowering my team to achieve strong goals, but it is important to stress that leadership exists at every level of An Garda Síochána and the community. Michelle Obama described this well: 'True leadership often happens with the smallest acts, in the most unexpected places, by the most unlikely individuals.'

Getting to know my team and giving them a clear sense of what I expect is very important to me. I look for opportunities to develop their skills and improve performances, and I work hard at building consistency and trust by ensuring that 'what I say is what I do'. I cannot speak highly enough of my team; the work performed during the COVID-19 pandemic, for example, in reaching out to the vulnerable and isolated, was exemplary. Never had Gardaí had to undertake such tasks in such volumes, and I believe for many it has changed their understanding of what policing is all about. Improving the quality of life of the community is my goal, and I strive to achieve this every day in my role as an Inspector.

As a woman, juggling a busy career and family life has certainly been challenging. What has stood to me through my years in An Garda Síochána is the ability to reflect and utilise the positive influences in my life to inform how I deal with people daily. The core values of fairness, hard work and decency instilled by my parents have been honed through ongoing training, education and experiences. My role as an Inspector is very rewarding with an array of further possibilities.

THE SERGEANT

Detective Sergeant Dara Kenny, Clondalkin Garda Station

As a Detective Sergeant attached to the District Detective Unit (DDU) at Clondalkin Garda Station in West Dublin, I supervise the work of nineteen members across both Clondalkin and Rathcoole Garda Stations. From 2006 to 2016, I was a Garda attached to Pearse Street Station in Dublin's city centre. The latter seven of those years, I worked in plainclothes – initially in the Street Crime Unit, and then the DDU.

I don't remember ever seriously considering a different career. I applied to join An Garda Síochána within weeks of receiving my Leaving Cert results. The following year, I was in

Templemore. In between, I passed the time at University College Dublin. My grandfather, Daniel Kenny, served in An Garda Síochána between 1946 and 1988, and his wife – my grandmother – made it clear that she wanted me to follow in his footsteps. When I was a small boy, her observations on how I had grown since she last saw me would be accompanied by a half-joke about my progress toward reaching the now-obsolete height requirement.

Although my grandfather did not tell 'war stories', I know that his career in policing was anything but quaint. In the early 1970s, he worked on the border, leading operations at ground level against the Provisional Irish Republican Army (IRA) and bringing suspects before the fledgling Special Criminal Court, in many cases following significant seizures of firearms, ammunition and explosives. Some of those he prosecuted are now household names because of their involvement in legitimate Northern Ireland politics in the decades that followed.

This was a perilous and uncertain time for the State and those who defended it. My grandfather worked punishing hours and had to carry a firearm even when off-duty. Growing up I was inculcated with a strong sense that policing was an important and honourable profession. It is.

Clondalkin is a fantastic place to work. There are criminals here, for sure, but they are vastly outnumbered by decent salt-of-the-earth members of the community. My workload is varied, stimulating and unpredictable – that is why I was always attracted to detective work. We investigate all sorts of crime, from murders down. One of the advantages of entrusting the investigation of even the most serious crimes to local detectives is that they know their area and its people. It is a system that works well.

We can be frenetically busy for long periods, and at other times things are more manageable, but we are never idle. Because I am the only Detective Sergeant in our DDU, I am effectively on call around the clock. The phone is always on, and at bedtime the volume is turned up. While the main threat to my sleep is two young sons, serious incidents rarely seem to happen in the middle of my working day. When a violent death occurs, it is all shoulders to the wheel. Work becomes home, meals come wrapped in paper, and caffeine is key. We need supportive loved ones to work like this.

Firearms crime, serious assaults, robberies, burglaries, and economic crime are ever present, in peaks and troughs. In a six-month period in 2020, we had six violent deaths in the district. In contrast, in 2021, we used a period when we had no homicides to reopen a historical murder case, and we will do our best to bring about a resolution to it and, I hope, bring some comfort for the deceased's family.

All our major investigations are coordinated from an Incident Room, with the sometimes hundreds of individual tasks being completed mainly by members of the DDU, but generally supplemented by other local units. Detective Inspector Dan Callaghan is in overall charge. A policeman of immense experience, he is a consummate professional and a gent. We also enjoy generous support from our District and Divisional management.

Some cases are straightforward. Other times, you need a bit of luck, and when you get it, you flog it hard. Nowadays, we exploit technology to solve crimes, for example through analysis of CCTV and other forms of digital evidence. But a core function of a detective is getting people – all kinds of people – to talk to you, trust you, and tell you things that they may initially not want to tell you. This is a vintage policing skill that should always be prized. It is as relevant now as it was in 1922.

Detective Sergeant Dara Kenny at his desk in Clondalkin Garda Station.

I find huge satisfaction in cases where I turn up at a crime scene having no idea what happened, and then I see an investigation progress to a point where I know 'who' did 'what' and 'why', and I can prove it. To do that, we use every opportunity to obtain evidence, then work through it methodically and see where it leads. The fruits of our labour are to be found in courtrooms. There is nowhere to hide in there – if your work is substandard, you will be found out. Criminal trials can be bruising, but they breed great camaraderie.

There is no such thing as the quintessential detective. As a baseline, all my people are hard-working and trustworthy. After that, they are a diverse group of individuals notable for their different fortes – those with unrivalled local knowledge and contacts; those whose files are works of art; the technical geniuses; the master interviewers; the thief-catchers on the street. No one is ever all these things at once. Detective work is a team sport. Like in the classic GAA line-up, the sticky corner-back is every bit as vital as the stylish centre half-forward. I have a great team of players, so my job as *bainisteoir* is an easy one.

THE GARDA

Garda Billy Horan, Sligo Garda Station

Being a Garda is a unique job that comes with many challenges and rewards. When I think of what it means, the first thing that comes to mind is a sense of the sacrifice that is part of the commitment I made when I joined the ranks of An Garda Síochána. After 24 years in the job, my role has changed many times, but the idea of serving my community has not.

Garda Billy Horan

Throughout my formative years, my idea of policing came from the television programmes shown on RTÉ 1 and RTÉ 2. *Hawaii Five-0* and *Chips* gave me a completely unrealistic view of what police did in the real world. I come from a small village in west Limerick, where the biggest crime of the day was being found after hours in the local pub. I did not always want to be a Garda. Barring my great-grandfather who served in the RIC in the late 1800s, it was not a family calling. In my teen years, I toyed with the idea of working in some area of forensic science. I was some way down this road, studying science in Galway, when I got the letter of acceptance for An Garda Síochána. I left my studies behind me to enter Templemore in January 1996.

During my Phase II training in Salthill, Co. Galway, I was fortunate to attend the opening night of TG4; this was my first glimpse of history in the making. Throughout my career, I have been given a front-row seat at many historical events that will be spoken about long after I have gone. The job has also afforded me the opportunity to travel the country and live different experiences in each area.

To date in my career, I have worked in three Divisions, starting in one of the most famous stations in the country, Hackballscross. Nestled in the rolling drumlins of Co. Louth, bordering with the Fews of south Armagh to the north, and Monaghan's Kavanagh Country to the southwest, 'the Hack' became well known by the hundreds of members who passed through on temporary transfer during various border campaigns over the years. I spent good years there, with some of the best colleagues I would wish to have. It was an exciting station with fresh batches of recruits coming to the district every few months, and I made lifelong friends. During my time there, the BSE and foot-and-mouth crises occurred, as well as the historic visit of US President Bill Clinton to Dundalk. They were busy and challenging times, but equally memorable and rewarding.

The next stop for me on my journey in the job was Achill Island, Co. Mayo, where the pace was the complete opposite. The summer I arrived was busy with tourists and the work was more community-based – getting out and about, meeting people and being seen, as opposed to serious crime investigations. There were, of course, some serious incidents which got the appropriate attention, but in the main, community policing was the order of the day. Achill has a rich and diverse history – from archaeological sites to the former residence of Captain Boycott – and I enjoyed my time there before moving on to Ballina, Co. Mayo.

During my 13 years there, I renewed some old friendships made on the border and I was also involved in policing events for the visit of US President George W. Bush to Shannon, which coincided with ongoing protests over the Gulf War at Shannon Airport.

While in Ballina, I was attached to the Traffic Corps for a few years, coinciding with the introduction of MIT (Mandatory Intoxicant Testing) checkpoints and a concerted effort to reduce the fatality numbers on Irish roads. MIT checkpoints had real success in reducing fatalities and serious injuries, and I will always be proud of playing my part in what was achieved in a few years. Those first years helped to bring about a change in the mindset of many of the country's motorists.

All good things come to an end, though, and because of downsizing I found myself on the move again – this time to Sligo. Although it was not a move I had been considering at the time, I was no stranger to the county, having lived there since 2002.

My first day in the station coincided with a murder, which occurred as Fleadh Cheoil na hÉireann was taking place in the town. This left me in no doubt that I had arrived at a busy station, and it remains so to this day. While I am now entering the closing chapter of my career, I have enjoyed the change. I was fortunate to work in Dublin for the Centenary Commemorations of 1916 – an experience I thoroughly enjoyed. In Sligo, eager probationers keep the station fresh, and with the Centenary Celebrations of An Garda Síochána, I find there's life in this old dog still.

I have learned many things over the course of my service, but long after I retire from this job, one thing that will stick with me will be the importance of camaraderie. Whether in good times or bad, our work colleagues are always there for us. Sometimes we laugh together, and sometimes we cry together, we fall in and fall out with each other, but our strength lies in how we manage to pull together in the face of adversity. We overcome professional barriers and occasional torrid working conditions to achieve positive results every day for the communities that we serve.

At the outset, I mentioned sacrifice, and in this job we do sacrifice. We miss time with family and friends, we work nights and holidays, we cancel social events at short notice to serve our communities to the best of our abilities. However, these are small sacrifices; there is no greater reminder of the ultimate sacrifice some have made than the Roll of Honour, which is one of the first things you see when you walk through the doors of the Garda College. It stands as both a testament to their courage and a stark reminder to all passing through that this is real life and the risks associated are very real. I have enjoyed my time as a member of An Garda Síochána. There have been ups and downs. I have met some wonderful colleagues, members who are always ready to serve – the reason we all joined the service to begin with.

CHAPTER 27

'SURE, YOU CAN'T BE DOING THAT!' A CRIMECALL STORY

Sergeant Kelvin Courtney

Hundreds of people have toiled admirably over the years to get *Crimecall* on the air. Everyone involved will have their own memories and unique experiences. Following an association with the programme for 20 years, this is mine.

GARDA PATROL

Garda Patrol first broadcast on RTÉ 1 on 28 October 1964. My family were avid watchers and, as a kid, the beat of the bodhrán and the flashing blue light had me hooked. I have a clear memory from the early 1980s of being shushed by my dad as an angular-faced man, with airy grey hair, began to speak sternly and earnestly. You couldn't interrupt Sergeant Tommy Burns!

You can still see Tommy in his pomp on the RTÉ website, introducing the twenty-first anniversary of *Garda Patrol*. He is joined on that edition by then Sergeant Terry Brady, who along with Sergeant Vincent Smith, Garda Ned Russell, and Garda Seamus McPhillips achieved the distinction of being the first Gardaí presenters on a Garda television programme. Many more Gardaí would present over the years, myself included. On their shoulders we stood, each of us bringing our own personalities and taking example from those who had gone before.

An Garda Síochána was an early pioneer of using television to assist in investigations. Other European police organisations and television producers soon came calling, and Terry Brady was invited to make demonstration programmes for a variety of television stations across Europe, who were considering a similar platform for their viewers.

A team in the Crime Prevention Office, then located at Dublin Castle and led by Sergeant Michael Sutton, selected content for *Garda Patrol*. At RTÉ, journalist Ted Nealon was

Far left: Tommy Burns and Catherine Clancy, presenters of Garda Patrol. *Left: Sergeant Terry Brady on the set of* Garda Patrol.

the very first scriptwriter. Each week, Garda presenters would appeal for information and champion crime-prevention advice. This simple formula is the bedrock of the programme we see today. There are only a handful of people who truly know the effort it takes to bring the finished article to the point of broadcast. Their reward is the thrill of creating a programme watched by thousands and responsible for solving or preventing hundreds of crimes.

Above: Early presenters of Garda Patrol: *Sergeant Vincent Smith (left) and Garda Ned Russell.*

Garda Patrol was often parodied over the years, with D'Unbelievables brilliantly observing 'Sure, you can't be doing that!' They must have been doing something right, though, as for over thirty years people tuned in; at its peak, it reached audiences of 800,000. 'That's right!'

CRIMELINE

In 1992, An Garda Síochána joined forces with RTÉ on a new production. *Crimeline* was positively turbocharged in comparison to its predecessor. It was box office TV. The reconstructions on *Crimeline* equalled any shown on *Crime Watch*, which at the time was the UK's most watched TV crime show.

David Harvey was both producer and presenter. Assisting him over the years with presenting duties were two RTÉ stalwarts, first Marian Finucane and then Anne Doyle. Both presenters brought their journalistic backgrounds to the programme, allowing them to ask probing questions on behalf of the viewer.

A panel of Garda presenters would assist them each month. The audition process to become a Garda presenter was tough. It was a big deal for us at home when a neighbour of ours, Garda Mary Liz O'Leary, popped up as regular presenter. The panel changed over the years as a plethora of Gardaí became household names, such as Jim Molloy, Siobhán Redpath, Francis Ferris, Mags Faughnan, Mick Miley, Sinéad O'Hara, Gerry Tighe, Emma Fox, Grace O'Connell, Ian Ferris, Laura Sweeney, Alan Roughneen and – my mam's favourite – Margaret Hession. Mam loved her no-nonsense common sense, all presented with a distinct Dublin accent which set her apart from most of her colleagues.

My introduction to *Crimeline* coincided with Anne Doyle's tenure. I had applied to join the panel of presenters soon after joining An Garda Síochána in 1997. My unit Sergeant had questioned why I would want to jeopardise my chances of joining a covert unit. 'You can never do undercover,' he sighed. I was undeterred.

However, my debut was a disaster. We were covering an appeal to return a recovered compressor to its owner. To this day, compressors remain a mystery to me. I would wave my hands over the property like a shopping-channel presenter while describing it to the viewer – easy, I thought. That was until David Harvey asked me live, on air, what uses the compressor might have. Silence. My pitiful facial expressions begged him to end my agony. He suggested that compressors might be used to clean down mushroom houses. 'That's right, David,' I agreed. I could not believe I had said, 'That's right!' Admonishing myself after the ordeal, I swore that I would improve and be prepared for future presentations. With preparation, my confidence grew. But I was never allowed to get too cocky, as my friends would often goad me: 'Here's TV Cop!'

In 2002, I ceased my presenting duties to go behind the scenes. The *Crimeline* Garda production team was then based at Community Relations, in Garda HQ, so it meant leaving the regular unit I was on in Donnybrook Garda Station. I was excited at the prospect of preparing a programme to which I was, by now, thoroughly committed. My Garda career was to be defined by the move.

My new Sergeant, Nuala Finn, remains the most influential person I have encountered in the job. She could see around corners and solve problems that no one knew existed. Her attention to detail was like nothing I had experienced before. Making a mistake in front of thousands of people was not acceptable and jeopardising a criminal investigation could not happen on her watch. We got off to a shaky start but after about two years she started to trust my instincts for the job. When we both moved on to other departments, our successors, Sergeant Dermot Nolan and Garda Vanessa Stafford, ably carried on where we left off.

It is difficult to convey the immense effort that goes into making a programme like *Crimeline*, but the variety and volume of work make it a great project for inexperienced production assistants to cut their teeth on. Facts and figures have to be accurate. Appeal points have to be carefully considered. The right interviewee has to be chosen. An interviewee who doesn't know the appeal well enough has to be prepared intensively or, failing that, behind-the-scenes chicanery has to be employed to replace the interviewee. Gardaí are trained to make purely factual statements when giving evidence in court. Straying outside those facts into more informal conversation can prove difficult under the pressure of a television interview. 'The male alighted from the motor-propelled vehicle and fled in a northerly direction' – only a Garda can say that with a straight face. One long-time producer for the TV production company, CoCo Television, coached several participants to use more common phrases and rejoiced whenever an erudite detective Inspector came along: 'It's OK to say car.'

A balance must be struck between telling the story of an event in a way that grabs the viewer's attention and not giving away too much information. Some things – things that only the offender would know – must be left out of appeals, to weed out time-wasters offering up false information or confessions.

In a programme that is viewed by hundreds of thousands of people, defamation and privacy must be considered. If a face is going to be broadcast on TV and certain things alleged, it is important to be correct. The investigators must show us that they have exhausted all local inquiries and they have all the necessary proofs to satisfy the solicitors.

By 2003, *Crimeline* had been on air for over a decade and was beginning to look tired. The last episode broadcast in October 2003.

Above left:
Awaiting an
interview on
Crimecall.
Above right:
Crimecall
presenters
Gráinne Seoige
and Philip
Boucher-Hayes.
Right: Keelin
Shanley and the
Crimecall *team*
in 2016.

CRIMECALL

In 2004, with its commitment to public service broadcasting, RTÉ sought to bring back a Garda television programme; CoCo Television was awarded the tender. I was unsure about the name 'Crimecall' at first, but it grew on me. The first presenters were Daíthí Ó Sé and Brenda Power, followed by Con Murphy and Anne Cassin. They were then succeeded by Gráinne Seoige and Philip Boucher-Hayes.

When Green Inc Film & Television and Rare TV Ireland took over, it was decided that there would be one presenter only; Keelin Shanley was first to try her hand. She did an amazing job keeping the programme flowing, ably assisted by regular Garda presenters like Greg Freegrove, Derek Cloughley, Edwina Cahill, Adrian Corcoran and Graham Kavanagh. When she left to present the *Six One News*, she was replaced by Sharon Ní Bheoláin.

DO THOSE PHONES REALLY RING?

The phones do really ring. *Crimecall* is the largest interface between An Garda Síochána and the public, and the calls our call-takers receive genuinely solve crimes and generate leads. The programme is a tool in the investigator's toolbox. An image of a criminal caught in the act can leave them with very little choice but to give themselves up. Investigators can put the pressure on suspects with an appeal. You will often hear an investigator appeal for information they 'know' is in the community where the crime occurred. In doing this, they are sending a warning out to the criminal: we know it's you; it's just a matter of time before the evidence proves it conclusively.

Crimecall has had regular contributors over the years. These investigators firmly believe that repeated highlighting of incidents on the programme will eventually lead to breakthroughs. Irene White, a mother of three, was murdered in her home in Dundalk in 2005. Detective Inspector Pat Marry and his team in Louth Division made many appeals on *Crimecall* over the years for information to apprehend those responsible for her murder. In November 2016, shortly before retiring, Pat, along with Irene's daughter, Jennifer, made a final appeal on *Crimecall*. This emotional plea for information finally led to a breakthrough in the case, with Anthony Lambe eventually confessing to her murder. Lambe later told Pat Marry that

Crimeline *first went on air in 1992 and had production values on par with the UK's* CrimeWatch, *which at the time was the UK's most watched crime show.*

hearing Jennifer's voice on *Crimecall* reminded him of Irene and brought him straight back to the time of the murder. Niall Power was also found guilty of Irene's murder and confessed to having hired Lambe to carry out the heinous act. Whilst these men were eventually imprisoned for Irene's murder, investigations into the case are still ongoing.

In 2005, Chief Superintendent Christopher Mangan was a detective Inspector leading the investigation into the murder of Farah Swaleh Noor, whose dismembered body was found in a suitcase in the Royal Canal. The incident was shocking at the time and the investigation team had to appeal for information just to identify Noor. A viewer to the television appeal recognised his T-shirt and ultimately Noor was identified, leading to the arrest of the Mulhall sisters, labelled by the press as the 'Scissor Sisters'. According to Chief Superintendent Mangan, Linda Mulhall, who was found guilty of the manslaughter of Noor, confessed because she could not take the constant media appeals for information into the killing. Her sister Charlotte was found guilty of Noor's murder.

When Mangan became Superintendent in charge of the Cold Case Unit, he saw the power of the programme and sought to have several appeals into cold cases highlighted on *Crimecall*. The appeals showed the families of murder victims or missing persons that their cases were never closed. They had a chance to show the viewer what their son or daughter, brother or sister, or husband or wife meant to them, and to let it be known that they would never give up searching for answers.

Crimecall is not and never will be a current affairs programme like *Prime Time*. We ask different questions. We are an extension of a criminal investigation. We are advocates for victims and their families.

'SURE, YOU CAN'T BE DOING THAT!'

An Garda Síochána also uses the programme as a platform to promote safety campaigns. We try to be informative and not too preachy: 'Sure, you can't be doing that!' When traffic Sergeant Jim 'Scotty' McAllister pronounced on the programme that speed limits were not 'targets', he did so to inform viewers rather than scold them. Our 'Lock Up, Light Up' campaign was a simple but effective initiative, which did see a large drop in burglaries. *Crimecall* does not want to scare anyone; the programme wants to empower people to protect themselves and their property.

I am very proud of our 'Use Your Brain Not Your Fist' campaign. While promoting the initiative, I met Rosie and Joe Dolan, whose son Andrew died as a result of an unprovoked assault. Rosie made a powerful appeal on *Crimecall*, imploring people to walk away from violent situations. The Dolans have been great supporters of the campaign, promoting the message to students all over Ireland, even going as far as getting young people to make a video, encouraging personal safety. This video has since been placed in an assault-prevention module on the Garda Secondary Schools Programme, and Andrew's story will be told for many years to come.

In an age of streaming and hundreds of channels of choose from, *Crimecall* continues to be one of the most watched programmes in Ireland, with an average audience of 350,000 per episode; this means that, on average, one in three Irish people watches *Crimecall* live when it is broadcast ten times a year in its prime-time slot.

Whatever changes come, *Crimecall* will continue to seek answers and promote advice. I know first-hand the cathartic effect it has on families when they can tell their story and describe their loved ones to an audience they will never meet. I am back behind the scenes of *Crimecall* again now, in a smaller capacity. Even if I were not contributing to the programme I would still be watching, along with the hundreds of thousands of loyal viewers. Here's to another sixty years. That's right!

CHAPTER 28

OPERATIONAL SUPPORT SERVICES

Garda Stephen Moore
Garda Alan Cummins

In May 2000, the Garda Dog Unit, Garda Water Unit, Garda Mounted Unit and Garda Air Support Unit were officially amalgamated. The four-unit combination was initially known as the 'Operational Support Unit' but in recent years was renamed 'Operational Support Services'. Throughout the years, senior management attached to the section have been supported by a small cohort of office staff who have proved to be steadfast in support, professional and dedicated to the section. All four units have grown in strength since their initial inception and have become an integral component of An Garda Síochána.

THE GARDA WATER UNIT

The Garda Water Unit, previously known since the time of its establishment in 1974 as the 'sub-aqua unit', later expanded its location base at Santry in Dublin to include Athlone in Co.

Members of the Garda Water Unit at work.

Westmeath. The unit comprises two highly trained teams of members of An Garda Síochána who provide an operational support and search capability in marine environments and hazardous locations. This support is provided to both their colleagues within An Garda Síochána and external agencies, 24 hours a day, all year round.

Members of the unit search for missing persons and vital evidence relating to crime in Ireland's waterways. The significance of the unit finding a missing person and returning them to their loved ones, recovering vital evidence in serious criminal investigations, and other community support cannot be overestimated, and it is often carried out in the most difficult of circumstances. In addition to dive operations, the unit provides a surface capability throughout the country and around the Irish coastline; here they patrol regularly and enforce marine legislation. The Garda Water Unit plays an integral part in policing state security, organised and serious crime, major events nationally and community-focused engagements.

THE GARDA MOUNTED UNIT

The Garda Mounted Unit, based at Áras an Uachtaráin in the Phoenix Park, was established in 1998 and comprises both members of An Garda Síochána and Garda staff (grooms). Policing on horseback is ideal for high-visibility policing. Over the years, the Mounted Unit has played an integral part in policing public order and crowd-control events, the search and recovery of missing persons in terrain that is inaccessible to vehicles, high-visibility checkpoints, crime prevention and detection patrols, policing major events, public relations, and community engagement.

Temperament and physical attributes are very important characteristics of a police horse, and a commonly used breed by the unit is the indigenous Irish Draught. In addition to

policing duties and providing support to their colleagues nationally, the members of the unit care for the horses and take part in regular refresher training. The success and professionalism of the unit throughout the years is evident in the widespread interest received by them on a national and international basis.

THE GARDA AIR SUPPORT UNIT

The Garda Air Support Unit was established in September 1997. Its base is at Casement Aerodrome in Baldonnel, and it has a national remit. Initially the unit was established with two aircraft – a Eurocopter AS355N Twin Engine Squirrel Helicopter and a Britten Norman 4000 2T-4S. In 2000, the unit acquired an additional helicopter, an EC135T2+. In 2007, the AS355N helicopter was replaced by an EC135T2+, and to date these are the aircraft utilised by the unit. Garda aircraft are maintained on the Irish Military Aviation Register and piloted by Irish Air Corps personnel.

The unit provides a quick response call-out nationally all year round and monitors live

incidents, enabling its members to give invaluable information to their colleagues on the ground. They assist in investigating all types of crime, searching for high-risk missing persons, traffic management, event management and state security. In addition to this, the Garda Air Support Unit members assist their colleagues with aerial photography, escorts, and the carriage of various specialist teams. The unit assists with Cross-Border/EU/Joint Agency policing initiatives. It is also involved in land-based search-and-rescue, providing support to the Irish Coast Guard. The Garda Air Support Unit crew members are highly trained and have proved to be an invaluable support service to An Garda Síochána since its inception.

THE NATIONAL GARDA DOG UNIT

Garda Alan Cummins
DOGS AND POLICING

The first tentative steps at using dogs for policing in this country were taken on 20 September 1935, when the first Civic Guard Police Dog Championships were held in the grounds of what is now the Royal Hospital Kilmainham (RHK). At the time, the RHK was being used as Garda Headquarters and was overseen by the then Commissioner, Colonel Eamon Broy. The idea of the event was to showcase the abilities of the German Shepherd dog and how these dogs could be used to assist Gardaí in their duties. The handlers were members of An Garda Síochána, and they used their own private dogs for the event. The main competition was won by a Sergeant from Nenagh, with his dog, 'Wolf of Nenagh', who, according to *The Irish Times* of 21 September 1935, 'lived up to his fearsome name'.

The Garda Dog Unit was established in 1960. Pictured here are founding members (L to R): Brendan Maher, Mick Hayden, John Kelly and Patrick Slevin.

The years between 1935 and 1960 did not lead to any further progress being made in the introduction of dogs to assist in policing matters in Ireland. The use of dogs at that time was ad hoc at best, and certainly done on an informal basis. There are varying reports of 'Station dogs' being kept at some city-centre stations and being brought out to break up public disturbances.

In 1960, however, a decision was made to set up a Garda dog unit formally. The unit was to be based in an unused building to the rear of Kilmainham Garda Station. Initially four Garda handlers and a Sergeant were sent to the UK to train with British police dog handlers. The dogs they trained with were supplied by our British colleagues. After three months, the handlers returned to take up their new duties and formally begin their 'pawtrols'. The unit is still based at Kilmainham Garda Station.

In 2005, the Dog Unit was extended to the Southern Region, with bases in Limerick and Cork; owing to its success, it later became a permanent unit. Garda dogs attached to the unit are trained in a number of disciplines: Drugs/Cash/Firearms (DCF) detection, Explosive Detection (ED), and General-Purpose duties (GP). Operating as a part of a Garda dog team involves 24-hour care of the dog all year round. This includes regular refresher training in the above disciplines, in addition to normal operational policing duties. The most common breeds of dog used by the Garda Dog Unit are German Shepherds, Belgian Malinois, Labradors and Springer Spaniels. The dedication and commitment of the team at the Garda Dog Unit throughout the years has played a critical role in supporting and assisting uniformed operational units and national specialist units with the policing of organised and serious crime, state security, drugs crime, public order, searches for missing persons, community engagement and major events.

Today's Garda Dog Unit is relatively small by international standards. It does not have a high turnover of staff, but it is not the type of job that lends itself to a high staff turnover. Anyone who loves working with animals and who enjoys policing as a career could not ask for a better job. Nonetheless, it is a unit that punches above its weight in a modern and often challenging policing environment. The unit is constantly evolving to meet new needs and requirements as and when they arise; the recent establishment of a dedicated training school at the unit reflects this. Dog-training methods and techniques are constantly evolving and there is a high degree of co-operation on this with our European partners.

THE 'GENERAL PURPOSE DOG'

When people think of police dogs, they often think of 'sniffer dogs' for drugs, but that is not the entire picture. Most handlers will be asked to handle at least two different dogs, for two different roles, at any one time. Most will have a 'General Purpose Dog', which is generally a German Shepherd or Belgian Malinois. This is a day-to-day patrol dog, trained to protect and defend the handler, track and locate concealed suspects, search for missing persons, or retrieve items of evidence that contain recent human scent. This is the dog that gets put into the building to search for the burglar at 2 a.m., that searches the forest with its handler in the middle of the night for the violent offender, and that assists in finding vulnerable missing persons. This dog puts itself in harm's way to protect society. Each handler relies on their General-Purpose dog to return home safely at the end of each shift, because nobody ever knows what a tour of duty will entail on any given day.

The trust between handler and dog works both ways. A handler cares for the animal on a 24/7 basis – the dog lives with the handler, becoming part of the life of the handler's family; the handler gets up in the middle of the night if the dog is unwell or injured. A handler would never unnecessarily put the dog in harm's way, but when they do, it is to protect others – either Garda colleagues or the public at large. The dogs we use are not pets. They are highly driven and intense working dogs; they enjoy doing what they do, and they do it because their bond with their handler is so strong.

Garda Dogs are involved in a wide range of operational activity including assisting in searches.

SPECIALIST DOGS

Other specialist search services that the Garda Dog Unit provides include DCF (Drugs/Cash/Firearms)-detection dogs and EDD (Explosives Detection Dogs). The breeds normally used for this sort of work are Labrador or spaniel types and are of strong hunting lines. To these dogs, life is one big game, and they love nothing more than encouragement, affection, and a reward of play upon completion of a successful search. As the criminals' methods of concealment become increasingly elaborate, the demand for these specialist search dogs is ever increasing. Time and time again, the natural abilities of the dogs have shown themselves to be unbeatable. Their acute sense of smell is unparalleled. An analogy I use when describing their talents is of a human walking into a kitchen where a stew is cooking and being able to smell the stew. A dog's nose is so sensitive, however, that it will be

able to smell each individual ingredient contained in that stew – although, of course, the last thing any of my dogs would do if they got close enough to an unsupervised pot of stew would be to smell it!

DOG HANDLERS

Because of the nature of the job, including the travelling involved, dog handlers are widely known across the service. For the handler, attending any job in any given district is just another job – a chance to use the dog, a chance to put into practice the months of hard training it has taken to get the handler and this animal to the point where the handler has full faith in the dog's abilities. To the Gardaí on the ground, the handler is there to assist. It might be the first time they have seen a Garda dog work, and they are fascinated. I remember being that junior Garda and being full of annoying questions once I had seen a dog locate a quantity of cash hidden by drug dealers from nearly 30ft away. I was in awe.

As a handler, you get as much of a kick from the dog getting any kind of find if they have worked hard for it. To you and your dog, a find is a find – €30 worth of cocaine is the same as €3 million worth. Obviously from an organisational point of view, the two are vastly different!

Below left: Garda Alan Cummins with Garda Dog Roxy at the St Patrick's Day Parade in Dublin in 2022. Below right: Garda dogs are a big hit with the public. Garda Anne Cunnane with her dog Toby at an event in Dublin Castle in 2022.

Pictured at the St Patrick's Day Parade in Dublin in 2022 are (left) Sergeant Seán Pender with Garda Dog Uri and Inspector Mary Crehan of the Operational Support Unit.

The real joy, though, comes from incidents where it was the dog that made the difference in the call – the missing person, the drugs, the criminal or the explosive that could not have been found but for the abilities of the dog. This is where the real work satisfaction comes from, and it is why you keep doing what you do.

The highs are high, but there are lows, too. To get the most out of the dog, the handler must have a strong bond with them. You have to be invested in them: you want them to do well; you want them to excel. This is acutely felt in the early stages of training a new dog, a dog you have bonded with but that may be finding the training difficult. A trainer's mood can be affected if their new dog has had a bad day or is struggling to progress. If a dog is failed off a course, that dog is rehomed; a handler may have to start the process all over again with a new dog. The standards are high for a reason: the public's safety can depend on how well that dog is trained. On a live explosive search, you need to have full faith in your dog and its training.

THE SUCCESSES

In our ever-changing times, the Garda Síochána Dog Unit deserves all the plaudits it receives. Millions of illegal drugs have been removed off the streets; millions in cash have been recovered; criminals have been located by the dogs and evidence retrieved; violent disturbances have been quelled and broken up; vulnerable persons have been located and helped; thousands of hours of patrols have been conducted; but most importantly, lives have been saved.

Everything we do in the unit is built on the knowledge and experiences of those handlers and their dogs that served before us. The handlers and their dogs who have served in the Garda Dog Unit since 1960 have done so proudly and will continue to do so into the future – hopefully for many years to come.

Chapter 29

'The House of Horrors'

Retired Sergeant John Hynes

* Reader discretion advised as this chapter contains graphic content that some may find upsetting.

'What are you going to be when you grow up, young fella?'

This question was posed by the same man every time my father and I met him. From the age of four, I always gave the same answer: 'A guard.'

I was born just outside Kilkelly, Co. Mayo, a quiet, crime-free area. I remember my father tipping his hat whenever we met the local Gardaí. It was a sign of respect that I will always remember, and possibly one reason why, from such a young age, I wanted to become a Garda. Throughout my school years, I never changed my mind. On hearing about the murder of two Gardaí – Detective Garda John Morley and Garda Henry Byrne – at a bank robbery in Ballaghaderreen, Co. Roscommon, on 7 July 1980, I made up my mind that I was definitely joining. I entered Templemore on 6 October 1982, and 22 weeks later I arrived at Kevin Street Station.

A Sergeant in the College had told me that Kevin Street was one of the finest stations in the country, and I would not disagree with that. I met my wife, Catherine, there – she had joined in 1980 – and the vast experience I gained there, mainly in the investigation of crime and court procedure, stood to me until my retirement. I was attached to Unit B as an official driver and, in 1991, I went into plainclothes. In 1993, I was promoted to Sergeant and transferred to Keadue, Co. Roscommon. It was a lovely quiet station – too quiet for me – and I transferred to Castlerea nine months later.

A File for Investigation

In November 2004, I received a file from the Superintendent's Office to investigate a case of child sexual abuse following a referral from the Western Health Board (WHB). A 15-year old, the eldest of six children, had made an allegation on 23 September 2004 that his father had systematically sexually and physically abused him over several years. The child had been in the care of the WHB since June 2004 at his own request. Following this complaint, the WHB had applied to the District Court and been granted an Emergency Care Order for the remaining five children, who were then taken into care. A few days later, interim care orders were granted for these children; on 16 November, these were extended for a six-month period.

Following receipt of the referral, I requested a case conference with all WHB personnel involved with this family. At the conference, I listened as each person related their dealings with the family. I soon formed an impression of a very dysfunctional family with extremely manipulative parents. As the meeting went on, a horrendous picture emerged, of heavy drinking, squalid living conditions, neglect and cruelty, prostitution by the mother with children present, and, of course, the reason we were all there – the allegation of sexual abuse by the father. I asked the same question that Judge Reynolds would ask during the mother's trial: 'How could this not be noticed?'

I learned that in early October 2000, due to the terrible living conditions and the lack of co-operation by the parents, a shared parenting plan had been drawn up between the WHB, the parents and close relatives of the family; all parties had agreed to this, and it had been signed off on 24 October. The following day, the mother called to the WHB offices and served an ex-parte order – which she had obtained in the High Court – on one of the social workers. Her affidavit asserted that the shared parenting agreement had been forced on her and that the children were properly cared for by the parents.

The order restrained the WHB from removing the children from the parents' custody. It transpired that the parents had been assisted and advised by a Dublin-based religious group. The WHB did not challenge the order.

At the conclusion of the conference, I was aghast at what I had heard, but one thing I knew: this was going to be a prolonged and difficult investigation. It would involve each of the children being interviewed and, given their young ages and what they had endured, I would need professional help. At my request, two WHB childcare workers were assigned to assist me with interviewing the children. We would interview the four eldest children, but not the two youngest children due to their tender years.

THE ELDEST CHILD'S STORY

During September and October 2004, the eldest child, who was 15 years old when he asked to be taken into care, made three statements to Garda Paul Keane, who was based in Salthill. These statements led to the remaining five children being taken into care. He alleged sexual abuse and serious assaults by his father over the three previous years. Feeling that he had a lot more to tell, I interviewed him in early December 2004.

The boy detailed a litany of systematic rapes by his father from September 2001 to June 2004. He said that he was in such fear of his father that he slept with a butcher's knife under his mattress. He painted a horrific picture of the place he called home – a house that was always cold, dirty and overrun with rats and mice. The children seldom got a cooked meal, instead receiving stale bread and sour milk for breakfast, and bread and butter for lunch. Only on Mondays and Wednesdays, when home helps were engaged, did they have a dinner. He described the house as a 'kip'. Clothes were thrown everywhere. The beds just had quilts – no linen – and the children slept on urine-soaked mattresses. Every evening, the boy was forced to get what meals he could for the other children while his parents went to the pub. Mayhem would invariably break out when the parents returned home drunk, and he was subjected to constant beatings.

I brought on board the late Detective Garda Colm Horkan to assist in the investigation. Hardworking and reliable, Colm was fully dedicated to the pursuit of justice on behalf of victims; I relied on him a lot. He excelled under pressure and his attention to detail in criminal investigations was exemplary. Had it not been for Colm's dedication in leaving no stone unturned, convictions – including the one in this case – would not have been achieved as frequently as they were. (Alas, Colm's career in An Garda Síochána was cut short when he was confronted by a man on Main Street, Castlerea, on 17 June 2020, was overpowered and fatally wounded with his own gun.)

On 21 December 2004, having arrested the father, Colm and I interviewed him. This was the first time we had met the man. He denied all the allegations and painted a picture of loving parents and a happy household. However, he did admit to knowing that his son slept with a butcher's knife under his mattress. On leaving the station, he said to me, 'You have nothing.' His arrogance beggared belief.

On 5 February 2005, the mother called to the station to ask how the investigation was going. We had a long discussion and I told her that I was there to listen and to help. She left the station, but within two hours she rang and asked that I meet her at an agreed location, saying that she had left her husband. Colm and I collected her and brought her to the station, where she made a statement in which she corroborated her eldest son's allegation of regular rapes by her husand. She agreed to talk to us again and I arranged accommodation for her through the WHB.

On 27 May 2005, I interviewed the mother further in the presence of a social worker. It seemed that the fear she had of her husband was now gone. She made an extraordinary statement that told of living in the most appalling squalor, in a house that her husband ruled with an iron fist, instilling fear into every member of the family. She again reiterated the rapes by her husband on her eldest son, but also said that the same child had been severely beaten by his father for years. She described a chilling incident when this boy had fallen in school, breaking both wrists. He had been brought home by his teacher, but when the teacher left, the father grabbed the boy by his wrists, twisted and bent them, before firing the child across the kitchen floor, leaving him in excruciating pain. Both parents stopped for drinks in a pub before bringing their son to the hospital for surgery.

Her description of the house was more detailed than that of her son. She described how rubbish was piled up everywhere except in the hall and sitting room – the only places the social workers would see when they visited. The children were never washed, except when home helps visited. Most of the parents' income was spent on alcohol, which left the children short of food, clothing and heat. Both parents hit the children, especially when drunk. The two eldest were left to babysit the younger children when the parents went to the pub, which was seven nights a week. The mother stated that she was forced by her husband to have sex with men in the locality; her son was sent to phone these men to set up a meeting place. Sometimes the children went with her and witnessed these encounters. She described incidents that are too shocking to relate here, but which gave a true insight into the family's living conditions.

Interviewing the Children

By this time, interviews with the children had commenced. I was gradually introduced to them, with a view to gaining their trust. Initially, things were frightfully slow. In a meeting with WHB officials, I discovered that the children had been given mobile phones through which they maintained contact with their parents, and they also had supervised visits with them. Deciding that the children would not open up as long as this contact continued, I brought an application to the District Court to have all access by the parents terminated. The application was successful. It would later transpire that the parents had been threatening the children during phone calls

The children now began to talk more about their experiences. Between May and December 2005, together with childcare workers from the WHB, I interviewed the four eldest children. All four described being starved, neglected, beaten, and left on their own to fend for themselves while their parents were out drinking. They described their home as a 'scary' place, especially when the parents returned from the pub. Beatings were regular. One child described crawling into her bed as she turned up a radio to drown out the noise. They described a house that was overrun with rats and mice and spoke of head lice so big that they were crawling down their faces. They spoke of regularly having sour milk and blue-mouldy bread for breakfast and of wearing the same clothes for weeks at a time.

Throughout this prolonged investigation, I found interviewing the children extremely difficult. Nowadays, there are trained specialist interviewers to carry out such tasks, but no such training was available back then. I would go home at night exhausted and watch my own children sleeping peacefully. Our children had everything – loving parents, a beautiful home, warmth, nutritious meals and loads of friends – things every child should have. Unable to sleep, many nights I would mull over the things the children had told me: their prolonged suffering; the physical, emotional and sexual abuse that they had endured. Their childhoods had been stolen by people who called themselves their parents. It was simply the stuff of nightmares.

QUESTIONING THE PARENTS

On 19 January 2006, I arrested the mother for an offence under Section 246 of the Children Act, 2001 (Cruelty to Children). In interview, she fully admitted the offences for which she had been arrested. She also incriminated her husband in the sexual abuse of the eldest child and told how he had pimped her out to numerous men.

On 6 February 2006, I arrested the father for the rape of his eldest son. A crime photographer photographed the house. They say a picture paints a thousand words, but this photo album would bring a whole new meaning to that cliché. The volume of allegations was such that the 12-hour period of detention was insufficient. While detained, the father refuted all the allegations. Following his release, we asked him to meet us again at the Garda station on a voluntary basis, but we insisted that the interviews would be taped and recorded. He agreed to these terms, and we met him one week later. Again, he denied all allegations put to him.

In March 2006, the investigation took another turn when I received a message that one of the children wanted to speak to me. Together with one of the childcare workers, I met the child. He alleged that he had been raped by his mother. It was a bombshell and I was flabbergasted. The young boy described being raped by his mother on four occasions in the family home, while the other children were in the house. He cried as he related what had occurred. He was so upset that we had to suspend the interview, which was completed at a later date.

On 1 May 2006, I arrested the mother again, this time for the rape of her son. Colm and I interviewed her several times. To our amazement, she admitted to the alleged offences. She also admitted that a fifth rape had taken place when the family were on holidays. This was the woman who should have been protecting the child – the same child that she had given birth to on her kitchen floor in 1990, in such a drunken state that she did not even know she was in labour. Towards the end of one difficult interview, I said to her, 'Wouldn't it be a fair comment for us to say to you today that your house was a House of Horrors?'

She replied, 'John, it was a House of Horrors with bells on.'

And so, the title the media would later use to refer to this case had been coined. She also described herself as 'the worst mother in the world'.

At this stage, we had conducted over fifty hours of interviews with the parents. We believed that we had already obtained as much information as we could from the children, and we did not want to put them through any unnecessary trauma.

I had never encountered two individuals so manipulative as the parents. The father blamed the children, especially the eldest son, for the barrage of 'lies' they were telling. He said he found the allegations filthy and disgusting, and he was adamant that he would clear his name. What surprised me about the mother's interviews was the ease with which she agreed with the serious allegations made against her.

During our investigation, it came to light that the WHB had been involved with the family for 15 years, during which time 19 case conferences had taken place. The family had dealings with countless members and sections of the WHB, yet the children had not been rescued by anyone; they had rescued themselves. Colm and I put together an airtight investigation file. In our disclosure to the defence, we handed over more than 1,000 documents from the WHB alone. A very full and comprehensive file was forwarded to the Office of the Director of Public Prosecutions who directed the following: in the mother's case – four counts of rape, four counts of sexual assault, and six counts of neglect and cruelty to children; in the father's case – 23 counts of rape and 24 counts of sexual assault.

Arrest, Trial and Sentencing

On 19 October 2007, I arrested both parents. They appeared in the District Court and were remanded on bail with strict conditions. On 6 June 2008, the book of evidence was served.

The mother's trial in the Circuit Court began on 21 January 2009. She pleaded guilty to all charges, so the children did not have to give evidence at her trial. I spent all that day in the witness box relating the horrific details of the case to Justice Miriam Reynolds, who sadly passed away two months later. As I gave my evidence, I could see the distressing effect the details of the case were having on all present. The mother sat motionless as the courtroom heard the extent of the wilful neglect and sexual exploitation. When I finished, senior management from the WHB were called to give evidence as to how this could have happened.

The following day, Judge Reynolds in her summing up asked why nothing had been done to save the six children: 'No right-thinking person could or should stand idly by and watch, without doing anything. Any possibility of having a normal life has been stolen from them by this woman who calls herself their mother.' She was also critical of the legislators. A male abuser could have received a life sentence; however, the harshest sentence she could hand down to a woman was one of seven years.

Judge Reynolds noted the mother's plea of guilty, thereby preventing the children from having to give evidence, describing it as 'the final act of mercy and the only act of kindness she has bestowed on them since they were born'. She handed down the harshest sentence the law would allow and directed that the mother be placed on the Sex Offenders Register for life. This was the first woman in the history of the State to be both charged with and convicted of incest, and the first woman to be placed on the Sex Offenders Register.

Following an application by the defence, the father's case was delayed. When it commenced on 5 February 2010 at the Central Criminal Court, the father pleaded not guilty to all 47 counts, thus forcing his son to spend almost two days in the witness box. The mother gave evidence against her husband, while the father himself gave evidence, denying the charges. However, on 15 February, in an emotional atmosphere, he was found guilty on all counts. For the first time in my career, I cried as a verdict was given; some of the jury wept openly. At the conclusion of proceedings, the man's son came over and hugged and thanked Colm and me. It was the first time I saw members of a jury hug and converse with an injured party.

On 5 March 2010, the young man gave a powerful victim impact statement. Mr Justice Barry White imposed a 14-year term in respect of each count of anal rape, ten years for each count of oral rape, and a three-year term on each of the sexual assault charges, the sentences to run concurrently, with the final 18 months suspended. The father was to be put on the Sex Offenders Register for life.

CONCLUSION

The case was widely reported and caused immense national concern, leading to the establishment of the Gibbons Inquiry, chaired by Ms Norah Gibbons, which examined the management of the case from the care perspective of the Health Service Executive (HSE).

Today, having completed their sentences, both parents are free to carry on with their lives. However, their children's sentences continue, and the scars inflicted by their parents remain. I hope that the intervention of An Garda Síochána and the satisfactory conclusion of this case will in some way help them to live with the memories. Knowing how they have moved on with their lives, I believe that some of that has been achieved.

CHAPTER 30

POLICING WITH DIVERSE COMMUNITIES

Inspector David McInerney

I joined An Garda Síochána in 1980, and went on to serve in Terenure, Crumlin, the Garda National Drugs Unit, and Irishtown. During these postings, I served with the UN in Croatia, Bosnia Herzegovina and Mozambique, and on promotion to Sergeant I went on to lead the Garda Racial, Intercultural and Diversity Office (GRIDO) from 2001 to 2019. In 2019, I was promoted to Inspector and returned to my first station in Terenure. During my period in GRIDO, I witnessed unprecedented success for initiatives that were recognised as best practice throughout Europe and the US in policing diverse communities. In 2011, I received a Recognition Award from the Federal Bureau of Investigation (FBI) for co-operation in combatting international terrorism. In 2016, the Al Maktoum Foundation Award was granted for excellence in building friendship and positive relations with Ireland's Muslim community over a 15-year period. In 2017, my proposal, on behalf of An Garda Síochána, to develop positive relations with minority communities through anti-profiling technique training for Garda Ethnic Liaison Officers received an award of €1 million from the European Integration Fund.

INTRODUCTION

In the past three decades, Ireland has undergone an unprecedented and unique level of inward migration. The Census of 1991 indicated that 0.5 per cent of individuals in the State were born outside of Ireland, rising to 3 per cent in 2001, to 10 per cent in 2006, and to 17 per cent in 2016. This immigration trend was among the most important changes to policing in Ireland since 1922, in relation to its practices, policies, and the perception of An Garda Síochána.

Migrants to Ireland are made up of approximately 188 different nationalities; however, Albanian, Algerian, Bangladeshi, Bosnian, Chinese, Congolese, Egyptian, Filipino, Indian,

Iraqi, Latvian, Libyan, Lithuanian, Moroccan, Nigerian, Pakistani, Polish, Romanian, Sudanese, Somalian, and Zimbabwean nationals featured in greater numbers from the mid-1990s to date. These migrants were further categorised as asylum seekers, refugees, bearers of work permits, bearers of student visas, persons illegally trafficked into the State, and others classed as illegal immigrants not having leave to land. Until the mid-1990s, all such persons were categorised as 'aliens'.

Up until then, Gardaí had limited daily contact with migrants, apart from in the normal course of immigration law enforcement, and crime control. So regular frontline Gardaí knew little about immigrants, their culture, and their reasons for coming here. This was a complete change from what characterised the previous 70 years of policing in Ireland, when Gardaí had a good local knowledge of all those in the immediate community.

Monumental challenges were encountered daily by our frontline members, who came face to face with individuals of different ethnic and religious groups, speaking myriad different languages, and had no idea who these people were. Getting to know migrants' ethnic make-up, and to understand their religion, cultural traditions, and practices pertaining to their life, was crucial for these members. According to accounts of Garda frontline experiences at that time, factors such as traditional and religious practices, inter-ethnicity, male domination, child obedience, family honour, witchcraft, female genital mutilation (FGM), and arranged and forced marriage caused 'culture shock' among members.

An Garda Síochána had to adopt a change in its policing response to Ireland's expanding diversity. This new paradigm was about integration, not segregation; equal protection, not domination; and mutual respect, not deference. Enforcing the law was still important, of course, but maintaining racial and ethnic harmony was essential to the new order.

An Garda Síochána's Policing Model in the United Nations

In May 2001, while stationed in Irishtown, I received a call from Garda Community Relations, inviting me to take up duty at the newly formed Garda Racial and Intercultural Office (GRIO). Having served on three UN peacekeeping missions, it was felt that I would be ideal to lead the unit in building relations with Ireland's new arrivals. From my experience on UN service, where An Garda Síochána excelled in post-conflict crisis policing, I could see the potential to pioneer a completely new way of policing. Regardless of reports about local people's acts during periods of war and conflict, and irrespective of their ethnic status, our members' respect for individuals as human beings was never diminished. We were sought out to instil peace and stability through our tactful good-humoured mediation techniques that exhibited fairness and understanding. I was confident that this template would be perfect to transpose to the new unit as An Garda Síochána set about developing positive relations with the new arrivals on Irish soil.

NEW SPECIALIST UNIT – GARDA RACIAL AND INTERCULTURAL OFFICE (GRIO)

It was clear from the outset that our members would need to develop an understanding of the experiences that guide individuals through life, such as: language, gestures, personal appearance, social relationships, religion, philosophy, values, courtship, marriage, family customs, family honour, dress, food, recreation, education, work and government. Such cultural details are learned through face-to-face interaction with people. Therefore, our members would need to engage in a positive way at frontline level, to learn how to develop culturally appropriate friendly responses when communicating with minorities. This was accomplished through training and 24-hour back-up support from GRIO regarding questions concerning intercultural communication techniques during routine policing and investigations.

TAKING UP THE CHALLENGE

With the support of Garda Mary-Liz O'Leary – the only member of staff at GRIO at that time – I set about making contact with representatives of new migrant communities throughout Ireland, by phone and by attending any meeting that touched on integration, anti-discrimination and anti-racism. I also visited places of worship and venues where large groups of migrants would congregate. My first point of contact was to meet with the Sheikh at the Sunni Mosque on South Circular Road, Dublin. I knew that at the mosque I would encounter a vast diverse congregation from all walks of life and from every nation, and every colour, from the nearly 1.8 billion Muslims from every corner of the world. I enrolled in lessons in Arabic, which is spoken in 28 countries worldwide. Knowledge of languages (even just conversational) is essential to building trust and confidence with minority communities.

One contact led to another. All were told about the new unit that had been set up with the sole purpose of building relations and learning about our minority ethnic communities, so that we could provide a non-discriminatory professional police service, based on respect for difference. We explained that any member of their community nationwide would have the complete co-operation of the GRIO and An Garda Síochána at any time. Most were surprised by this, and a positive relationship with our new minority ethnic communities grew at a rapid rate. This flowed from visible action through immediate responses to requests for Garda assistance from members of these communities, many of whom had hitherto been

Representatives of minority communities attending the Garda Memorial Day.

apprehensive in seeking Garda assistance because of negative experiences and perceptions emanating from police relations in their home countries.

The work of GRIO accelerated daily, and An Garda Síochána embarked on the road to becoming one of the most prominent organisations involved in building positive relations with immigrants to ensure their safe integration into Irish society. A programme of widespread consultation with minority and key stakeholders took place throughout Ireland, with Garda management listening to concerns of minority communities, and taking appropriate action attuned to cultural and religious sensitivities. This trust-and-confidence-building strategy was enhanced by the arrival of Garda Jonathan O'Mahony, Garda Darren Coventry-Howlett and Mr John O'Hara (Clerical Officer) at GRIO, under the leadership of Chief Superintendent Karl Heller.

ELO CONCEPT

I quickly observed that this stand-alone unit based in Dublin could not possibly deliver services at local level without appointing specifically trained Gardaí with a direct link to the office. I proposed that the role of a Garda Ethnic Liaison Officer (ELO) be considered by the Commissioner, to facilitate the delivery of a professional policing service to rapidly increasing ethnic communities, including our own Traveller Community.

In 2002, 145 members of An Garda Síochána were appointed as Ethnic Liaison Officers with their defined role being to 'liaise with representatives of minority groups including the Traveller Community and to reassure them of the Garda services available'. This was a starting point in coming to terms with the policing realities associated with Ireland's changing demographic environment. ELOs would receive intensive appropriate professional anti-discrimination and cultural awareness training by the Garda Racial and Intercultural Office.

In effect, ELOs were to be regarded as 'change agents' within An Garda Síochána, and by minority groups. By facilitating ease of access to the Garda institution, they would instil confidence in minorities that Ireland's police service was non-discriminatory and was dedicated to openness, fairness and transparency in the delivery of service. Through positive interaction with minorities in performing their role, they would acquire skills while at the same time increasing their understanding of difference and vulnerability. Garda first responders, in contrast, did not have an opportunity to build relations with those seeking assistance.

ELOs were also charged with reaching out to local communities to provide information about the new arrivals, their background and reasons for coming to Ireland, and to a particular town. It was envisaged that this would prevent any hostility that could arise, especially in the light of anticipated collateral damage from negative public commentary from some about migrants being 'scroungers', 'criminals', and 'terrorists'.

TRAINING OF ELOS

Prior to embarking on preparation of a training course for the 145 newly appointed ELOs, I ran a pilot survey of eighty Phase V probationer Gardaí during their final phase of training at the Garda College, to elicit from them what they had witnessed during their frontline policing phase, in relation to contact with our new minority communities.

Of the probationers surveyed, 70 per cent said that their primary contact with non-Irish nationals was through arrest and crime investigation, while only 20 per cent reported having had positive contact through daily patrolling; 10 per cent indicated that they had met a non-Irish national through being the victim of a crime. The figure for the arrest and investigation of crime categories was high, tending to indicate that negative stereotypes could become entrenched from the outset of these probationers' careers.

They were asked for their views, from recollection, of their experience from their first station posting. In response to a query regarding their thoughts about the attitude of local communities to new migrants coming to live in their towns and villages, none of the probationer respondents believed that local communities would be enthused at the prospect.

Finally, all those surveyed indicated that they had no real understanding of diversity, and needed to know about the use of interpreters, cultural and religious traditions of newly arriving migrants, and how to deal with reports of racism and hate crime.

The results were crucial in steering the development of an appropriate, practical, cultural-awareness and anti-discrimination training course, in conjunction with local minority expert trainers identified by GRIO. A central feature of the training focused on anti-profiling techniques. Police officers usually make decisions based on assumptions derived from their previous dealings with different people, so the importance of neither creating stereotypes nor making ill-informed assumptions was an area of priority in developing ELO skills.

GRIO and ELO Initiatives at Local Level

On encountering ELOs at regional training sessions, I was impressed by their enthusiasm, although this role was in addition to their normal duties. These members were on the front line of social change, negotiating with ethnic minorities through initiatives that stemmed from an inclusive approach to policing and ethnic diversity.

The ELOs ensured the safe integration of minorities in the community through visiting Refugee Reception Centres, meeting, greeting, and reassuring newly arriving immigrants. Female ELOs held separate sessions for groups of ethnic women, bearing in mind gender sensitivities. ELOs visited schools and places of worship to advertise the services of An Garda Síochána, and to encourage engagement with local Gardaí. They organised sports events with ethnic-minority children the length and breadth of Ireland, ranging from hurling and football to basketball and cricket.

Ireland's Muslim population exceeded 100,000 in 2020 and continues to grow.

ELOs attached to Kevin Street and Donnybrook Garda Stations played a huge role in developing relationships with the Muslim community through Friday 'After Prayer Clinics'

in the mosques, where advice was given to those seeking Garda assistance. The positive feedback from this initiative has been remarked upon by Muslims from all over the world.

Based on their frontline learning experiences, ELOs gave freely of their time to advise their colleagues on approaches to adopt when dealing with local minority community members. The contacts they had made became invaluable in diffusing inter-cultural communication difficulties that could have developed in the course of prevention and detection of crime.

Open-Day Initiative

In 2002, GRIO was asked by the Garda Commissioner for proposals to coincide with 'Anti-Racism in the Workplace Week', the first week of April. I saw it as an ideal opportunity to invite members of minorities to get to know their local Gardaí through a Garda station 'Open Day'. I proposed that ELOs would invite community contacts to visit their local Garda station to meet with the Superintendent over tea. A Headquarters Directive issued with instructions to ELOs in this regard. The initial invitations to new immigrants in the community caused alarm, and many organisations called GRIO explaining that there was a perception among invitees that this was a ruse designed to deport immigrants from the State. All callers were reassured of the thinking behind the initiative and the 'Open Day' is now a regular feature in Garda stations throughout the country – not just for minorities, but for all in the community.

CONCLUSION

The role of the ELO came about as an emergency response to a massive demographic change not witnessed anywhere else in the world. The ELOs' frontline role in fostering trust and reassuring minorities has built the foundation for a cohesive society such as has not been witnessed in any nation with a similar demographic make-up.

Under the Garda Diversity and Integration Strategy, which was launched in 2019, a number of measures have been introduced to strengthen this further. This includes the introduction of a working definition of hate crime along with online hate-crime reporting, the establishment of the Garda National Diversity Forum, and ELOs upskilled and given a wider remit to reflect Ireland's changing society by becoming Diversity Officers.

The next hundred years will witness the role of the community Garda becoming even more crucial, as Gardaí face the transition from first-generation immigrants to second and third

An Garda Síochána was one of the first police services in the world to establish a specialist section to engage with diverse communities.

generation. Minority communities now have a secure legal basis on which to make decisions about their life perspectives.

Notwithstanding the rapid digital transformation of the world, face-to-face respectful engagement in the local community by Gardaí must remain a priority. Having served for more than four decades, I will always look back on my first day parading in Terenure Garda Station where I was fortunate to encounter Sergeant Philip Cahill and Sergeant George Oliver who quipped that policing was simply about communication and respect. Their guidance and example were invaluable and reflected the highest level of respectful ethical policing for both members of An Garda Síochána and the public.

Through An Garda Síochána's expertise in policing a multicultural society, built on the foundations of respect for all people, I am hopeful that Ireland will be a safe and cohesive society for people of every colour, culture, and religion throughout the next century and beyond.

CHAPTER 31

G-FORCING CHANGE

Superintendent Paul Franey

'Y ou've no business joining the guards,' a college mate laughed as we waited for a bus in Belfield. My final exams were approaching and my commencement in Templemore had been deferred until July. It was the year 2000, and even my more open-minded mates thought the idea of an openly gay man joining An Garda Síochána was laughable. Funnily, I had never thought about it that way. Having wanted to be a Garda since I was a young boy, I was sure it would be fine. Ireland was coming of age, after all, and the Celtic Tiger was starting to roar. A few months later, I drove through the gates of the Garda College for the first time. Then I began to wonder if I had been a little naive.

A HEAVY VEIL

'A few of the lads have had a meeting about you. They said they had a right to know.' This was said to me during a phone call a few weeks into my training, as I was driving back to Templemore one dark Sunday evening. Apparently, some of my fellow students were not as open-minded as I thought. A palpable fear hit me as I walked back into the College. All I had ever wanted was to be a Garda. Why this? Why now? The fear that seeped into me that night affected my relationship with the organisation for almost two decades. With the support of a few good friends, I got on with it. I worked hard and did well as a student. But I was never truly able to be me.

Going out to a station was a new start. I had no idea at the time that my student years were subject to so much scrutiny, with some senior managers recommending that my services be disposed of – all because I drank in a gay bar. Ignorance sometimes is bliss. In many ways, I wish I had never found out.

I loved being a Garda. Police cars and utility belts full of torches and tools, prisoners, and court – that youthful enthusiasm, which I still love to see in my staff today. My immediate colleagues were always supportive and probably a little protective, but the homophobia was never too far away. There was a sense of isolation being openly gay in that environment. It took three years before I found a second member who was gay. And a year after that before I found two more. In an organisation of approximately 11,000 members, the invisibility spoke volumes. Only a heavy veil of secrecy could hide that many people.

OUT FROM THE SHADOWS

In 2005, we organised a night out. Five gay Gardaí who had managed to find each other met mid-week at the Porter House in Temple Bar. It was emotional for those who for decades had been hiding who they were– something that they never imagined could happen. It was just a few pints and some chicken wings, but it was the start of something. The same year, I was asked to attend a European Gay Police Association (EGPA) conference in London. Shortly afterwards, the request was withdrawn. A step forward and a step back. It was the start of a pattern of institutional resistance, the start of a frustration that would persist for over a decade.

However, the next year, thanks to the assistance of a brave and progressive manager, I attended the EGPA conference in Stockholm, which started me on a singular career journey. I saw what professional support for both LGBT (Lesbian, Gay, Bisexual and Transgender) victims of crime and police employees looked like. While there was an element of the grass looking greener, I was aware we had a long way to go in Ireland. In my excitement, I under-took to organise the EGPA conference in Dublin, scheduled for 2012 – a strategic but sensible six years away. We would surely have made amazing progress by then, I thought, and I decided to push for change at home.

Members of An Garda Síochána at the launch of G-Force.

The move from a small group meeting for a pint to setting up an employee support network was harder than expected. We could not seem to move forward. In 2007, at our first formal meeting, we outlined what a brighter future could look like for gay and lesbian Gardaí. Half of the attending members signed the minutes with an X or just their initials. This was in a diary that nobody was ever going to see. There was no trust for the institution and there was a lot of fear.

The Garda Representative Association (GRA) and Association of Garda Sergeants and Inspectors (AGSI) turned out to be a huge support at that point. The editor of the *Garda Review*, in particular, saw an opportunity for change. The staff associations gently coaxed a statement of support for the group at a meeting with senior Garda management. While the support may not have been explicit, we used it to launch G-Force in the *Garda Review*. G-Force is an unofficial support group for LGBT members and staff of An Garda Síochána. While many were unhappy with the concept of openly LGBT people in An Garda Síochána, the cat was out of the bag, and it would not be put back in. We had passed a point of no return.

SLOW PROGRESS

However, in G-Force's efforts to make progress from a staff-support or community-engagement perspective, things moved slowly. We approached each engagement professionally and built relationships where we could, but our frustration was growing. A more open-minded middle management supported us as much as possible. Things were shifting, but we had to be patient. We were young, though, and wanted to change the lived experiences of people we cared about – patience did not come easy.

As 2012 approached, G-Force commenced planning the Sixth European LGBT Police Association conference – the conference I had undertaken to organise six years earlier. We

Members of G-Force at Áras an Uachtaráin in 2012.

garnered support from the Government, obtained the use of Dublin Castle for the event, and arranged a reception at Áras an Uachtaráin, with the Minister for Justice to attend the launch. Sadly, the institution we worked for was not as supportive. What should have been the highlight of the group's achievements was marred by strong organisational resistance.

A key battle was fought over our right to wear our Garda uniforms, not only at the Dublin Pride Parade, which would be held the weekend of the event, but also at Áras an Uachtaráin where we had been invited by the President, and at the conference itself in Dublin Castle. Symbolically, An Garda Síochána was not yet ready to have its uniform associated with gay and lesbian staff. On 30 June 2012, police officers from across Europe and beyond marched in the Dublin Pride Parade in a wide array of police uniforms. The Garda contingent could not be seen. An opportunity to reach out to a large, marginalised community in Ireland was lost. One newspaper reported that the members of An Garda Síochána mixing with the crowd looked like ushers in their non-Garda-branded polo shirts. Despite this, the conference was a great success. It forced a cultural examination in an organisation that had not yet been subject to intrusive oversight. However, the personal damage done to the members who put themselves on the line was significant.

G-Force went through a rocky period after 2012. Ireland had grown up a little and the work environment changed with it. A new generation of gay and lesbian Gardaí could go to work, do their job, go home, and suffer little, if any, homophobia in the process. The central team who had fought for years to improve things were more than a little tired, though, and a lack of trust made working with the organisation difficult.

G-Force did make great strides working independently. We provided community policing services to LGBT people. We provided comprehensive training programmes to members of An Garda Síochána, free of charge. And we developed hate-crime training materials first with University College Dublin and later with the Council of Europe. We also built relationships with LGBT staff in other organisations and became leaders in the employee resource group space, most notably with the Irish Prison Service. In 2018, human resources (HR) sections across Government departments started launching LGBT employee networks. It was well over a decade since a group of brave (or slightly mad) young Gardaí and Sergeants had challenged culture and supported each other in what was an environment where survival meant secrecy. We were well ahead of the pack.

A MORE POSITIVE SPACE

In 2019, under the leadership of Commissioner Harris, a large contingent of Gardaí in uniform and Garda staff took part in the Pride Parade for the first time. After such strong

Above left: International police officers marching in the Dublin Pride Parade, 2019.
Above right: Watching the Dublin Pride Parade, 2019.

opposition to our efforts in 2012, it was bittersweet, but it was progress. An Garda Síochána had moved into a more positive space. It was a hugely emotional day for many of us who had struggled for so long, but that is often how change comes. One day, things are simply different – fortunately in this case, better.

Despite this, there are still many people in hiding today, people who struggle to be authentic in the place they spend significant amounts of their lives. As Commissioner Harris has said, An Garda Síochána needs to be more representative of the people it serves.

Visible difference in an increasingly polarised world will make being the face of diversity in An Garda Síochána testing. In the mid-noughties a group of young Gardaí and Sergeants fought to improve the internal working environment and reached out to vulnerable minority communities. It was a daunting task. It should never have had to happen that way.

The Garda LGBT network started a conversation some time ago on building a respectful work environment. The next hundred years will require a significant evolution of this conversation. It has never been so important to be respectful of each other, to listen to and to understand different perspectives. Our legitimacy in a modern Ireland depends on it.

CHAPTER 32

THE FIRST FEMALE COMMISSIONER

Nóirín O'Sullivan

Although I wanted to be a vet and travel the world, when I left school, my first job was in a vegetable shop in Ballymun. From there, I had several different jobs, all of which I loved but none of which was exciting to me. One day, a pal of mine was looking for moral support in going to Coolock Garda Station to apply to join An Garda Síochána. I went along as a favour but also out of curiosity. The Sergeant we met encouraged me to apply, and in June 1981, I went into Templemore as the 219th woman. Six months later, ten days after my twenty-first birthday, I arrived at Store Street along with three classmates, and was given the shoulder number 109C. Three days later, I had my first court appearance with a prisoner in District Court Number 4.

MY INTRODUCTION TO POLICING

No amount of training could prepare you for the 'C' District – a bustling shopping and business district by day, the docks with ferries and container traffic constantly coming and going, big match days, protests, parades, and huge throughputs of people; communities striving to survive in the face of high levels of unemployment, social deprivation, and everyday challenges.

'Banners' (Ban Gardaí) were still a curiosity in 1981. We wore skirts and Cuban heels and were conditioned to work different tours of duty, with different mess facilities. We dealt primarily with women and children and provided administrative support. Having pushed to go on a 'regular unit', I was assigned to Unit 'A', where I met my husband, Jim McGowan. The marriage ban had been lifted only a few years earlier, so a married operational woman – and in due course one with children – was a rarity. My three sons were born in the early days of my career, and I could not have continued my operational career without significant sacrifices being made by my parents, my husband and my children who encouraged me and supported me all the way.

On the beat, it was clear that heroin was taking a grip. Injecting and sharing of needles were commonplace, as were HIV/AIDS and lethal overdoses devastating communities and families. A network of street dealers and mini-fortresses was emerging, and new role models were setting themselves up, with easier money to be made from drugs than from traditional crime. An Garda Síochána had to respond quickly and come up with a new approach. I was one of six Gardaí handpicked to act as mock drug dealers/addicts, infiltrating the drug gangs and spearheading the first undercover unit in An Garda Síochána. (See also Chapter 23: The War on Drugs.)

Over the next two decades, I worked at the coalface in the fight against organised crime, becoming the first woman to serve at all five ranks in Detective Branch, up to Detective Superintendent in the Drug Squad and the Garda National Drugs Unit, and as Detective Chief Superintendent in the Garda Technical Bureau. As the Irish organised crime world became more transnational, profitable, dangerous and ruthless, the Garda response adapted, and I was at the forefront of forging European and international law-enforcement co-operation and efforts to combat organised crime, leading and participating in several international operations and operational fora.

PATH TO PROMOTION

Having been advised that if I wanted to be considered for promotion, I would need some academic qualifications, I successfully completed the first BA degree in police management, when I was allocated to the Garda College in 2000, as Superintendent in charge of specialist training. I went on to complete the first Advanced Leadership Programme and an MBS at the Smurfit School of Business. I was then selected by the Federal Bureau of Investigation (FBI) to complete their most senior executive leadership programme at the National Executive Institute in Quantico. My education allowed me to expand my network and develop external partnerships, including with the Garda Inspectorate and the Garda Síochána Ombudsman Commission (GSOC), to try to create more openness and introduce new thinking and fresh ideas to the organisation.

This was particularly relevant in my roles in Human Resource Management (HRM), where I was able to support new structures and initiatives to create greater inclusivity for civilian colleagues, acceptance of changing family structures, and recognition for LGBTI (Lesbian, Gay, Bisexual, Transgender and Intersex) colleagues. I was also able to put a renewed focus on dignity in the workplace and the development of the welfare service, including the introduction of counselling services for members. In 2007, I was the second woman to be appointed Assistant Commissioner, and I served in the Western Region and HRM.

In 2009, I was the first woman to be appointed as Assistant Commissioner Crime and Security, taking the lead for national security and intelligence-led operations to disrupt and suppress threats from domestic and international terrorism and organised crime. A key focus was on real-time sharing of information and intelligence with international partners, and building trusted partnerships. Participating in international law-enforcement and security fora, I was reminded how few women were in leadership and decision-making roles in the law-enforcement and security arenas.

Nóirín O'Sullivan became the first female Commissioner of An Garda Síochána in November 2014.

In 2011, I successfully competed for the position of Deputy Commissioner and became the first woman in the role. This was an exciting opportunity to step into a strategic command role and take leadership on all national policing and security operations. Two of the most high-profile and challenging events were the back-to-back visits of Queen Elizabeth II and President Barack Obama. In addition, I pioneered an intelligence-led approach to tackle volume crime and strengthened the Garda Analysis Service so it could better contribute to serious and organised crime investigations. I also spearheaded training initiatives for members of An Garda Síochána to upskill and professionalise approaches to crime investigation.

In March 2014, I was appointed acting Commissioner on an interim basis and found myself, in a 'caretaker' capacity, at the helm of an organisation that was punch drunk and reeling from years of controversy and crisis. A decision was made by the Government to hold an international open competition to fill the role on a permanent basis for the first time. I applied. Following a rigorous interview process and series of psychometric testing, I beat off the national and international competition. In November 2014, I was appointed as the twentieth Commissioner of An Garda Síochána – the first woman to hold the role in the 92-year history of the service. It was a proud moment and a significant first that enabled me to tackle some of the deep-rooted cultural and structural reforms that were needed.

ACHIEVEMENTS AS COMMISSIONER

I went on to lead the biggest reform programme in the history of An Garda Síochána, which took the lessons of the past and the recommendations of the Garda Inspectorate and GSOC since their inception in 2005, to develop the Modernisation and Renewal Programme (later subsumed into the Commission on the Future of Policing), which focused on strengthening the organisation and providing greater development opportunities and supports for our people to do their job, including investment in information and communications technology (ICT) and transport. I negotiated and secured Government commitment and significant investment to support the programme, including increased recruiting of Garda and civilian staff to increase the strength of the organisation significantly to 21,000.

Through the establishment of the Economic Crime Bureau to tackle white-collar and cybercrime, I restructured the organisation to be agile and responsive to more sophisticated crimes. To respond to increases in organised crime, I expanded the Armed Support Units and established the Strategic and Tactical Operational Command Unit (STOC) and the Drugs and Organised Crime Bureau (DOCB). Working with non-governmental organisation (NGOs) and victim-support groups to put victims at the heart of the Garda service, I established Victims Service Offices in every Garda division and established the Garda Protective Services Bureau to support the most vulnerable victims.

Placing an emphasis on valuing our people, I encouraged an environment of 'commitment v. compliance', where staff would be listened to and valued for their input; structures were put in place to support those who wished to speak up, including engagement with Transparency Ireland, and 24/7 counselling services were put in place to support members.

After my retirement, I was invited to compete for the position of United Nations Assistant Secretary General with responsibility for Safety and Security. I was successful and relocated to New York, serving with the UN at one of the highest ranks achieved by an Irish citizen. It was a fascinating opportunity to contribute at the highest levels on the global stage, especially at a time of heightened geopolitical tensions and a push-back against multilateralism, not to mention the backdrop of a global pandemic. I have now relocated home to Ireland, turning the page on the next career chapter.

I was not always lucky. Sometimes I was seriously unlucky. But I learned resilience and realised that the challenges I faced provide case-study material for those who follow. With luck, the next female Commissioner will have some of the problems ironed out before she starts. She will need to understand that doing the best you can do, no matter what the opposition, delivers huge pride and allows you to survive and thrive – even through the bad times that happen in every career.

CHAPTER 33

CYBERCRIME

Garda Stephen Moore interviews Chief Superintendent Paul Cleary

For the first hundred years of the existence of An Garda Síochána, our organisation has in the main kept people safe by investigating traditional crimes, but as we move into the next hundred years of policing, the crime landscape is changing with the increased digitisation of society. Criminals are on the lookout all the time and are coming up with more innovative ways to make money, to steal data or to cause disruption. Cybercrime, especially over the last 18 months, spurred on by the consequences of a global pandemic, has risen significantly, and I don't see it slowing down…. Cybercrime in all its manifestations is going to be a very significant part for us as law-enforcement officers; we have to ensure that we have the capacity and the capabilities to keep people safe online. We also need to be able to investigate those people who are responsible for cybercrime.

Those are the words of Detective Chief Superintendent Paul Cleary, Head of the Garda National Cyber Crime Bureau (GNCCB), with whom I discussed the rise in cybercrime both

Detective Chief Superintendent Paul Cleary, Head of the Garda National Cyber Crime Bureau.

in Ireland and internationally. A native of Ronanstown in west Dublin, Cleary has 29 years of policing experience. Head of the Garda National Cyber Crime Bureau (GNCCB) since July 2020, he also has responsibility for two other Organised and Serious Crime (OSC) Bureaus – the Garda National Technical Bureau, and the Garda Operational Support Services.

Cleary has always been involved in investigations, but the area of cybercrime was almost new to him on his arrival at GNCCB. He continues:

> My eyes were opened. I can now see that there is a digital footprint in almost all headline crimes. Whether it be in the planning, preparation, execution, or the cover up – with all headline crimes, there is potential digital evidence. An example would be if a stabbing occurred at a public order incident – you can be sure that somebody recorded something on a phone and that it will appear on social media.

It is estimated that cybercrimes cost $6 trillion in losses to the worldwide economy in 2021, but the projected loses for 2025 rise significantly to $10 trillion. Cleary believes that everyone will be a victim of an attack at some point, and that the best prevention is being prepared.

Cleary's teams provide top-tier digital forensics for investigations. They seize digital devices and extract from them what they believe may be required for the evidential threshold. They prepare evidence packs for individual investigators; they provide very detailed statements of evidence, and expert testimony in court. Cleary explains how this work has increased in recent years:

A new state-of-the-art decryption suite allows the bureau to stay up to speed.

The work we do is very resource intensive, and this is growing by the week. In past years, maybe one or two devices would be associated with a case, but today you could have anything like forty or fifty devices per case.

Cybercrime can be separated into two components: cyber-enabled crime and cyber-dependent crime. Cyber-enabled crime is traditional crime, such as theft, harassment, child exploitation or fraud. Such crimes can be committed without a computer but are enabled by a computer in certain circumstances. Cyber-dependent crime includes hacking, ransomware, DDoS (distributed denial of service, i.e. a malicious attempt to disrupt the usual traffic of the targeted service, server or network) attacks and malware.

While cyber-enabled crime is generally investigated by colleagues across An Garda Síochána, the GNCCB is entrusted with digital forensic examination of computer media seized as part of investigations, including phones, laptops, desktop computers, SD cards, memory sticks and hard drives.

Meanwhile, cyber-dependent crime falls under the GNCCB's proactive investigations, and different sections within the Bureau ensure that it has the capacity and capability to investigate all types of cybercrime. According to Cleary:

> This is where we as a bureau get to be proactive; as these crimes can only be committed by using computers, we are the bureau tasked with investigating these crimes for the organisation. A very important part of our ability to investigate these crimes revolves around stakeholders both internally with the ICT (information and communications technology) and externally with private industry and reputable bodies who represent the tech industry. We also work very closely with UCD (University College Dublin) on an academic front. They provide training programmes that are tailored to our needs, and the needs of top-tier cyber law-enforcement investigators around the world.

The Garda National Cyber Crime Bureau

The GNCCB comprises two top-tier digital forensics units known as Computer Forensics 1 (CFE1) and Computer Forensics 2 (CFE2); the Cybercrime Investigations Unit; the Cyber Intelligence Unit; the Cyber Security Unit; and the Cyber Safety Unit

In addition, four satellite GNCCB hubs have been established, in Galway, Cork, Mullingar, and Wexford. As part of its expansion, in conjunction with its partners in UCD, the GNCCB has trained almost 200 digital first responders across every district in the country. Whereas the GNCCB and its satellite hubs provide top-tier digital forensics, the digital first responders are trained to assess, triage, and preserve evidence on devices that they examine. Issued with specialist equipment, they are attached to district detective units around the country. Cleary explains:

> We have them trained to a level at which they can be brought on searches by detectives. If they come across devices, they can have a look and analyse it to determine whether it contains data of evidential value. They are a very important component of the GNCCB's expansion plan.

An Garda Síochána is currently investing resources in the cybercrime area. Cleary elaborates:

> For the first time in July 2020 a Detective Chief Superintendent was allocated to head this bureau, and it was made into a bureau in its own right. That was a significant step because it gave cybercrime the recognition it deserves, and it was certainly an indication of how serious the Commissioner and the Garda organisation view it.

RANSOMWARE ATTACKS

In discussing the 2021 ransomware attack on the Health Service Executive (HSE), Cleary maintains that the response was good:

> The NCSC (National Cyber Security Centre) took the lead; they pulled together all the relevant stakeholders. Their priority was to restore the HSE systems safely, limiting the damage. Once that was complete, we moved in and began our investigation. Our job is to work with the criminal justice system. We have a different agenda but we [different agencies] all work together well. There were a lot of lessons learned through this attack that made us more prepared in the future…. There was some level of preparedness there already … it was great to be able to demonstrate how we can immediately come together to act and make tangible progress.

Despite the challenges, including pursuing cybercriminals across multiple borders, Cleary believes that there is a realistic prospect of justice being served:

> We always have to be optimistic because – yes – while it does present challenges, I know from my experience that criminals will always make mistakes somewhere along the line, and we will always be there to capitalise on those mistakes. We are collaborating with INTERPOL and EUROPOL on a concerted effort to use our combined law-enforcement skills and resources to mutually beneficial aims. If you consider how we are already doing this with drug trafficking and importation and human trafficking investigations, you will see the same standard being applied to cybercrime investigations as is assigned to those other investigations. Yes, it is

difficult. Yes, there are some areas of the world which are not as receptive to our inquiries as others. However, we keep going.

In response to a question regarding what might be in store for these cybercriminals when they are tracked down, Cleary says:

> Sanctions do not always come in the form of putting handcuffs on someone. There are a number of alternatives … I am cautiously optimistic that we will see attribution and sanction against those involved in these cybercriminal gangs.

CHILD SEXUAL ABUSE MATERIAL

The Detective Chief Superintendent is quick to praise the staff working at the bureau:

> I want my team to know I value them, and I want them to feel supported. The type of work that is done by the bureau – in particular, with child sexual abuse material – is unique in the area of policing. You need very strong public service values, and you need to show great resilience all day, every day whilst doing your job.

Child sexual abuse material makes up the majority of digital forensics work, today. It is a job within An Garda Síochána that would not suit everybody. Cleary continues:

> The work can be emotionally and psychologically demanding. The welfare of my staff is my top priority, with enhanced counselling and 24-hour support services available to all. Staff in the bureau genuinely want to protect the vulnerable and target those committing these hideous crimes.

CONCLUSION

Cybercrime is a developing story. As the next century of policing begins for An Garda Síochána, it is imperative that we stay ahead of the criminals. A new state-of-the-art decryption suite allows the bureau to stay up to speed, and to move to the top-tier of digital forensic examinations worldwide.

CHAPTER 34

— GARDA STAFF —

Andrew McLindon

From the start of An Garda Síochána's existence the need for civilian personnel to provide expertise in the running of the new police service was recognised. In 1923, among the senior management team based in Garda HQ were a C. Monks, who was in charge of Finance, a Chief and Assistant Chief Surgeon, and the Secretary to the Commissioner. This was followed by the appointment of two Assistant Secretaries from the Department of Justice as Commissioners successively from 1938 to 1965 – Michael Kinnane and Daniel Costigan respectively. However, it would be over forty years before civil servants occupied any other senior positions, and civil servant numbers remained low for decades.

The greater use of civil servants began in the 1970s. At that time, there were approximately 300 civil servants working in An Garda Síochána. In the 1980s, this had grown slightly to about 400, and by the early 1990s, it was around 700. Of course, not all civilian personnel employed in An Garda Síochána were civil servants. For example, in 1992, there were also 168 traffic wardens; 220 tradesmen, labourers, gardeners, boilermen, storemen and cleaners; as well as 565 part-time cleaners.

CHANGES IN THE TWENTY-FIRST CENTURY

Despite many external and internal reports over the decades recommending increased civilianisation, it was not until the late 2000s that there was significant change. At the time, there were no civilian managers in key senior posts.

In 2006, reports by the Garda Inspectorate and an advisory group to the Commissioner, chaired by Senator Maurice Hayes, recommended a new role of Chief Administrative Officer (CAO) at Deputy Commissioner level to oversee Finance, Legal, human resources (HR), information and communications technology (ICT), Housing, and Fleet, with additional senior civilian managers in charge of Legal, HR, ICT, and Communications. They also recommended the employment of civilian specialists in areas such as Analysis, Scenes of Crime,

Garda staff are an integral part of An Garda Síochána.

Finance, HR, ICT and Forensic Support. And, again, they cited the need for further civilianisation to release Gardaí to frontline duties. In addition, in October of that year, the Minister for Justice under the 2005 Garda Síochána Act transferred responsibility for all civilian staff from the Department of Justice to the Commissioner.

Changes to the senior management structure began to happen. The first CAO was appointed in 2007, and key positions started to be filled by personnel from inside and outside the civil service.

It has not always been an easy journey for Garda staff in the organisation. At times, they were seen as peripheral to the organisation's mission and more part of the civil service than of An Garda Síochána. However, this has changed in recent years. For example, in 2018, there was a change in terminology, with Garda civil servants now designated as Garda staff. In addition, eight members of the nineteen-strong Garda Senior Leadership Team are Garda staff responsible for areas such as Legal, ICT, Finance, Communications, Analysis, HR, Health and Wellness, and Strategy and Transformation.

By early 2022, there were 3,389 Garda staff involved in a range of activities to support operational policing, such as processing vetting applications; handling crime-reporting calls from Gardaí; dealing with fixed-charge penalty notices; developing and running IT systems to aid crime investigation; keeping Gardaí informed of the latest policing developments; supporting the mental and physical health of Gardaí; and providing analysis of crime trends.

This civilianisation over the last number of years has resulted in over 800 Gardaí returning to frontline duties, and Garda staff are due to take on more functions to release further Gardaí. It has taken a long time, but Garda staff are now central to the delivery of keeping people safe through the support provided to our operational colleagues.

CHAPTER 35

THE GARDA RESERVE

Garda Stephen Moore
Garda Reserves Sean O'Sullivan, Mick Kenneally and Ravinder Singh Oberoi

T he Garda Reserve consists of voluntary unpaid members, drawn from the community to assist the existing service. Although Garda Reserve members have limited Garda powers while on duty, they have become a very welcome addition to An Garda Síochána. They perform policing duties as determined by the Commissioner under the supervision of and accompanied by full-time members of An Garda Síochána.

The first intake of Garda Reserve members began training at the Garda College in Templemore on 30 September 2006. They became fully operational on 15 December and were assigned to Pearse Street and Store Street Stations in Dublin, Anglesea Street in Cork, Galway City and Sligo Town Stations.

For this chapter, I spoke with three members of the Garda Reserve – two based in Cork, and one in Dublin – to get their thoughts and insights into an area of policing that has become an integral part of our organisation. These are their stories.

SEAN O'SULLIVAN, 80570L

I joined the Garda Reserve for several reasons. Firstly, I wanted to be a role model for my children, my family, and friends; I firmly believe that you must give something back to society as you go through life, and I saw the Garda Reserve as the conduit for this. I also wanted to keep my family ties to An Garda Síochána; this was very important for me and for my family as my late grandfather was a Garda Sergeant. I saw the Garda Reserve as an ideal opportunity to continue this proud family tradition. My son Kian is now a full-time member with An Garda Síochána, and so our ties continue.

I joined on 14 April 2009, initially training in Anglesea Street Station in Cork, where I was attached to Unit D. After attestation, I continued to work with Unit 'D', working side by side with many fantastic people. I was regularly detailed for work on busy Friday and

Reserve Garda Sean O'Sullivan.

Saturday nights to support members. My duties involved beat patrol, CCTV monitoring and checkpoints. With many events on in the city, my other duties involved support at large crowd events such as St Patrick's Day parades, football matches and concerts – working right across the city.

When COVID-19 hit the country in March 2019, I was seconded to Community Engagement as a method of supporting vulnerable members of our community. I supported both the Togher Station and the Blackrock Station – where I am now based – as part of the Community Engagement team.

A highlight for me will always be representing the Garda Reserve from the Cork City Division at the 2016 Centenary Commemoration of the 1916 Rising in Dublin. I am grateful to Superintendent John Deasy for that terrific opportunity.

Experiences on the job can be very diverse. What I have learned is that every situation is different, everyone you meet has a story behind them, and everyone's story is different. You need to be a good listener with a good level of common sense. You need to be calm in your approach and make the call as you see it. It is important to have good social skills for interactions with people – this, along with a good sense of humour, goes a long way.

Being a Reserve Garda is a way of life. It absorbs you, and you get a kick out of achieving good results. We do it because we are dedicated and professional, and sometimes we are the only ones available to work with a full-time colleague. I would rather be there to help colleagues wrestle with drunk people who are fighting than leave them on their own. I would like to stop the car with the uninsured drink driver, who might otherwise end up killing someone on the roads. Being a Reserve Garda is a job like no other.

MICK KENNEALLY, 80020A

I joined in September 2006, having previously spent over twenty years serving with the Military Police in the Army Reserve as a Quartermaster Sergeant. I was in the first class of Reserves to enter Templemore. Following my training, I was attested with thirty-six other colleagues on 15 December 2006.

Having been assigned to Unit 'D' in Anglesea Street, I worked mostly late shifts on Friday and Saturday nights, providing additional support to the unit at weekends. My duties were varied and included beat patrol, MIT (Mandatory Intoxicant Testing) checkpoints and station duties, such as monitoring CCTV from the main control room. I was also on duty at the visit of Queen Elizabeth II, in addition to various concerts, and large sporting events.

At the outbreak of the COVID-19 pandemic, I was assigned to the Community Engagement team, to help in supporting local communities and vulnerable people within the Cork city area; I am still performing my duties with the team there.

Reserve Garda Mick Kenneally.

Over the years, Reserve Gardaí in Cork have received great support from our liaison Inspectors, especially in relation to integration within An Garda Síochána. This support has been extremely beneficial and has helped to streamline the whole process.

Through experience I have learned that each incident Gardaí encounter is different, and how each incident is handled can also be vastly different. However, the professionalism and attention to detail must always be the same. One word can change a very positive outcome into a not-so-positive one. Being a good listener and using common sense are key in most situations. It is critical that each person is treated with dignity and respect.

I have learned a huge amount during my time working as a Reserve Garda. Whilst dealing with the public, I have met some lovely people, and occasionally I have met the other kind as well. I take pride in being a Reserve Garda and a member of An Garda Síochána. I do it because I enjoy it: I enjoy working alongside my colleagues; I enjoy helping vulnerable people. I take pride in helping people who are in distress and who are in need, and I hope to continue doing so for some time to come.

RAVINDER SINGH OBEROI, 80060M

As a young Sikh from India, I came to Ireland in 1997, working in the IT industry. There were not many Sikhs in Ireland at the time, and I was asked about my turban everywhere I went. As people started to become aware of what the turban represented, I felt more at home here. However, after the tragedy of 9/11, a different face was brought out. Sikhs were misidentified as Muslims, and we started to receive a lot of attention in a bad way. This brought on a new set of challenges for Sikhs. We now had to elevate and respond – rather than react – to people's ignorance.

When the position of Reserve Gardaí was opened, I saw a great opportunity to accomplish one of my dreams, as well as to serve the community and bring about acceptance of the turban. I had always wanted to serve in the armed forces and had once imagined myself serving in the Indian defence forces. I strongly believed that Sikhs in Garda uniforms would send a powerful message that An Garda Síochána is committed to the idea of unity through diversity.

In November 2006, I applied to become a Garda Reserve, and was successful in my application. Being the first Sikh ever to apply, I didn't know if my turban would become an issue. In 2007, having successfully completed three of the five phases of my training, I was provided with my uniform, without the hat, but with a badge for my turban. However, to my disappointment, in July 2007, it was decided not to accept my turban as part of the uniform. It was at this point that I realised I needed to escalate matters further and fight for my right to wear the turban. We tried many avenues and brought the matter to the High Court, using the Equality Tribunal. Although the rejections kept coming, I did not lose hope, as I had the support of my family and community, and I had my faith. Finally, in April 2019, Garda Commissioner Drew Harris announced the inclusion of both the turban and the hijab in the uniform of the service. This was a landmark decision.

Those who don't know the importance of the turban for a Sikh might ask why someone would fight so hard for an article of clothing. However, for a Sikh, the turban is equivalent to a crown. Historically in India, only kings wore turbans. As a symbol of equality, our gurus gave us all turbans to wear. This also helps us to stand out in a crowd so that we can be identified and approached for help. A practising Sikh cannot remove his turban in public, and it is considered a grave insult to touch or forcefully remove a Sikh's turban – the turban is at the core of our identity. I fought for it not only for myself but for all Sikhs who may want to join the service. The colour, fabric and design of the turban are left to the individual and can be adapted based on the task at hand.

The inclusion of Sikhs in An Garda Síochána was announced in April 2019. However, it took over a year before I could complete my training and be on the streets of Ireland as a serving Reserve Garda. In the summer of 2020, 13 years after originally completing my training, I commenced my training once more.

From this point, it was all very positive; even the COVID-19 cloud did not affect it. Sergeant Gerard McGrath (now retired) spent more than sixty hours providing the classroom training over a couple of months at Blanchardstown Garda Station, including PULSE (Police Using Leading Systems Effectively) and FCPN (fixed-charge penalty and notice) training at Kevin Street. In parallel with Sergeant McGrath, we worked in coming up with the colour and fabric of the Garda turban, which was to match the Garda uniform. I was then assigned with Sergeant (now Inspector) Ian Lambe with the Community Garda Unit at Kevin Street to complete my 40 hours of operational training. It was the start of the journey; the Dublin streets for the first time saw a Sikh, with a turban as part of the Garda uniform. Following this, there were a couple of short visits to Templemore to complete my training. Finally, on 19 January 2021, I was sworn in as a member of the Garda Reserve of An Garda Síochána. With COVID-19 restrictions, it was a very solemn and private affair, but history had been written, and a more diverse and inclusive police service was the result.

For my first assignment I was posted and assigned to Unit 'A', Pearse Street Garda Station. I was paired with Sergeant Billy Quinlan who was very supportive and welcoming, as were all the other members at the station. I got to see a different side of Dublin and how Gardaí deal with the public to make it a safer place. My experience overall has been very positive and pleasant. The public has welcomed me, and I have often been stopped by people asking to take pictures of me. I also distinctly remember the day I was helping at an anti-COVID-19 restrictions protest on Grafton Street when trouble erupted. People often forget that at the end of the day, Gardaí are also people behind the uniform; fortunately, order was restored quickly before things got too out of hand.

Public acceptance and respect for the Garda uniform – whether or not a turban forms part of it – have always been there, and I am grateful to be able to experience it. I am so glad to be part of the frontline workers of the community and to support them in making our city and country streets safer. I look forward to continuing in this role over the years and to more challenging moments that will surely come my way as part of my role as a member of the Garda Reserve.

Reserve Garda Ravinder Singh Oberoi.

CHAPTER 36

POLICING A PANDEMIC

Retired Deputy Commissioner John Twomey
Detective Sergeant Brendan Tighe

POLICING A PANDEMIC

Retired Deputy Commissioner John Twomey

This meeting with Government ministers and senior civil servants was different. The room was quieter than usual and there was an eerie feeling amid the uncertainty of what was to come. We all knew about what was going on in China, and we had read that there was a concern of it spreading – but what had this really got to do with us?

The meeting started and all was about to change. Change like we had never experienced before. We knew what the word 'pandemic' meant, but what did it mean from a practical perspective and what would we, in An Garda Síochána, have to do?

Commissioner Drew Harris and I were told that the country was going into lockdown. A few short minutes later, it became clear that An Garda Síochána would have a critical role in community engagement, ensuring a high-visibility presence in every community in the country. We would be required to assist the elderly and vulnerable and to respond to various demands made of us. The challenge was in how we were going to do that and how we were going to do it straightaway. There was no lead-in time, no time to prepare – this was a pandemic and action was needed now. As Commissioner Harris and I left the room, we asked ourselves what we needed to do and how we would achieve it.

Despite the unprecedented nature of the situation, I was clear in my mind that, in the true traditions of An Garda Síochána, we would respond to every request and demand made in the best interests of the State and its people. There was no doubt that we would need to be highly visible in every community to provide reassurance to a public that would have significant worries and concerns following the lockdown announcement.

If ever we needed confirmation that An Garda Síochána is a community-based policing service, our response to the pandemic confirmed that fact quite clearly. It was a great lesson to our younger Gardaí in what is meant when we say that we are a community-based policing and security service.

Later that evening, a meeting was held in Garda Headquarters with the Garda Senior Management Team and the initial plan was agreed. Some critical changes would be required within the next 24 to 48 hours. In general, it was agreed that policing of the pandemic would be our sole strategic imperative for the immediate future and the entire focus of all resources would be on 'policing the pandemic'. The four Es would be our key principles: 'Engage, Explain, Encourage, Enforce'.

It was agreed that the Garda College would have to close, and the staff be re-deployed, while an emergency roster was introduced to increase significantly the policing hours available. In tandem, all Gardaí were re-deployed to operational units. While the need to be 'agile' was considered critical, our mobility was also essential, and we needed to obtain suitable transport as a matter of urgency.

Equally, support staff would now work from home and our IT section was tasked with making this happen. We would have to utilise our entire estate to try to avoid cross-contamination across different units.

A key concern for the Senior Management Team in providing our policing response was to ensure organisational resilience and protection of our own people. The decision to use our entire estate was part of this, as was the need to purchase large quantities of protective equipment at short notice.

Communication was critical, and timely and accurate information would be required both internally and externally. The Director of Communications was tasked with preparing

Garda Commissioner Drew Harris announces measures to respond to the COVID-19 pandemic, 13 March 2020.

There are many examples of great community work by Gardaí who helped those most in need. Here a local Garda shops for someone cocooned at home.

a communications strategy as a matter of priority. To support this, a COVID Coordination Centre was opened in Garda HQ and the Assistant Commissioner with responsibility for Security and Intelligence was tasked with developing and overseeing this operation.

A meeting was held with the Garda Associations the following morning. Their overwhelming response was that they would do whatever they could to help. A partnership-type approach was agreed, with a promise that all issues arising could and would be addressed swiftly.

This 'can do, will do' attitude ensured that the organisation responded as positively as it did. Garda personnel reached out all over the country to the elderly and the vulnerable and assisted them in whatever way necessary or possible. There are many examples of great community work by Gardaí who helped those most in need and provided comfort and assurance when needed. That visible presence was so critical. For the many who were cocooning, local Gardaí did their shopping, collected their pension, or just stopped for a very valued socially distanced chat.

I think it is fair to say that we did what we said we would do.

SPECIFIC OPERATIONS

Several specific operations were introduced to help support the vulnerable and to ensure public compliance with health guidelines and regulations. Again, these were all implemented based on our tradition of policing by consent.

With people largely restricted to their homes, we knew that there would be an increase in domestic abuse. **Operation Faoiseamh** was launched to provide enhanced proactive support and protection to victims of domestic abuse. Designed to supplement ongoing Garda activity

Launched in April 2020, Operation Fanacht involved large-scale checkpoints on main routes and thousands of mobile checkpoints on secondary routes.

on domestic abuse, it resulted in thousands of contacts being made with victims of domestic abuse and many charges against perpetrators.

Operation Fanacht commenced in April and was rolled out on several occasions throughout 2020 in support of public health guidelines and regulations relating to travel restrictions. It involved large-scale checkpoints on main routes and thousands of mobile checkpoints on secondary routes.

Operation Navigation commenced in July 2020 to ensure that licensed premises were in compliance with public health regulations.

Operation Treoraím commenced in October 2020, with members of An Garda Síochána conducting checks on retail premises across the country to ensure compliance with public health regulations. The vast majority of retail premises were compliant or came into compliance when requested to do so.

CONCLUSION

The Irish people needed a visible presence to provide comfort and assurance. I believe that An Garda Síochána fulfilled that role while also ensuring that normal policing and security duties continued.

A number of independent public surveys showed high levels of satisfaction with how An Garda Síochána was operating during the COVID-19 pandemic. According to one, An Garda Síochána ranked second, only behind the HSE, in organisations

Deputy Commissioner John Twomey.

leading and making a positive contribution in response to the crisis. Meanwhile, the Policing Authority said that the policing response to COVID-19 was characterised for many by greater Garda visibility, engagement and proactivity within communities.

Internally, there was considerable upheaval regarding work practices. Remote working was introduced without delay and support staff continued to provide the necessary back-up to operational policing. Our Procurement Section worked tirelessly to ensure that staff had the necessary equipment to go about their work safely. Our human resources (HR) team ensured that the necessary policies and procedures were in place to maintain staffing. The Vetting Bureau faced increased demands from the HSE and were not found wanting. Our Legal Department issued numerous updates, often at very short notice, to ensure that staff were aware of the latest regulations – a considerable challenge in the face of ever-changing rules. The Communications team kept the public and our own personnel regularly informed of the work we were doing to help protect them, and the COVID-19 Centre fielded a huge volume of calls and e-mails 24/7 to help our people to navigate the rapidly changing environment in a safe manner.

It was a team effort and one of which we can be extremely proud.

Life in Ireland grew quiet during lockdown. Here, a lone Garda patrols the normally bustling streets of Dublin's Temple Bar.

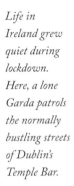

A POLICEMAN'S VIEW

Sergeant Brendan Tighe

At first it seemed to be a Chinese issue – a distant disease that would probably never affect us. But as the situation progressed, the world as we knew it came to a halt. Never in our lives had we seen such a dramatic change in our society – our lives on pause, our previously bustling Irish streets empty, roads eerily lonely and our homes empty of the bustle of visitors. Life in Ireland grew quiet, and we lived within a short radius; holidays abroad were dreams for the future and there was nothing on the horizon, only hope.

In these historic and unprecedented times, we underwent one of our era's most significant and dramatic transformations. The nuclear threat that had been our parents' biggest enemy was replaced by microorganisms that penetrated our elderly and vulnerable and sent them hurtling towards their graves. We lived in a state of concern, fear and anticipation, learning every night at 6 p.m. how many precious lives had been lost to the devastating infection – in so many cases alone and without their loved ones around them.

We waited with bated breath for delivery of what we hoped would be lifesaving vaccines and the inoculation of our population. However, as the disease spread, so did its parameters, and variants of the deadly infection appeared, calling into question the efficacy of the vaccines that were soon being mass produced.

With all the despair and frustration, the pandemic taught us the importance of life and of being there for one another, even if it was just a quick phone call or checking in on someone. It taught us about the vulnerability of the elderly, their children trying to protect them by not visiting them. It was a strange time, too, when we embraced changes like working from home, children going to school in their pyjamas, business deals being done after beans and toast, workout videos replacing trips to the gym, and ordering more than just takeaways to the door. With local amenities becoming part of everyday life, the world seemed generally a quieter and safer place to be.

Our old normal had changed and our world had taken a leap forward into a new digital normal.

THE NEW NORMAL

These unprecedented times showed us the qualities of the emergency services and frontline workers – the people who braved danger and presented themselves at the frontline when huge efforts were being instituted to control the population's movements and to minimise the spread of the infection.

The country was dotted with COVID checkpoints and Gardaí had never had so much interaction with the public. Engaging locally as community police offers, we illustrated our

A lockdown visit. By visiting the elderly and the vulnerable, Gardaí strengthened their already close bond with local communities.

skills of listening, talking, and asking questions. In doing so we not only obtained information but also built up a rapport with our local communities. By visiting the elderly, delivering groceries and medication, we reconnected with our clients, our communities, and with the people who really needed us when they were lonely, afraid, and isolated from their families and friends.

At the same time, Gardaí continued to engage with criminals and their everyday undertakings. The huge number of checkpoints acted as a deterrent and created problems for drug mules. Burglaries were significantly reduced as people stayed at home. More people were looking out their windows and reporting suspicious activity. However, while some criminal activity might have been reduced, online frauds and domestic violence increased.

PERSONAL TOLL ON GARDAÍ

An Garda Síochána's 'Jerusalema' video, which was produced by the Garda Office of Corporate Communications, has been viewed over 19 million times and gave people a much-needed lift during the COVID-19 lockdown period.

Many members of An Garda Síochána have underlying health conditions, many have elderly relatives living with them, and many grandchildren were being babysat by grandparents while their parents were at work. On every police officer's mind was the worry that they might bring home this deadly disease to their family. What car on the approach to a checkpoint had an asymptomatic driver at the wheel? What call would we be dispatched to next? What sudden death or suicide? Who was going to call into the station to make a complaint? Sometimes, COVID-19 attacked Garda stations in their entirety, effectively shutting down epicentres of communities.

The burden of responsibility weighed heavily on the shoulders of our boys and girls in blue who relentlessly and courageously engaged with the public on 12-hour shifts daily.

But throughout it all, in keeping with the 100-year ethos of An Garda Síochána, we continued to do our absolute best, taking pride in our uniform. This is the cost that police officers pay in their service of the State.

CHAPTER 37

— AN GARDA SÍOCHÁNA — A CHANGING FORCE

Conor Brady
Journalist, novelist and academic

P olice organisations, by their nature, are slow to embrace change. In most western societies, they reflect prevailing social values and expectations, and they tend to respond to changes in these after the event, rather than in anticipation. They embody the status quo. The late Deputy Commissioner T.J. O'Reilly often observed that in contrast to the military, there is probably no instance in history of a police force leading a revolution.

Nor are there many instances of police organisations initiating reforming change from within. When they do change, the process tends to be driven by outside influences – commissions of inquiry, judicial or political direction, media pressure or new social demands. But when pressures for change can no longer be resisted, police organisations often prove themselves pragmatic and adaptable. The history of An Garda Síochána offers not a few instances of this.

It can be difficult to describe to outsiders the service's somewhat unique role in this society. Most western countries have multiple layers of policing. The concept of a single, unitary policing system would seem bizarre to many mainland Europeans as well as to Americans. No less curious would be the notion that the Irish national police operates in parallel as the State's primary security and intelligence service.

SHAPING AN GARDA SÍOCHÁNA

The history of the State and, indeed, the earlier history of Irish policing, have shaped this unusual organisation. Today, An Garda Síochána has many fewer stations than on foundation, while motor transport has largely eliminated the foot patrol down the village or along the main street. Yet the service remains generally well-engaged with the community, as it has been from the days when the first recruits went out to their posts in 1922.

Some of this is attributable to its early and enlightened embracing of structured link-ages such as the original neighbourhood watch and local policing committees. But it is also grounded in the things that made for early success after foundation – sport, Irish culture, community movements and locally based social interaction. Before immigration in the 1990s impacted on the demographics, there was hardly an Irish family that had not had a relative or close friend in 'the Guards'.

This degree of police–community integration is not universal, even in countries with advanced and well-developed civic values. It requires nurturing because the country's ethnic minorities are still underrepresented in the service.

When the architects of the new Irish State decided, 100 years ago, that the Royal Irish Constabulary (RIC) was to be disbanded, they had to create a replacement. The approach to the task was hurried, clumsy and naïve. Building a new state out of the ruins of civil war required much improvisation. Departments of government were established and hastily staffed, even as the departing officials of the British administration were heading for London.

Myriad challenges presented themselves. Some may seem relatively trivial now. But they were of immense practical importance at the time. For example, the new state had no post-age stamps, so in order to prevent the collapse of the postal system, British stamps had to be franked with a 'Saorstát Éireann' mark.

Shaping a new police force was important but it was not at the very top of the ministers' priority list. They had a dirty war to win against determined opponents and they had to find funding for an impoverished state. The task of creating a new police force was mainly left to a committee of former members of the RIC and the Dublin Metropolitan Police (DMP) who had been surreptitiously working for Michael Collins. Unsurprisingly, the new police system proposed by this group was to be a mirror-image of the RIC in organisation and rank struc-ture. The nomenclature and the uniforms were to be changed. Otherwise, it was to be armed, organised, deployed and led from the Phoenix Park Depot by senior officers, appointed by central government.

But what must have appeared to the new government as simply another administrative challenge – albeit on a large scale – turned out to be anything but that. As civil conflict spread across the country, the newly recruited 'Civic Guard' mutinied, evicting Commissioner Michael Staines at gunpoint from the temporary depot at Kildare and emptying the armoury of its weapons and ammunition. The concept of the unarmed Garda Síochána, with Eoin O'Duffy as Commissioner, came into existence only after a hastily established 'commission of inquiry', comprising two senior civil servants, O'Sheil and McAuliffe, directed that the service be disarmed and disbanded, with hand-picked, loyal men being re-enrolled.

It was a remarkable turnaround from a potential disaster – an early lesson to the fledgling force that it could be required to adapt, perhaps dramatically, to change. In modern business parlance, it would have to 'pivot', to square up to changing realities, while hopefully adhering to the values and principles it proclaimed. It was at this stage that the ideology, if one may use the term, of the unarmed Garda Síochána, embedded in the community, began to form.

As Commissioner Staines departed the scene, he delivered the oft-quoted declaration that the members of the service would succeed 'not through force of arms or numbers' but on their 'moral authority as servants of the people'. It would be 'Irish in thought and action', O'Duffy insisted. It was to be presented as the guarantor and the servant of the new Irish democracy, enforcing Irish law on behalf of the people of Ireland. The 'guards' were to be the physical embodiment of the Irish state in every town and village.

Nothing would be as powerful a symbol of change as taking down the RIC's harp and crown from over the barracks doors – and replacing it with J.F. Maxwell's Celtic sunburst, the emblem of the new Civic Guard or An Garda Síochána, the 'Guardians of the Peace'.

REALISING THE IDEALS

These were profound ideas, succinctly expressed in stirring language, providing the moral bedrock upon which the new police force was to be established. The success of the unarmed Garda Síochána would promulgate the new state as stable, safe, law-abiding and well-run. It embodied the best civic values – what would today be called 'policing by consent'.

Commissioner O'Duffy and the Minister for Home Affairs, Kevin O'Higgins, proved themselves to be masters of public relations. Understanding the power of sport in winning respect and affection for his force. O'Duffy instituted 'Aonach an Gharda', an annual festival of field and track athletics, boxing, hammer, and javelin. The Gardaí would 'play their way into the hearts of the Irish people', he declared. He organised regular 'garden parties' around Aonach events, hosting receptions at the Depot at which Scott Medals would be presented, and invited guests would be regaled with stirring accounts of Garda successes around the country.

The 1922 mutiny, followed by disbandment and re-formation, was the first of many challenges that might be described as transformative of the Irish policing system. With the accession of Éamon de Valera's Fianna Fáil to power in 1932 and the emergence of the Blueshirt movement, An Garda Síochána faced another great test. Now they had to serve with loyalty and integrity those who had been their political enemies and detractors. Key leadership like O'Duffy and Special Branch chief David Neligan were removed, and the original membership was diluted through the recruitment of the so-called 'Broy Harriers', tough men who were loyal to de Valera, many of whom had fought in arms against the Treaty.

The forced integration of pro- and anti-treaty elements and O'Duffy's replacement as Commissioner by Eamon Broy were traumatic. Yet, by the time of the next great test – the outbreak of the Second World War and the declaration of a state of national emergency – these changes had served to make An Garda Síochána stronger and better suited to discharge both its civil policing and its security roles. The major threat to the State was from an Irish Republican Army (IRA) emboldened by German military successes and happy to throw in its lot with the Nazis if it meant defeat for Britain. The IRA and the Fianna Fáil Gardaí were essentially from the same political gene-pool. Thus, the quality of Special Branch intelligence was much higher than it would have been without the presence of the Broy Harriers. Under Fianna Fáil's appointee, Detective Superintendent Michael Gill, the Special Branch never failed to stay on top of the IRA threat right through to the end of the war.

The most problematic period for An Garda Síochána was yet to come, however. While the service adapted to political change in the 1930s and the myriad challenges of the Emergency, the reality was that no coherent processes of renewal were in hand to meet the future.

A NEED FOR CHANGE

In the 1950s, Ireland was impoverished. The economy was shrinking. The population was in decline. Investing in the police force, in a society almost free of crime, was not a priority. By now, most of the men who had joined An Garda Síochána in the early years were moving towards retirement. The officer corps was tired and worn out, mostly coming into their sixties. The force continued to operate under administrative systems and a disciplinary code that belonged to another era. Recruitment opened in 1955, initially at the Depot and later in Templemore. But educational standards were undemanding, and training was basic. Many of those advanced to promotional ranks had no formal preparation for these roles. Equipment was primitive by comparison with forces in the United Kingdom. Stations were dilapidated. Pay had fallen behind that of other state employees.

This was now an organisation advancing rapidly in decay. Two Commissioners, Michael Kinnane and Daniel Costigan, had been appointed from within the senior ranks of the Department of Justice, spanning the years from 1938 to 1965. They were competent men but the effect on the service's morale over time was incalculable. The grip of the Department of Justice tightened over every aspect of its operations. The civil servants expected total subservience from the Depot. It was widely accepted that promotion and preferment were dependent upon political patronage or connections through family, the GAA, county associations, and sometimes the Church.

An Garda Síochána was saved by the Conroy Commission (1967–69), which tentatively set the service on a pathway to modernisation, as a desperate political response to a series of ever-deepening crises within the service. The Conroy Commission was appalled by what it found. It urged nothing less than a radical reshaping of the relationship between the service and the Department of Justice, a complete overhaul of training, the establishment of a research-and-development unit, and the creation of a press relations office. Gardaí were now to be paid overtime, while selected members would be sent to university to study at the State's expense.

Not all of Conroy's recommendations were implemented. The Departments of Justice and Finance fought bitterly against reform. But a change dynamic had been initiated that would prove sufficient to enable the service to make a response to the tempest that struck in 1968–69. The onset of the Northern Ireland Troubles, the consequent series of security threats to the State, and the parallel emergence of organised and violent crime created the perfect storm. These combined challenges were no less daunting than those faced in the early years after foundation. This writer would argue that future historians will realise that the State owed its stability, if not, indeed, its very survival to the efforts and the dedication of the Gardaí of this period.

CRISES, REMEDIES AND REFORM

The decades since Conroy have witnessed a cycle of crises, remedies, and half-reforms, almost invariably driven by scandal or the revelation of systemic abuse, perhaps most seriously in Donegal in the 1980s and 1990s. Political manipulation and interference continued and not a few senior officers found their careers blasted. It was not until the passing of the Garda Síochána Acts, 2005 and 2015, that any serious attempts were undertaken by the political establishment to introduce the service to twenty-first century values of accountability, transparency, and independent oversight.

It goes without saying that An Garda Síochána of the 2020s is infinitely more effective than the poorly equipped, often poorly led and poorly trained organisation that was required to face up to the violent challenges of subversion and organised crime from the start of the 1970s. It functions now at extremely high levels of professionalism and integrity. Deservedly, it enjoys widespread public confidence and is consistently rated as among the most trusted institutions in the country.

It is important to acknowledge, nonetheless, the extraordinary personal sacrifices, dedication and courage displayed by so many in those earlier troubled years. It was these qualities, grounded in the experiences of earlier decades, that enabled the service to persevere and succeed.

It is also important to recognise that many of the evils that beset the service for decades have been measurably diminished. Promotion systems are more transparent. Improper political interference, always likely to remain a threat, has been greatly reduced. Favouritism in law enforcement and misuse of authority by ill-motivated members are now less likely, thanks to improved data systems. The service has learned to adapt to independent oversight by the Garda Síochána Ombudsman Commission and to external scrutiny by the Policing Authority. The Garda Inspectorate has been an important 'friendly critic' of the service's operating procedures. The Commissioner is now the accounting officer for the service. Considerable progress has been made towards civilianisation. The Department of Justice itself has undergone transformation for the better.

The extent to which the full benefits of these reforms will endure is unclear. The recommendations of the Commission on the Future of Policing have at least the potential of significantly undermining them. Many of the 2005–15 reforms were designed to give the appearance of independent oversight and accountability while leaving ultimate power in the hands of the political powers that be and of the civil servants.

FUTURE ROLE IN SOCIETY

The next great test for An Garda Síochána will probably come if there is a changed political landscape with the advent of a radical left-wing government. It must be hoped that the lessons of 1922 and 1932 will guide the thinking of those who find themselves in positions of political authority at that point. The discharging of its role as Guardians of the Peace by generations of An Garda Síochána is a long story. And it is far from over.

The views expressed by the author are his own.

CHAPTER 38

GUARDIANS OF THE PEACE – AN ASSESSMENT

Myles Dungan
Writer, Historian and Broadcaster

T he building was already burning and the crowd below the steps had begun to pull back as the small cohort of Gardaí drew their batons and advanced. As the beautiful Georgian building began to succumb to the flames, the Gardaí were being subjected to a barrage of abuse and a few random missiles. You could sense that each of the men in the blue uniforms was debating with himself whether a baton charge would be necessary. They were waiting for the order. Thankfully it never came.

At least that is how I remember the burning of the British Embassy in February 1972, a few days after the atrocity of Bloody Sunday in Derry. I was a first-year student at University College Dublin, so I wasn't exactly unaccustomed to protest marches. I had come along with my older brother – for all I know, it was his first. We stood at the rear of the crowd with our backs to the Merrion Square railings and watched as a few nimble activists climbed up to one of the balconies of the Embassy, broke windows, and tossed in a couple of petrol bombs. No fire engine was going to get close enough to save the burning building. The crowd cheered raucously as the Embassy caught fire. I have no doubt that I did, too. Those were very different times. Fourteen innocent Irishmen, on a protest march not unlike this one, had been gunned down in Derry by British paratroopers. To my teenage way of thinking, there had to be some response. This would do nicely.

However, had it not been for the restraint of the Gardaí on duty that night, I would probe ably not be writing this piece. Just as the Gardaí advanced, the Merrion Square railings gave way, and my brother and I toppled backwards. At least half a dozen people fell on top of me, and I found myself at the bottom of a life-threatening crush. Thoughts of the Ibrox disaster the previous year – where sixty-six Rangers fans were crushed to death after an Old Firm clash with Celtic – flashed through my mind. Probably because a calm and experienced police Sergeant at the front could see the potential result of a baton charge, nothing happened. The Gardaí stood, taking the abuse and the odd missile, until the crowd – our thirst for revenge satisfied – got bored and began to disperse. I had never been happier and more relieved to disperse in my life. I forgave all the official reprimands for cycling on an unlit bicycle.

That's the end of the declaration of interest. But it says something about policing in the Republic of Ireland, about the capacity for restraint of our largely unarmed police service. Policing is often as much about what you don't do as it is about your active response to a hazardous situation.

Having lived in the USA a lot in recent years, I know parts of northern California as well as I do much of Dublin (I must confess to being a culchie Meathman). Whenever I see a Garda or a Garda car, I tend to do an immediate inventory. Am I jaywalking? Speeding? Engaging in anti-social behaviour (though at my time of life that would amount to something like kicking leaves into the gutter). In California, when I see a policeman, my mindset is radically different. First, they are armed. Second, there will be no small talk or exchange of pleasantries. Third, there will be no use of discretion. It is very clear that they are very much a police force and not a police service.

When you are stopped by a member of An Garda Síochána – even though you might be well-deserving of a trip to the naughty step – there is something consoling in the fact that s/he is not carrying a gun and won't take exception should you try and reason with or plámás him/her.

LOOKING BACK

In the aftermath of the War of Independence and, more particularly, the Civil War – bliss it was *not* in that dawn to be alive – Ireland needed a house-trained civic police force to replace the paramilitary and highly politicised Royal Irish Constabulary (RIC). The less obnoxious Dublin Metropolitan Police (who never quite surmounted the images of brutal suppression during the 1913 Lockout) were allowed to linger for a few years. The RIC had been targeted mercilessly during the War of Independence by bullet and boycott, and its precipitate demise was an inevitable consequence of the Anglo-Irish Treaty. In its place we got a template intended to be an 'anti-RIC', an almost entirely unarmed, non-political force, the Civic Guard. By the time it was renamed Garda Síochána na hÉireann in August 1923, Michael Staines was in charge, the Civil War had come to an emphatic but bitter conclusion, and it was decided to equip the new force with recruits from the victorious Free State Army. Many, especially those from areas that had escaped the worst violence of the War of Independence, already had a background in 'Republican' policing; they had been adjuncts of the surprisingly efficient alternative Sinn Féin administration of law and order in parts of rural Ireland where the RIC dared not venture after early 1920 without at least a sprinkling of Tans and Auxies in Crossley Tenders to stiffen their resolve.

Since then, eighty-nine members of the service have given their lives for the communities they served – most of these deaths the wilful cold-blooded murder of unarmed policemen (thus far all fatalities have been male). Self-discipline, service, sacrifice. That's all on the credit side of the ledger.

Of course, there are two sides to most narratives.

An Garda Síochána has – like most police services – not been immune to malfeasance and venality in its 100-year history, but it has avoided some of the almost institutionalised corruption evident in other law-enforcement units around the world. While there have been notable Garda whistle-blowers who have been treated terribly, there has been no Irish equivalent of the NYPD Frank Serpico's testimony to the Knapp Commission in the 1970s of rampant 'graft' at all levels of 'New York's finest'. While some whistle-blowers were treated abominably by a Garda service in self-defence mode, none were lured into a police raid where they were exposed, abandoned, and almost fatally injured – as happened to Serpico in February 1971.

CULTURAL LEGACY

The culture of a service that still, in certain quarters, deifies and waxes nostalgic about the excesses of the celebrated/notorious Detective Sergeant James 'Lugs' Branigan during an era where scrutiny and accountability were virtually non-existent, is also highly questionable. That was the same dominant culture that countenanced the activities of the 'Heavy Gang' in the 1970s, activities highlighted in an era where press scrutiny was less pusillanimous than when Branigan was in his pomp. That culture was also exposed, and some members were called to account for their actions.

An uncomfortable number of sworn tribunals of inquiry have centred directly or largely on controversial Garda investigations or actions. The Kerry Babies scandal of the 1980s resulted in financial compensation for the family of Joanne Hayes and a belated apology from (among others) An Garda Síochána. The Disclosures Tribunal, chaired by Justice Peter Charleton, based on the disclosures of (retired Sergeant) Maurice McCabe, had reprehensible Garda behaviour front and centre. The Morris Tribunal, which reported in 2008, was scathing in its condemnation of the unconscionable activities of members of the service in Donegal. Morris expressed himself as being staggered by the levels of indiscipline and insubordination he found among members of the service there. Just below the level of full-scale tribunal was the 1982/83 inquiry into the illegal tapping of the phones of journalists. The entire scandal was joined at the hip to the treatment of another Garda whistle-blower at that time, Tom Tully, who highlighted abuses in Roscommon and suffered the consequences. His experience – he was fortunately protected by his association, the Association of Garda Sergeants and Inspectors (AGSI) – could not have been overly encouraging for whistle-blowers such as Maurice McCabe who came after him.

So, it is clear that, in these and other instances, the service has often deviated from the policing protocols articulated in the Garda Síochána Act (2005) which holds that policing must be provided:

- Independently and impartially,
- In a manner that respects human rights, and
- In a manner that supports the proper and effective administration of justice.

The rubric continues with the injunction that 'Effective and efficient policing depends on securing the confidence, support and co-operation of local communities and engaging with those communities.' (The rubric can be found on the Garda website.) Clearly, the service has not always enjoyed the entire confidence and support of at least some geographic communities (Donegal, Baileborough) and cultural/social/political communities (immigrants, Travellers, the far left).

Within the ranks of the service itself, there are also tensions that don't necessarily impinge upon the consciousness of the general public. There were more than seventy allegations of bullying, harassment or sexual harassment (96 per cent related to bullying) within the service itself in the five years up to 2022. Worryingly, according to the *Irish Independent* of 2 November 2020, there is a significantly higher rate of these complaints coming from female officers and civilian staff. It should, however, be pointed out that, in a service of 15,000 members, that represents an incidence of 0.1 per cent per annum in a service where institutionalised hierarchical structures might well have been expected to lead to a far greater prevalence of victimisation and mistreatment.

CONCLUSION

An Garda Síochána has been around for 100 years. It has had its bad apples and malevolent players at all levels of the service. But it has also had its whistle-blowers; the Sergeant who told you to go and get your rear light sorted and waved you on; the Garda who arrived in the nick of time to save your skin when you were about to become the victim of a drunken Friday-night shindig; the officer who patiently suggested that you might need to consider doing something about your faulty burglar alarm as he didn't want to be knocking on your front door a third time that night. (Obviously none of the above comes from personal experience.) Because, for all the bad apples, these are the members of the service that most of us encounter on a daily basis. They are not pulling us over because they don't like the colour of our skin; they are not taking backhanders from dodgy journalists for inside information on newsworthy investigations; and they are not putting our lives in danger because they are shiftless parasites intent only on feathering their own nests.

I imagine, if you were an examiner marking the performance over the last century of An Garda Síochána, that you would be likely to come up with an A- or, if you were in a particularly grumpy mood, perhaps a B+. As a consistent C+ or B- student myself over the years, I would be happy with that.

The views expressed by the author are his own.

Inclement weather. Garda Brendan Fennell stands watch outside the Special Criminal Court in the early 1990s. Gardaí patrol no matter what the weather may be.

CHAPTER 39

An Garda Síochána Roll of Honour

REFLECTION

Fr Joe Kennedy

On Thursday, 17 August 1922, the first Garda Commissioner, Michael Staines, led a party of Civic Guards through the Palace Street Gates of Dublin Castle. In the words of retired Chief Superintendent John O'Brien, that entrance 'was a symbolic transfer of power from the Royal Irish Constabulary (RIC) to the new police force'. Dublin Castle has had a very special place in the 100-year history of An Garda Síochána. Michael Staines's idealistic exhortation to his Garda colleagues about succeeding not by force of arms or numbers but on their moral authority as servants of the people is often quoted, including elsewhere in this book.

In celebrating the huge contribution that our Gardaí have made as servants of the people for the last 100 years, we also pay our respects to those who have died in the line of duty. On the third Saturday of May each year, we gather in the Garda Memorial Garden – opened on 15 May 2010 – and we pay tribute to our Garda colleagues who have given their lives in the service of our country. Their names are individually inscribed on the granite walls in the garden. 'In the rising of the sun and in its going down, we remember them.'

The Roll of Honour has a special place in the hearts and minds of all our Gardaí, serving and retired. As Guardians of the Peace in our country, they gave their lives guarding the peace. The French philosopher Paul Ricœur once said, 'To be forgotten is to die twice.' Our Gardaí who have made the ultimate sacrifice will never be forgotten within the Garda family. Their memory will continue to inspire all our Gardaí as we look back on 100 years of service to the people of Ireland and look forward to the future. May God bless all our Gardaí, now and in the years ahead.

For those named on the Garda Roll of Honour: *Ar dheis Dé go raibh a n-anamacha dílse.*

REFLECTION

Archdeacon David Pierpoint

Walking through the Dubh Linn gardens at Dublin Castle, you cannot help but notice that small area set aside to remember the members of An Garda Síochána who died while serving their country and their communities.

As we take time out to look through the eighty-nine names on the Roll of Honour, we are called, not to remember in order to celebrate the events which caused so many deaths, but to remember so that history does not repeat itself. We remember in order to honour those who gave their lives in the hopes of achieving a greater good: peace, safety and freedom. While we look at the names on the Roll of Honour, we must always remember the families and colleagues left behind who continue to grieve.

As a Christian in today's secular society, I believe that we are all called to love our neighbour; that is something which these eighty-nine men believed in and worked towards while on duty to serve the people of this land.

We are confronted not only with the sacrifices they made, but also with our response to those sacrifices. The whole concept of anyone making sacrifices for us, much less dying for us, makes us uneasy. If we confront their sacrifices, then we must feel gratitude and humility. Even worse, confronting their heroism forces us to stop and examine our own lives. Would we have done the same?

The people we remember today, like many who have died for others, were heroes. But what makes a hero? Heroes are people who make history. The qualities of heroism are eternal: self-sacrifice, courage, honour, duty. And in the gospels, Jesus adds the integral ingredient – love. In these verses, Jesus gives us a new context for heroism:

> My command is this: Love each other as I have loved you. Greater love has no one
> than this, than to lay down one's life for one's friends.

May God continually watch over the eighty-nine inscribed on the Roll of Honour and their families and may we never forget their heroism. We pray that all who serve in An Garda Síochána may be kept safe in their daily duties.

We remember with affection the members of An Garda Síochána killed in service:

John Brennan	John Flynn	Brian MacNeill	Timothy O'Sullivan
Henry Byrne	Ambrose Fogarty	Sean Masterson	Michael Padden
James Byrne	Patrick Foley	Jeremiah McCabe	Henry Phelan
Andrew Callanan	Patrick Forde	Robert McCallion	Seamus Quaid
Nathy Cawley	Sean Gantly	Eugene McCarthy	Paul Reid
Michael Clerkin	Tony Golden	Patrick McGeehan	Michael Reynolds
Richard Cody	Conor Griffin	James McIntyre	Patrick Reynolds
Paul Colleran	Thomas Griffin	Patrick McKeown	George Rice
Denis Connolly	Frank Hand	Gary McLoughlin	John Roche
Noel Conroy	Garreth Harmon	Patrick McLoughlin	William Roche
John Curtin	Denis Harrington	John McMahon	Declan Roe
Desmond Dixon	Walter Hennelly	George Mordaunt	Patrick Ruttledge
Samuel Donegan	Cyril Hickey	John Morley	Vincent Ryan
Adrian Donohoe	Colm Horkan	Patrick Morrissey	Gary Sheehan
James Doody	Richard Hyland	John Murrin	Tony Tighe
David Dowd	Ciarán Jones	Arthur Nolan	Michael Walsh
Thomas Dowling	Michael Joyce	Richard Nolan	Hugh Ward
James Downey	Brian Kelleher	William Nolan	Patrick Waters
John Eiffe	Michael Kennelly	Denis O'Brien	Joseph Wilkinson
Richard Fallon	John Lally	Declan O'Connor	James Woods
Eoin Fitzgerald	Michael Lawless	John O'Donnell	
James Fitzsimons	Thomas Lawn	Thomas O'Driscoll	
John Fitzsimons	John Linehan	Patrick O'Halloran	

May their courage, dedicated service and sacrifice be an inspiration to us all.

The funeral of Detective Garda Colm Horkan who was killed in the line of duty in Roscommon in June 2020.

A FALLEN COLLEAGUE

Written after the murder of Adrian Donohoe

I cried when I heard the news
A feeling deep inside
The thoughts of your weeping wife
And your children asleep inside

A fallen colleague on the news
A Garda shot and killed
A robbery gone wrong, they said
Awaiting TV crews

A senseless killing in every way
The ultimate sacrifice paid
To think you were just doing your job
Like thousands every day

I cried when I thought again
How my wife would take the news
And of my unborn child in her
How much I have to lose

Tonight another hero made
The statistics will have to change
A man I could not call my friend
But who I knew in many ways

I will pray for you tonight
And wish your family hope
Knowing that the thin blue line
Will endeavour to help them cope

Please remember behind the uniform
There is a person just like you
A mother, father, husband, wife
A son, or daughter too.

Ar dheis Dé go raibh a anam.

S. Moore

ABOUT THE CONTRIBUTORS

Retired Sergeant Tim Bowe 17202B is currently the secretary of the Cork City Garda Síochána Retired Members Association (GSRMA) branch. He served 13 years as Sergeant in charge in Ballincollig, Co. Cork.

Conor Brady is a former editor of *The Irish Times*. He was editor of *The Garda Review* 1973–75 . He was a founding Commissioner of the Garda Síochána Ombudsman Commission 2005–11. From 2003 to 2005, he was Visiting Professor at John Jay College of Criminal Justice, City University of New York. He is author of two histories of An Garda Síochána. Since 2019, he has chaired the State's Top-Level Appointments Committee.

Sheelagh Brady provides security-related research and risk-management consultancy services for international organisations and corporations. She has over 20 years' experience in policing and security and is a former member of An Garda Síochána.

Áine Broy is daughter of the third Commissioner of An Garda Síochána, Eamon Broy. She is currently working on a book of her father's memoirs.

Retired Detective Superintendent Michael Byrne 17501C retired as Detective Superintendent with the Technical Bureau.

Serving Detective Chief Superintendent Paul Cleary 25879B has, since July 2020, been assigned Head of Bureau as Detective Chief Superintendent in charge of the GNCCB (Garda National Cyber Crime Bureau). He also has additional responsibility for two other OSC (Organised and Serious Crime) Bureaus – the Garda National Technical Bureau, and the Garda Operational Support Services.

Mark Condren is an award-winning photographer working with the Independent Group.

Serving Sergeant Kelvin Courtney 27319H, a direct descendent of Harry Phelan, the first Garda killed on duty, is currently working with the Garda National Crime Prevention Unit.

Retired Detective Garda John Cribbin 23987K has over twenty-five years' experience working as a detective in Kevin Street, Ronanstown, Lucan and Leixlip Garda Stations.

Serving Garda Alan Cummins 31583D is currently stationed with the Garda Dog Unit in Kilmainham with his dogs, Roxy and Bran.

Serving Garda Tom Daly 25612K is stationed in Macroom, Co. Cork. He is a historian and columnist with *The Garda Review*.

Retired Inspector Tim Doyle 16784C is author of the books *Changing of the Guard* (2021), *Get Up Them Steps* (2001), and *Peaks and Valleys* (1997).

Retired Sergeant Martin Drew 23942K is a former curator of the Garda Museum.

Geraldine Du Berry is a Clerical Officer currently working in the Garda College in Templemore.

Serving Garda Damien Duffy 29853B is currently working with Dublin Metropolitan Roads Policing and is based in Dublin Castle.

Retired Inspector John Duffy 18309A is a former curator of the Garda Museum.

Myles Dungan is a broadcaster and author. Since 2010 he has presented *The History Show* on RTÉ Radio 1. He has many book titles to his name and in 2011 he fronted RTÉ Radio's coverage of Queen Elizabeth II's visit to Ireland.

Serving Superintendent Paul Franey 28661C is currently stationed in Balbriggan Garda Station, Co. Dublin.

Serving Superintendent Chris Grogan 26057F is currently stationed in Carrick-on-Shannon, Co. Leitrim.

Retired Inspector Edwin S. Handcock 16229K is a historian and writer with nearly thirty years' experience working in the Technical Bureau.

Retired Assistant Commissioner Tony Hickey 16070K was responsible for the Dublin Metropolitan Region and National Support Services.

Serving Garda Billy Horan 26635C is currently stationed in Sligo Garda Station.

Retired Sergeant John Hynes 23028F retired from Castlerea Garda Station in Co. Roscommon.

Serving Member of the Garda Reserve Mick Kenneally 80020A is currently part of the Community Engagement Team in Cork city.

Fr Joe Kennedy is a Garda Chaplain.

Serving Detective Sergeant Dara Kenny 32028E is currently stationed in Clondalkin Garda Station, Dublin 22.

Retired Assistant Commissioner Pat Leahy 22644M is a former Assistant Commissioner with responsibility for the Dublin Metropolitan Region.

Stephen McDonagh currently works in the Office of Corporate Communications in An Garda Síochána, in media production.

Retired Inspector Phelim Patrick McGee 18979M is a former curator of the Garda Museum.

Serving Inspector David McInerney 22052C is currently stationed in Terenure Garda Station, Dublin 6W.

Andrew McLindon is the Director of Corporate Communications for An Garda Síochána.

Serving Inspector Paul Maher 26291K is a former curator of the Garda Museum and chair of the Garda Historical Society.

Serving Detective Garda Darren Martin 27426G holds advanced diplomas in Data Protection Law and Applied Employment Law. He is a fellow of the Association of Compliance Officers in Ireland.

Retired Garda Commissioner Fachtna Murphy 16920L served as Garda Commissioner from 2007 to 2010. Prior to his appointment, he was Deputy Commissioner with responsibility for Operational Policing Strategies.

Serving Inspector Ailish Myles 00945H is currently stationed in Nenagh Garda Station, Co. Tipperary.

Serving Member of the Garda Reserve Ravinder Singh Oberoi 80060M is currently stationed in Pearse Street Garda Station, Dublin 2.

Serving Garda Brendan O'Connor 26725B is the Vice President of the Garda Representative Association and is stationed in Dunfanaghy, Co. Donegal.

Retired Garda Pat O'Donoghue 18510H is the author of the book *A Border Beat – Policing in Dundalk*.

Retired Sergeant Fachtna O'Donovan 21981K is a local historian and secretary of the Beara Historical Society.

Serving Assistant Commissioner John O'Driscoll 22317D is the Assistant Commissioner with responsibility for Organised and Serious Crime.

Retired Assistant Commissioner John O'Mahony 20477C was responsible for the Crime and Security Branch of An Garda Síochána.

Retired Assistant Commissioner Michael O'Sullivan 20808F is a former Assistant Commissioner. He was the head of the precursor to the Garda Drugs and Organised Crime Bureau and has recently retired from leading the influential Maritime Analysis and Operations Centre Narcotics (MAOC-N) in Portugal.

Retired Garda Commissioner Nóirín O'Sullivan 00219D became the first female to hold the post of Garda Commissioner when she was appointed in 2014.

Serving Member of the Garda Reserve Sean O'Sullivan 80570L is currently part of the Community Engagement Team in Cork city.

Former Minister for Justice Nora Owen served as Minister for Justice 1994–1997 and as Deputy Leader of Fine Gael 1993–2001.

Archdeacon David Pierpoint is a Garda Chaplain.

Serving Sergeant John Reynolds 24283G has a PhD in policing history and is the author of two books, *46 Men Dead: The Royal Irish Constabulary in Tipperary, 1919–22* and *The Templemore*

Miracles, 1920. His son **Michael Reynolds** holds a BA in history and is studying for an MA in the same subject.

Retired Chief Superintendent Paul Smyth 15068A is the author of the book *The Commissioners*, published by Carrowmore.

Retired Detective Superintendent Tony Sourke 15794E retired as Detective Superintendent from Blanchardstown Garda Station, Dublin 15.

Serving Detective Sergeant Brendan Tighe 28138G is currently attached to the Special Detective Unit working out of Harcourt Square.

Retired Deputy Commissioner John Twomey 23565B retired in 2021 after 39 years in An Garda Síochána. He was Deputy Garda Commissioner with responsibility for Policing and Security.

Retired Chief Superintendent Lorraine Wheatley 00404K is a former Chief Superintendent of the Dublin Metropolitan Region, South Central Division.

A new contemporary Garda uniform has been issued for all frontline members and will be worn for the first time in the second half of 2022. This will be only the third uniform change in the 100-year history of An Garda Síochána. Pictured above are Garda Aisling Gralton (Store Street) and Garda Ailish McBride (Kilmainham).

ACKNOWLEDGEMENTS

Garda Stephen Moore

This book would not have been possible without the co-operation, help and support I received from so many people. Firstly, I would like to thank all at The O'Brien Press for having faith in this project from the very beginning; their professionalism and dedication throughout has been exemplary.

I wish to show my appreciation to the editorial board with whom I have worked closely throughout and who have always been available for advice; they kept me going throughout, and for this I'd like to thank John Reynolds, John Twomey, Andrew McLindon and Shona Dennis.

I wish to thank Garda Management for their belief in me and for choosing a Garda to write the centenary book for the organisation; this was a brave move and I thank them for the faith shown in me. I hope this publication repays that faith. Special thanks to Deputy Commissioner Anne Marie McMahon and Assistant Commissioners Anne Marie Cagney and Orla McPartlin.

To my own immediate superiors and supervisors, thank you for the time allocated to me to get this book completed. Retired Chief Superintendent Wheatley and retired Superintendent Gannon, thank you for your patience, and to Chief Superintendent McElgunn and Superintendent McKenna, thank you for your continued patience.

I would like to thank the previous curators of the Garda Museum – Martin Drew, Pat McGee, Paul Maher and John Duffy – for their friendship and support, and I am delighted that each one features in this book. Thank you to Fiona, who is currently working in the museum, for all assistance provided.

To all in the Garda family who have contributed to this publication, thank you; it is only because of you and all who submitted articles and photographs that this book exists. To those who submitted material that does not feature, I apologise; unfortunately, it was impossible to include all material received. In truth, another volume could have been produced.

Thank you to Myles Dungan, Conor Brady and Sheelagh Brady who so willingly submitted chapters to this book. It was important to get opinions from outside the Garda family, and I was delighted with the quality of each piece received.

A special thanks to the following who were always at hand to advise me: Tony Sourke, Mick Byrne, Tony Hickey, Edwin S. Handcock, Tim Doyle, John Cribbin, Gregory O'Donnell, Jim Herlihy, Darren Martin, Nóirín O'Sullivan, Bronagh McCrystal, Julie Greene and Paul Smyth.

Thank you to Sergeant David Conway, Ian Redican and all at the Garda Photographic Section for opening their archives to me, and thank you to Mark Condren, Stephen McDonagh, Damien Storan and Niall Kinsella for providing fantastic photographs for publication.

Finally, I would like to thank my own family – my wife, Emer, and children, Matthew and Michael, for their patience shown and support given. I dedicate this book to my mother, Rita, who as I write this is entering palliative care and will not see the book when printed. Not a day passed when my mother did not enquire about the book's progress. Her love and support will always be treasured, and she will be sadly missed.

April 2022

Garda Stephen Moore.

BIBLIOGRAPHY

Allen, Gregory, *The Garda Síochána, Policing Independent Ireland 1922–1982*, Dublin: Gill & Macmillan, 1999

Brady, Conor, *Guardians of the Peace*, Dublin: Gill & Macmillan, 1974

Brady, Conor, *The Guarding of Ireland*, Dublin: Gill & Macmillan, 2014

Brewer John, Bill Lockhart and Paula Rodgers, *Crime in Ireland 1945–95: Here be Dragons*, Oxford: Clarendon, 1997

Campbell, L. 'Responding to Gun Crime in Ireland', *British Journal of Criminology*, vol. 50, no. 3, 2010: pp. 414–34

Commission on the Future of Policing (2018), *The Future of Policing in Ireland*

Condren, Mark, *The Guards: Behind the Scenes with the Men and Women of An Garda Síochána*, Bray, Co. Wicklow: Ballpoint Press Ltd, 2011

Conway, Vicky, *Policing Twentieth Century Ireland: A History of An Garda Síochána*, Abingdon, Oxon: Routledge, 2014

Doyle, Tim, *Changing of the Guard: Jack Marrinan's Battle to Modernise An Garda Síochána*, Dublin: Currach Books, 2021

Garvan, Tom, *Judging Lemass: The Measure of the Man*, Dublin: Royal Irish Academy, 2009

Herlihy, Jim, *The Dublin Metropolitan Police: A Short History and Genealogical Guide*, Dublin: Four Courts Press, 2001

Herlihy, Jim, *The Royal Irish Constabulary*, Dublin: Four Courts Press, 2016.

Hogan, Gerald and Clive Walker, *Political Violence and the Law in Ireland*, Manchester: Manchester University Press, 1989

Irish Human Rights and Equality Commission (IHREC), 'End Ireland's Special Criminal Court and Use Standard Courts to Ensure Fair Trials, 19 November 2021

Kilcommins, S., I. O'Donnell, E. O'Sullivan and B. Vaughan, *Crime, Punishment and the Search for Order in Ireland*, Dublin: Irish Academic Press, 2004

Lee, J.J. in John Crowley, Donal Ó Drisceoil, Mike Murphy and John Borgonovo, *Atlas of the Irish Revolution*, Cork: Cork University Press, 2017

Loader, I. and R. Sparks, 'For an Historical Sociology of Crime Policy in England and Wales since 1968', *Critical Review of International and Political Philosophy*, vol. 7, 2004: pp. 5-32

McCarthy, Brian, *The Civic Guard Mutiny*, Cork: Mercier Press, 2012

McEntee, P., *Commission of Investigation into the Dublin and Monaghan Bombings 1974*, Dublin: The Stationery Office, 2007

McGarry, Fearghal, *Eoin O'Duffy: A Self-Made Hero*, Oxford: Oxford University Press, 2005

Manning, P.K., *Police Work: The Social Organisation of Policing*, Boston: MIT Press, 1977

Moore, Garda Stephen, *A History of Kevin Street Garda Station*, Dublin: Monument Media, 2018

Moore, Garda Stephen, *Pearse Street 100*, Dublin: Monument Media, 2015

Mulcahy, A., 'The Impact of the Northern "Troubles" on Criminal Justice in the Irish Republic' in P. O'Mahony (ed.), *Criminal Justice in Ireland*, Dublin: Institute of Public Administration, 2008

O'Brien, Gerard, *An Garda Síochána and the Scott Medal*, Dublin: Four Courts Press, 2008

O'Brien, John A., *A Question of Honour*, Dublin: Choice Publishing, 2021

O'Donoghue, Pat, *A Border Beat*, 2021 (self-published)

O'Donnell, Ian, 'Criminal Justice Review 1998', *Administration*, no. 4712, Summer 1999, pp. 175–211

Ó Drisceoil, Fachtna, *The Missing Postman: What Really Happened to Larry Griffin?* Cork: Mercier Press, 2011

O'Halpin, Eunan, *Defending Ireland: The Irish State and its Enemies*, Oxford: Oxford University Press, 1999

Patterson, H., *Ireland's Violent Frontier: The Border and Anglo-Irish Relations During the Troubles*, London: Palgrave Macmillan, 2013

Reynolds, John, *The Templemore Miracles: Jimmy Walsh, Ceasefires and Moving Statues*, Cheltenham: The History Press, 2019

Smyth, Paul, *The Commissioners*, Dublin: Carrowmore Publishing, 2022

Sourke, Patrick Anthony, *An Evaluation of Homicide Investigation in the Republic of Ireland*, 2006 (self-published)

Willoughby, Brian and Noel Hynes, *Guardians of the GAA: A Compilation of Garda GAA Players*, 2018 (self-published)

MAGAZINES AND PERIODICALS

Garda Review, The

Síochán Magazine

Daily Mail

Irish Examiner

Irish Independent

Irish News

Irish Press

Irish Times

Sunday Times

and Other Garda publications

Other Sources

Army Enquiry Committee Papers

Army Mutiny Records

Bureau of Military History, 1913–21

Dublin Metropolitan Police Letters Book

Military Archive Records

Oriel House Records

On 6 July 2009 Sergeant Larry Condren walks his last beat with his grandson Ben in tow. Larry is the father of award-winning photographer Mark Condren, who has supplied several photographs for this publication. Larry retired after 37 years' service and epitomised all that community policing stands for. He retired from Castletownroche Garda Station, and he knew everybody who lived in the village, and everybody knew him.

First published 2022 by The O'Brien Press Ltd.
12 Terenure Road East, Rathgar, Dublin 6, D06 HD27, Ireland.
Tel: +353 1 4923333. Fax: +353 1 4922777
Email: books@obrien.ie. Website: obrien.ie
The O'Brien Press is a member of Publishing Ireland.

ISBN: 978-1-78849-339-0

7 6 5 4 3 2 1
27 26 25 24 23 22

Printed by EDELVIVES, Spain.
The paper in this book is produced using pulp from managed forests.

*Front cover image: A Garda on the beat chats with members of the community in which he serves.
Back cover: Top: Garda Headquarters, Phoenix Park. Middle (L to R): Early members of the Garda
Traffic Corps; Assisting a member of the public with directions; Garda Memorial Garden, Dublin
Castle; Parade for the 2022 International Association of Women Police (IAWP) Conference, Dublin
Castle. Bottom (L to R): Assisting a child; Garda Band performing at Pride; Gardaí introduced
socially distanced 'chatting benches' in a number of locations during COVID-19; Members of the
Mounted Unit patrolling at Croke Park.
p. 2: Gardaí marching at the IAWP Conference, which was held in Dublin Castle in March 2022.
pp. 22–3: Group of the new Civic Guards at Collinstown, Dublin.
p. 167: A member of the Roads Policing Unit using a mobility device.*

Published in